Consider the Ravens

On Contemporary Hermit Life

PAUL A. FREDETTE
AND
KAREN KARPER FREDETTE

iUniverse, Inc.
New York   Bloomington

Consider the Ravens

On Contemporary Hermit Life

iUniverse books may be ordered through booksellers or by contacting:

iUniverse
1663 Liberty Drive
Bloomington, IN 47403
www.iuniverse.com
1-800-Authors (1-800-288-4677)

ISBN: 978-0-595-48294-8 (pbk)
ISBN: 978-0-595-51756-5 (cloth)
ISBN: 978-0-595-60380-0 (ebk)

Printed in the United States of America

iUniverse rev. date: 11/17/2008

Also by Karen Karper Fredette

    Clare: Her Light and Her Song

    Where God Begins to Be: A Woman's Journey into Solitude

Co-Authored with Paul A. Fredette

    The Legend of Lovada Branch

Consider the Ravens

On Contemporary Hermit Life

Paul A. Fredette and Karen Karper Fredette

To the Sentinels who await the dawn

Consider the ravens: they do not sow, they do not reap,
They have neither cellar nor barn—
Yet God feeds them.
(Lk 12:24)

Table of Contents

Foreword

I remember being deeply surprised when I heard that there might have been as many as fourteen hundred Franciscan-affiliated hermits in Europe in the year 1400 (friars, anchoresses, "third order", under rule and secular, men and women, clerical, religious, and lay)!

The exact same numbers made it easy to remember but, even more, the surprising fact itself. I had grown up inside of a Franciscan vision that was almost entirely communitarian. In fact, that was the test of whether you were a good Franciscan and could be professed: Could you live well in community, attend community prayer, serve the community by your skills, and resolve relational conflicts? These were the litmus tests of acceptable membership, and surely not all bad or unnecessary. But you could unfortunately do all of these without any actual transformative God experience.

I can understand why community was the starting place and even the grounding and testing place for an authentic spiritual life (How can you say you love God, if you do not love your brother or sister? (1 John 2:9)), but it was obvious that this school of community was not necessarily the place of continuance for many or the path for the second half of life. This is quite similar to the pattern that we find in Hinduism and Buddhism, by the way. Some form of community is often the container but does not always lead us to the contents.

Other scholars went further and tried to add up the days that Francis himself actually lived in community, and it was probably only a third of his active life, at best! The rest of the time, he was walking the countryside, off in caves and wattles, doing his "Lents" alone on islands and in forests, and living in reclusive places like La Verna (where he received the stigmata), with a strictly physically boundaried relationship with Brother Leo. Our notion of community might have much more to do with stability, security, economics, careers, practicality, accountability, and church work than actual Divine Encounter. Francis wanted that encounter and that abiding above all else.

Even the Shakespearean line "walking like a friar" referred to the common practice of Franciscans walking in single file when they moved about the world as preachers, mendicants, and spiritual migrant workers. The desire was not for social chatter but an ever deeper contemplation and a form of solitude, even on the road. Silence, even while together. "The whole world is our cloister," as Francis put it. One wonders how we ever lost all of this freedom, depth, and apparent joy.

After the defensiveness from all sides that proceeded from the Reformation, and after the heady rationalism of the Enlightenment, the older tradition of desert and monastic contemplation (the "pensar sin pensar" or "thinking of nothing" of Francisco de Osuna) was largely lost, even in the Religious Orders. Certainly, it was not taught in any systematic way after the sixteenth century, as Thomas Merton, and others since him, have so sadly uncovered. Thank God, "eccentric" (out of the center) individuals always discovered it by "accident," suffering, gift, and "infusion."

Once you lose that deeper understanding of contemplation, you also lose the desire, expectation, skill, or capacity to live this way twenty-four hours a day—alone! The fullness is no longer there that supports silence and solitude over long periods. Social and liturgical prayer, good as they are, became the common substitute for being alone with the Alone, and sufficient with the Sufficient. The wisdom way of knowing that continued all the way from Jesus and the desert fathers and mothers largely came to an end in any socially visible way. Perhaps something was gained by all the group organization, but something was surely lost too.

So you see why there is so much joy and hope in our time! We are rediscovering the fullness, the sufficiency, and the new kind of community that comes from living the inner life of the Trinity at new levels of depth and conviction. All over the world of Christianity, solitaries, hermits, and recluses are reappearing—and sometimes even appreciated. When not on the road, I myself live as a solitary and do Lent bi-annually in a hermitage, with the full blessing of my Franciscan superiors and a bewildered comprehension from bishops and those praying for more sacramental priests. These times are always, without doubt, my great spiritual breakthroughs and allow me to be sacramental in a wholly different way, I hope.

What drives us? Is it the desire to live on the far edge of both social and ecclesiastical contention? Is it the desire to bring a new depth to these conversations and institutions? Is it just the naked search for God? Is it the search for true joy? Is it the recognition that all of our saying must be balanced by unsaying? Is it just our vocation? All of these, I am sure, but mostly the *new self-confidence* to think that we can actually do it! And must do it! And deeply desire to do it! Because the Great Desirer has already done it in us! Suddenly, we are finding that "the now life," the sacrament of the present moment, as we once called it, is understandable at broader levels than ever before. And we are the blessed and lucky ones who get to actually live it.

This stripped-down, silent, stark, sensate, and oh-so-simple life seems to be saying at least three things that we know that we ourselves, the world, and even the church must hear anew:

All is from God.
All is toward God.
All else is not God.

April 23, 2008
Feast of Blessed Giles of Assisi, Hermit, and Vagrant

Richard Rohr, o.f.m.
Center for Action and Contemplation
Albuquerque, New Mexico

Acknowledgments

We offer heartfelt thanks to the Bogert Fund Committee for awarding us a generous grant; to Father James Finder for his outstanding support and encouragement; also to Reverend Marc Fredette, to Patti Wollenberg (Little Buddy), and to readers of *Raven's Bread* (particularly D and M) whose contributions, monetary and literary, have allowed *Consider the Ravens* to become a reality. We are also grateful for all the words of encouragement, assuring us of eager anticipation for this work on contemporary hermit life. Above all, we thank the silent pray-ers whose spiritual presence permeates the following pages.

Cover design and illustrations by Paul A. Fredette

Copyright permissions appear on page 251, which constitutes a continuation of these acknowledgments.

Elijah at the Wadi Cherith
1 Kings 17:1–6

Introduction

"Quark!" One day, as we were hiking the overgrown logging road that winds up the mountain behind our home, my husband, Paul, and I heard an unfamiliar cry.

"Wha-a-at?" we asked, scanning the trees around us.

"Quark!" The strange call was echoed from another direction. Suddenly, a heavy black bird lifted off from the top of a tulip poplar. Slightly larger than a crow, with a thicker beak and fan-shaped tail, our mystery bird was briefly silhouetted against the blue sky.

Once home, we pulled out our well-thumbed copy of *Birds of the Eastern United States* and flipped to the section on black birds. Our suspicion was confirmed. We had sighted a raven, uncommon in our part of the Smokies! The incident felt most fortuitous. Just a few days earlier, we had agreed to take over publishing a small newsletter for hermits titled *Marabou*, founded by Dominican friar, Father Bede Jagoe. Though enthusiastic about the periodical, the title bothered us. How many people, we wondered, knew that a marabou is a large, solitary stork native to West Africa? Or that "marabout" is an Islamic term (by way of French) for a hermit or holy person?

While considering a more comprehensible title for the newsletter, we recalled the story of the prophet/hermit, Elijah. At one point in his checkered career, Elijah needed to hide out from the king who was seeking his life. God directed him to a solitary glen with a stream and told him: "I have commanded ravens to feed you there." As the story goes, ravens dropped in morning and evening with bread and meat! The imagery seemed ideal, so *Marabou* morphed into *Raven's Bread: Food for Those in Solitude*.

Throughout the following ten years, the number of readers of the paper edition grew from two hundred to one thousand worldwide, while the number of hits the Web site received kept it near the top of the search engines. Hermits, real and would-be, were obviously looking for nourishment. We had set the traditional extra place for Elijah at our table, and lo, he and his disciples had joined us!

What is drawing people to partake of *Raven's Bread*? As we conversed with our guests (via the post office, e-mail, and phone), we heard many urgent cries for a calmer, more spiritually oriented, and yes, solitary way of life. Some of our contacts feared they might be called to "hermit life" and spoke of their anxiety in hushed tones, concerned that we might brand them as weird or odd. We accepted their confidence with respect and assured them that they were not alone in their desire; that in fact, there were hundreds, probably even thousands, of other people also drawn to solitude and silence. The sigh of relief we heard was nearly thunderous, and a typical example is the story this man from Virginia shared:

> "I'm a retired Episcopal priest, a robust sixty-six, theologically trained to seek the Face of God. I ended up in the religion business instead. I had to leave eleven years ago in a state of total exhaustion. All my pat answers and hymns and formulas for prayer no longer filled the gnawing emptiness that, over time, had seized my life. I learned that the only way out of my confusion was to go through the confusion ... allowing the rich, luminous darkness to be consciously present in a Silence so profound that all else in my life was brought into its embrace. I know the Silence is all I have now and all that engages me. It is boundless, wordless (for the most part), and filled with potential. It is a Silence that loves all just as it is. Such Silence is met only in solitude. Maybe I'm a solitary, a hermit ... or just weird? My interest in religious community life waned decades ago. I'm more the marrying kind, I'm afraid ... blessed with thirty years of wedded

grace and two grown daughters. I hear the stories from many of my monk friends who struggle with a Holy Rule that no longer brings the heart of the World alive for them. I live in a network (real and virtual) of others drawn to the solitary life and, at least for now, prefer to keep zealous "spiritual teachers" away. The contemplative calling ain't broke. Don't try to help me fix it. When I leave my house, I'm aware that the Silence goes with me ... at least until I melt down at some gathering or at Wal-Mart. I am that Silence, the Hermitage, the Seeker and That Being Sought. That's what I believe Jesus brought to the marketplace ... a glimpse of Life's compassionate depths that we overlook because we're too busy playing God."[1]

Raven's Bread is basically a "table ministry," sharing nourishment from the various life experiences of the guest-readers. It is a venue for asking and answering the questions and providing the fellowship that even hermits need. This ongoing discussion among the readers covers all the challenges inherent in a life of silence, solitude, and simplicity. Our readers share their struggles to develop an authentic lifestyle that will not only open them to the solace of God but will enable them to become a hidden channel of grace for others.

Over the years, letters to *Raven's Bread* have increased, arousing the curiosity of local postal workers. A hermit in Colorado wrote:

> "I laughed out loud to read that some local folks might think *Raven's Bread* is a bakery! Well ... in some ways it is, isn't it? You knead the dough that comes in as raw flour from all over the world; you roll it out, having added the special ingredients that only seasoned souls know about, and bake it, so that others can receive it as nourishment. It is special bread, one that shows others they can 'bake it' too!"[2]

Consider the Ravens: On Contemporary Hermit Life distills eleven years of exchange among the readers of *Raven's Bread,* including the data derived from the survey we circulated in 2001. The survey results are a rare collection of information, derived from the largest number of hermits ever contacted. As editors, we were both amazed and humbled by the willing cooperation the survey evoked. We were also surprised by what the answers to the questions revealed. The responses to certain questions were almost predictable, but other information proved downright startling. *Raven's* table has an astonishing variety of "dishes" served up with some spicy ingredients!

One reader has written:

> "I cannot stop thinking of the koan: 'the kiss of sunlight on stone' from the February 2006 issue. *Raven's Bread* gets better and better ... a collage reflecting many voices. You have given far more than a publication to the world. You have given a new way to celebrate life." [3]

The way of life we are celebrating is as old as civilization itself. Throughout history, many individuals have followed the mysterious "call of the raven" and sought their deepest, truest selves in solitude and silence. We hope to encourage those who today are rediscovering hermit life. As many of us now admit, status, security, and a surfeit of goods are insufficient to nourish our souls. We long for less rather than more. We flee a society that pursues us with ever-new means of communication. Turning off our cell phones invites guilt and a home without a TV in every room is an anomaly. Our headphones often become the only place of escape available to us!

Are hermits escapists? Yes. Is running away a bad thing? Like most choices, its value is determined by its purpose. There are men and women who are selfishly seeking a sanctuary untouched by human pain. But there are others who deliberately choose to be powerless, to live simply, and to use no more than their fair share of the world's resources. They elect to be unknown, hidden, forgotten. And their goal? To become transparent to the Divine or, as one supporter of *Raven's Bread* succinctly phrases it, *"to be always present to the Presence."*

People who make such radical choices can make us uncomfortable. They challenge us—and they give us hope. It is good to know that hidden among us are solitary seekers choosing to live each day in profound silence and solitude and by so doing, adding a spiritual dimension to our contemporary society. When the number of such fully alive human beings reaches a critical mass, this silent leaven will turn our planet into a table of plenty where everyone will be invited to the feast.

Hermits and solitaries are those who have dared the impossible in their own lives and thus have blazed a trail for others to follow, not necessarily into the desert but into the infinitely more frightening wilderness of their own souls. They believe and live the words of Barbara J. Winters:

> "When we come to the edge of all the light that we know and are about to step off into the darkness of the unknown, faith is knowing that one of two things will happen: either there will be something solid for us to stand on, or we will be taught to fly."[4]

During the more than ten years we have published *Raven's Bread* and corresponded with people living as hermits, we have discovered that individuals called to eremitical life are indeed that—individuals! There are no two hermits who define their goals alike or who share a wholly similar lifestyle. Some folk live on mountainsides and some in hidden valleys; others find their hermitage in a complex for seniors or on a houseboat. There are urban anchorites, rural recluses, and desert solitaries. Not all are recognized by Church authorities, and not all are Christians; some live an eclectic spiritual mix of their own devising. Perhaps the only thing that all hermits have in common is that they are most uncommon! As you will see, there are as many ways of being a hermit as there are people doing it.

It is certainly true that hermit life today (as always) is a lonely one by its very nature. Yet, it is also a vocation with an innate calling to spiritual hospitality. It is a lifestyle of simplicity but with in-built contradictions. It is as simple today as it was when Abba Hierax, one of the early desert fathers, answered the brother who asked: "Give me a word. How can I be saved?" With admirable brevity, the old man declared: "Sit in your cell, and if you are hungry, eat; if you are thirsty, drink; only do not speak evil of anyone and you will be saved."[2]

We hope this volume may introduce an ancient way of the life to curious readers; that it encourages persons who feel an attraction to solitude but fear to follow it; and that it may serve as resource for those who wish to become hermits, as well as for those already treading the "less-traveled road". This book looks at hermit life from all angles and offers helpful advice derived from the experiences of many hermits in our contemporary society.

Yet all our words cannot improve on this classic story of a Russian "staretzi" or "hermit-father":

> Abba Lot went to see Abba Joseph and said: "Abba, as much as I am able I practice a small rule, a little fasting, some prayer and meditation, and remain quiet, and as much as possible I keep my thoughts clean. What else should I do?" Then the old man stood up and stretched out his hands toward heaven, and his fingers became like ten torches of flame. And he said: "Why not be totally changed into fire?"[3]

Chapter 1

Solitaries: Psychotics or Sages?

It has been said (and quite accurately) that mystics swim in the same waters in which psychotics drown. Solitary life frequently proves to be the "waters" where sagacity or psychoses can surface quite dramatically. Many of us are haunted by this possibility and so view the desire to live alone, apart from maximum human interaction, with profound suspicion, even when this attraction rises in our own heart. *"It ain't natural!"* proclaims the censor within, and we quickly flee from the temptation to become (may God save us!) a *hermit*.

Yet some of us harbor a concern that we might just be running from the life-giving stream that once sustained that old Biblical hermit, Elijah. We can well understand the occasional desire to chuck it all and head for the hills where, at least for a while, we can just *be*. But what happens when such an attraction threatens to become a way of life? Are we skirting the edges of psychosis? Displaying symptoms of major depression? Or struggling with the mid-life nemesis of change for change's sake? At the very least, aren't we being profoundly selfish?

The one thing we are most certain about is that there is an aching void at our center. Traditional religious practices and conservative morals have (we believe) given earlier generations "blessed assurance." We may strive to recover such certainties by returning to our earlier beliefs, or we may seek out more esoteric spiritualities which seem to offer the key to meaningful living. However, even as we go about this search (and grow in the process), we are likely to discover that the fulfillment we want involves increasing chunks of solitude. Uh oh, here comes that *h* word again—hermit! Maybe it is time to stop running blindly and look more seriously at this phenomenon known as eremitical life. Just what is a hermit, anyway?

Curmudgeons and Other Misconceptions

There is a scruffy character in a patched robe and wild beard that turns up in every issue of *Raven's Bread*. Wood B. Hermit is a spoof on the popular stereotype of the hermit. Although he generally provides a chuckle for the readers, his underlying message is serious. Wood B. is everything that a hermit is *not*! Should he appear trudging along the road toward his tumble-down hut, he would attract the very thing genuine hermits abhor—attention. Hermits are not sideshow attractions with a neon sign flashing: "Hermit This Way!" In truth, most hermits, if they put up a sign at all, would have one pointing away from their hermitage!

An anonymous Camaldolese hermit wrote of his life in terms of hiddenness and concealment. Among the lessons, he describes: "The first is this: our departure for the hermitage is an eloquent rejection of the mentality of our environment. Our solitary life is not only a renunciation of the artificiality of a mundane existence based on appearance and efficiency, but it hides us from the eyes and the acquaintance of (others) ... in such a way that we live truly concealed in complete anonymity."[1] An interview with Sr. Carole Marie Kelly, a hermit living among the redwoods, illustrates a kind of "concealment in full view" that typifies most hermits today.

"Are you really a hermit?"

"Yes."

"Do you have a garden?"

"No."

"Where do you get your food?"

"I go to a supermarket."[2]

In a similar vein, Sister Maggie Ross, an Anglican solitary whose trips to the local grocery provoked cynical questions about the validity of her calling, remarked: "People don't endow hermits (as was often the case in the Middle Ages). I'd like to be an anchorite, like Julian of Norwich, with two maids and all the time in the world to get on with her writing."[3] Here, Ross is touching on another sensitive topic that serious hermits must deal with. Few are independently wealthy, and fewer still can make a living weaving baskets under a palm tree.

One of the tests that anyone seriously considering hermit life must pass is how they handle the practicalities of life while maintaining their solitude and spiritual focus. It is true that a hermit "does not live on bread alone" (even *Raven's Bread*!), but a solitary shouldn't count on finding a box of food on his or her doorstep at regular intervals or the electric bill always "forgiven" by the local utility company. On the other hand, excessive concern about finances is contrary to the freedom of heart that characterizes a genuine solitary.

Most hermits tell us that one of their biggest hurdles initially was cultivating the trust which allowed them to live without care for the morrow while doing whatever it took to provide for their own needs. There is a fine line between unhealthy expectations of support from on high and confidence that, if you do all you can, the Lord will provide the rest. Passing this test is part of sorting the "sages from the psychotics." An example of unrealistic expectations turned up in a letter to the editor from *Hermit Wannabe* posted in *Raven's Bread* a few years back.

> "I am considering becoming a hermit in the near future and realize one of the main obstacles is lack of funding. There is a possible solution to this dilemma which I would like to share with your readers. My idea is for a potential hermit to 'advertise.' For example: 'Serious Hermit desires benefactor to supply a monthly donation of $500. Will keep benefactor and their family in my daily prayers. Please contact, etc. Thank you' I believe

there are wealthy people with spiritual ideals who may be glad to sponsor a hermit in exchange for daily prayers. Local churches or religious orders may be another source of such support. In the Gospels, it states that Jesus and his disciples were provided for, housing and all, by the generosity of certain wealthy women. Are there currently hermits who have obtained this kind of patronage as well as a place to live?"[4]

We were not surprised to receive this response to *Wannabe*: It appears he or she is looking for a free lunch, which is so contrary to monastic ideals. Has he or she read any of the *Fathers of the Desert*? Or Thomas Merton, who wrote: "If a monk has abandoned the cares and distractions and burdens of life in the world, that does not mean he has renounced the society of other men or the responsibility of providing for himself by the labor of his hands; far from it!" Maggie Ross, Anglican Anchorite, writes: "To pay someone to be self-emptying is a contradiction in terms." I know of many senior citizens who by constraint live a hermit-like life and could well use the assistance from wealthy people, as *Wannabe* suggests. The suggestion is redolent of the selling of indulgences, hmmm?[5]

The most well-known hermit in the past fifty years is Thomas Merton. Thanks to his voluminous writings recording his every thought and doubt and desire regarding eremitic life, his very search for solitude catapulted him out of the isolation he sought! In June of 1959, he was musing in his journal about his growing attraction to solitude: "If only it were a simple question! I like less and less the term "hermit." I want to live alone—not become a member of a fictitious category ... I am more and more convinced that I have to settle this question somehow ...."[6] Five years later, he was still trying "to settle this question somehow," ruminating over and rejecting such a variety of hermit situations that his journals are a veritable manual on discernment!

Among other questions, Merton wrestled with the disparate images he and his superiors separately held about hermits and hermit life: "The fact is, I do not want purely and simply to 'be a hermit' or to lead a life purely and ideally contemplative. I truly seek a very solitary, simple, and primitive life with no special labels attached. However, there must be love in it, and not an abstract love, but a real love for real people."[7] In other words, Merton did not believe the curmudgeon myth. A real hermit would never utter the famous line from the *Peanuts* comic strip: "I love humanity. It is people I can't stand."

This quote evokes the popular image of a recluse. Is there a difference between a hermit and a recluse? Despite Merriam-Webster's apparent confusion, there *is* a difference. Understanding this eliminates many false expectations about how one can live as a genuine hermit in the twenty-first century. A total recluse is a rare bird and would seem to require both wealth and a support staff (shades of Howard Hughes!) supplying her or him with food, toilet paper, and other daily necessities; fetching and delivering these items to a place where the recluse may pick them up, preferably sight unseen; as well as arranging for private attention from doctors and dentists. Whence come the funds for such a lifestyle? It is a rare solitary that is independently wealthy! Thus, recluses are the exception, not the rule.

Fr. Paul Jones writes:

> "In the end, a hermit is not a recluse, defined by living alone, for many live alone but are not hermits in our sense. The hermit life is primarily defined by orientation, in which one's centering is internal, thus having minimal need for external recognition or sense of acknowledged accomplishment. Thus defined, a true hermit can live in the midst of society and be engaged with others, and still be a hermit, just as long as s/he draws their meaning and poised center elsewhere. A Christian hermit is not one who particularly loves being alone but is drawn to be emptied into the Divine Presence."[8]

Among the thousand-plus readers of *Raven's Bread*, only two people identified themselves as recluses and both belonged to monastic orders. These had followed a time-honored progression of many years' service in community life until, tried and tested, they were permitted to withdraw into a life of total reclusion. The community gave them a place to live on the monastery grounds and provided for the rest of their physical needs. There are more monastic hermits than just these two who subscribe to *Raven's Bread*. A life of reclusion and literal hiddenness marks the style of eremitism which they have embraced.

The hermits we are discussing generally do not belong to a religious order. Their lifestyle involves some interaction with the world, an exchange defined by simplicity and necessity, as well as kindness and concern. J. Leclercq comments that "sociability is a natural trait of the authentic hermit. He needs to meet others from time to time."[9] More than once, contributors to *Raven's Bread* have discussed the problem of how to limit the many people attracted to the kindly hermit who always has a smile and cheerful word. There could be an advantage in affecting to be the snarling curmudgeon who throws his or her hood up and stomps back into the woods!

Where did we get all these wild tales about hermits? We need only turn to the lives of the Desert Fathers and Mothers to discover the source of the stereotypical hermit that haunts us still. Hermits lived in strange ways and strange places. There were those who spent their lives in caves; others chose trees; and still others perched on pillars or in bell towers. What distinguished the divinely inspired from the merely crazed? What is the fine line which distinguishes the Spirit-called from the mentally impaired or the merely eccentric?

The bald truth is that one can be mentally or emotionally ill and still be very holy. Sanctity and mental balance are not necessarily companions. On the other hand, strange lifestyles and habitats do not a holy hermit make. As has been said, a genuine hermit is recognized by the reasons which determined that person's choice of solitude and the fruits that life produces. "He was loved by all" may not be true of every solitary, but all should be striving to grow in care, compassion, and concern for their brothers and sisters.

In today's world, not all hermits can live in physical isolation. As editors of *Raven's Bread*, we have come to admire the great ingenuity our readers exercise in finding ways to enjoy the "silence of solitude" wherever circumstances have placed them. The quality of hiddenness, essential to the hermit way, can be found in the heart of a busy city as well as at a suburban address or in a wilderness cabin.

What about this hermitage? What constitutes a true hermitage provokes as many questions as there are regarding the hermit who lives in it. Perhaps the following dictum, pronounced by the Buddha, can help to clarify what distinguishes a hermitage from just another house: "Wherever you live is your temple if you treat it like one."

A true hermit chooses his or her dwelling and consecrates it by the life she or he lives therein. A reader of *Raven's Bread* expressed this as follows:

> "My home is my main Spiritual Center, and from my backyard I meditate, find serenity by absorbing the stillness of the open fields, the ducks, geese, pheasants, quail, and wandering cats. I also have silently made my office (at my workplace) another spiritual workshop. I am aware of today's chaotic life but more and more my life is filled with peace, inner silence, purpose, and meaning. I have come to a deep realization that I am on The Pathway—what more could I ask?"[10]

Without doubt, hermits are different. The crucial question is the nature of that difference. One of the more noticeable traits most genuine hermits exhibit is their independence from popular opinion, activities, and choices. They live their own lives, happily indifferent to social norms. Fr. Cornelius Wencel points out that:

> "Such independence does not result from the passing whims of an unbalanced personality, from an excessive individualism or pride ... The hermit's

consistency and independence of action do not bear the stamp of haughtiness, vehemence, or stubbornness. They rather flow out of a heart that is strong, recollected, and also humble."[11]

Fr. Wencel goes on to point out that being free from the burden of public opinion, the hermit is able to resist popular points of view that are often simplistic and superficial, if not downright cheap and vulgar, even when applied to hermits! Yes, the hermit is somehow different, and almost everyone who meets him or her senses that difference right away. The hermit is not weird, however, as a crotchety bachelor, a neighborhood crank, or the odd person afflicted with complexes might appear to be. Quite the opposite!

"The hermit's peculiarity is rooted rather in his or her mature, extraordinary, and strong personality that amazes and attracts others because it is sincere, deep, and simple. Without a doubt, each authentic anchorite is a kind of sage for those who seek his or her help and support. His or her wisdom strikes a harmony between ideals and life; she or he lives what she or he preaches. The Good News is preached at all times; when necessary, with words. She or he has practical knowledge, based on many years of experience, which is impressive. The difference the hermit displays does not imply an alienation or remoteness. Rather she or he is "different" because of living his or her calling in a spontaneous and authentic way, because she or he indeed believes in truth, justice, and peace. His or her paths, way of thinking, and choices, particular as they are, positively radiate a special warmth and charm wherever she or he goes."[12]

In a word, the genuine hermit is a sage, not a psychotic, although a few in past ages chose to hide under the cloak of a "holy fool."

Hermit "Types"—Are There?

There have always been individuals who by nature are aloof and prefer to keep to themselves, limiting interaction with others to the minimum. Across the centuries, artists have realized the necessity of solitude to foster the development of their gifts. We are all familiar with the caricature of the artist barricading him or herself into their studio or the writer dipping his quill in his or her inaccessible loft. For them, retreat from society was a means to an end. The same is true for those who wish to develop and deepen their relationship with the Divine. If we are honest, we must admit that we all need a degree of solitude in our lives if we are to maintain our inner balance.

That being said, can we ask if there are "hermit types," individuals who are better suited for a life of solitude than others? Eremitical life is most definitely a case of "grace building on nature." However, not all people who are shy turn into recluses. Nor does everyone who prefers quiet space around them become a hermit. As we look for similar qualities or traits that all hermits should possess, we soon realize that we are trying to analyze fish swimming in various aquatic milieus. Each species is differently endowed, depending on whether they are freshwater fish or deep-sea creatures; intended for tumbling mountain streams or lurking in deep, still pools.

This is analogously true for hermits. Solitaries have various and differing ways of living. The natural gifts they have are subsumed into something greater than a "job," for eremitical life is a calling, not a career choice. The variety of hermit lifestyles is so bewildering that a new reader of *Raven's Bread* expressed some existential frustration over how to define a hermit. He had eagerly read advice that various readers were offering to a beginning hermit and had found it "so varied that one is not sure what is good or important and what is not. Is it just one more person's opinion?"[13]

Hermit life is indeed a slippery fish to define, and one could unprofitably spend much time trying to do so. This is just as true when we try to pin down what type of person would be called to such a marginal lifestyle. Hermit Fr. W. Paul Jones has pondered this question of what types of people might be attracted to hermit

9

life and who could live it successfully and offers the following reflection:

> "There are multiple reasons for being a hermit, and there are as many types as there are hermits. Those most likely to succeed are those who feel a calling to the life for positive reasons rather than negative ones; who have done well enough in their life thus far, but want more, who want to go deeper. Their choice to leave the world has about it a moral and spiritual base; a seeking of an alternative to a society built on the American Dream. They are disciplined individuals who have had some experience already of the solitary life.
>
> Those more likely to fail are those who are fleeing something; who are running away; who do not like people and are reclusive by nature; who see themselves as failures; who are compensating for something else; who retain a strong dose of the American free-enterprise: competitive, individualistic, materialistic ethos; who have made friends with their own obsessiveness, and who do not have a deep love for the simple, rustic, frugal pioneer spirit. Above all, they are those who have not yet dealt well with their own demons."[14]

Are introverts or extroverts more suited to solitude? One might initially consider that it would have to be introverts, but is it? A reader of *Raven's Bread* offered this "cautionary note from an experienced hermit":

> "It is often assumed or said outright that the solitary life is designed for psychological 'introverts.' My own experience of this life—over a period of forty years—together with reports from others, is that psychological introversion is not necessarily a

condition for fruitful solitary living and could result in serious harm to the individual and a compromise of the genuinely spiritual motivation required. For some, the purely natural fulfillment of living alone may not allow for the transition from the psychological to the ontological basis of a supernatural calling. The Syrian word 'ihidayutha' (solitariness) carries various connotations, including singular, undivided in heart, celibate. It is likely that ihidaya is the Syrian root for the Greek 'monachos' (monk) and came to connote a solitary or hermit monk. I do not wish to get into polemics over this. But the question deserves to be addressed." [15]

And the question is: who is called, fitted, or suited for eremitical life? Is there only one type?

My retreat director and I were discussing my budding attraction to solitude, which had awakened after twenty-five years spent in a monastery. He was well-versed in the Enneagram typology and had even co-authored some popular books on the subject. We agreed that I fit the description of a "Five in the Enneagram" schematic. Such types prefer books to people, are observers of life rather than participants, seek private space, and are often out of touch with their feelings. They are uncomfortable with small talk and appear to be loners, even in a group. The priest frowned and warned me that I was seeking the worst possible form of life for my type. Solitary life would only encourage all the unhealthy tendencies of a "Five." Told that, I hastily dropped any further thought of solitary life as if it were the proverbial hot potato.

Some years later, still wrestling with an attraction that just would not go away, I related my earlier discussion about eremitical life to another retreat director. This director listened thoughtfully and pointed out that being a "Five" *could* mean I was admirably suited to hold my own in solitude since it was a "natural" state for me. Suddenly, the light went on! A genuine call to hermit life (or any other vocation) takes into account a person's natural gifts and tendencies, not to destroy them, but to build on them.

Another reader of *Raven's Bread* commented on the topic of hermit "types" from the viewpoint of someone who had, on occasion, questioned her own balance:

> "I struggled as an undiagnosed adult with Autism/ Asperger Syndrome subtype for many years. I didn't know why I preferred solitude and didn't know why I didn't fit in with many groups of people. I lost many jobs because I just didn't 'fit in.' I guess a lot of people thought I was weird. Finally I found the reason why I was different and a loner. I really think that many or most contemplatives are on the autism spectrum. People with Asperger Syndrome prefer solitude. No, we are not all spiritual people. In fact, I believe the unibomber had Asperger's syndrome!"[16]

Fr. W. Paul Jones offers this observation:

> "I am particularly fascinated with introvert and extrovert personalities and the hermit life. My life is governed by Trappist spirituality, innately introvert in orientation, and yet I am a vigorous extrovert, in love with people and nature, with living and society, and with history. However, I have come to crave yet more—a radical interiority. Not as a place where meaning really is but more perhaps as a matter of growth by walking into my shadow. Therefore I am uneasy about introverts, for whom the hermit life is a 'natural' settling into their self-image in a comfortable manner that does not call them to stretch. Coming at the hermit life from any personality type needs to produce a creative discomfort and is at the heart of yearning, of reaching beyond one's grasp.

The hermit life requires 'conversion,' a catharsis regarding the social lifestyle in which one was raised. This task of emptying out the baggage, personal and societal, is an enormous one, but imperative if one is to 'make it.' To plunge in without some preliminary efforts involving sufficient support, is to find one's self in a nightmare. Monasteries are excellent training grounds in this regard. The danger is that one simply brings with her or him the very things one hopes to leave, yet this time it will be worse, for they come as unrecognizably internalized goals and standards. The temptation to, and the ability for, self-deception is enormous. Perhaps the greatest danger is for this new life to be sour grapes for failure elsewhere."[17]

What we see from the foregoing is that there are a lot of opinions about what psychological traits might be required for someone to have a genuine call to hermit life. To paraphrase a Scriptural passage: Many are attracted to solitude, but few are called to a hermit vocation. We should also begin to see that motivation and maturity are the diagnostic keys to whether someone has a genuine call or a spurious romantic attraction. An experienced director focuses on "why" a person desires a solitary lifestyle, rather than administering a battery of tests!

What is a healthy reason to seek solitude? In *The Forgotten Desert Mothers*, Laura Swan offers keen insight into what should be the goal for a seeker of solitude by elucidating a wonderful and ancient word—"apatheia."

"The goal of the desert journey is apatheia, that quality of the interior spiritual journey in which the inner struggle against inordinate attachments has ceased. Grounded in profound interior freedom, the ascetic is free of the strong pulls of worldly desires. Apatheia is a mature mindfulness, a grounded sensitivity, and keen attention to one's inner world as well as to the world in which one has journeyed. Strong emotions such as anger, fear, or anxiety do not dominate or control the ascetic's inner world—these are disciplined to serve the inner journey rather than disrupt it.

The 'ammas' (desert mothers) teach us to let go of feelings and thoughts that bind us, cravings and addictions that diminish our sense of worth, and attachments to self-imposed perfectionism. Apatheia is nourished by simplicity grounded in abundance of the soul. This simplicity is in balance and harmony with the human community and the created world. To cultivate apatheia, we must be uncluttered in mind and heart, watchful and vigilant about those 'seeping boundaries' where we can be deceived ..."[18]

This does not sound like a recipe for an unbalanced personality, but a rather wonderful formula for healthy living. Individuals who cultivate *apatheia* generally appear quite ordinary, so commonplace, in fact, that they achieve their goal of hiddenness even while living a "visible" life, fulfilling their ordinary duties towards family and friends but with extraordinary grace. If anyone notices something different about these hidden hermits, it is generally their serenity and lack of entanglement in the complexity of society.

Fr. Cornelius Wencel, author of *The Eremitic Life: Encountering God in Silence and Solitude*, writes:

"A person does not go to the desert just on a whim, in a moment of melancholy or boredom. But even if that could be the reason, such a trip would end only in a feeling of absurdity and loss. Somebody who is empty cannot stand up to the emptiness of the desert. Somebody who has not discovered the mysterious depth at the very bottom of his own heart cannot discover the mystery of the desert. So, you cannot discover the desert just by chance, just while running through your errands. The strict logic of the desert calls for your heart's generosity and your total devotion. Finally, it requires your brave decision to face it to the point of risking your life. Only then may you hear in the vast wilderness the echoing mystery that attracts and scares you, that is at the same time a source of fascination and horror. The desert, therefore, invites only those who have seen, at the most elementary level of their existence, that they are called to enter the mystery of their own hearts. The mystery's name is love."[19]

As far is we know, no one has done a precise "psychological study" of men and women who have chosen to live as hermits. However, Marsha Sinetar, in her book *Ordinary People as Monks and Mystics*, applied the observations and terminology of Abraham Maslow to individuals whom she termed "secular monks." She concluded that the traits most of these had in common were consciously cultivated qualities rather than characteristics they were simply born with.

Rev. Eugene Stockton tested Sinetar's work in the desert itself by talking with hermits he met while journeying through the British Isles, Australia, and New Zealand and corresponding with individuals in other English-speaking countries. He summarizes the most remarkable traits these solitaries had in common as follows:

1. All those interviewed evinced a *strong sense of call*. The solitaries spoke of a personal attraction toward the desert, a robust belief in this intimate calling, which for some went back to their childhood when they were content to be "loners."

2. *Passion* characterized many. They spoke with energy and enthusiasm about their call. Phrases such as "a relentless fire," "a primal urge to be one with God," and "a craving to be alone with God alone" characterized their discussion of

their vocation.

3. Though generally warm and welcoming, the hermits interviewed displayed an *emotional distance from society.* They evinced freedom from the pressure of both civil society and "church" concerns. By "emotional distance," Stockton meant that they were not so much *against* the social order as *for* a life that transcended its limits and interests.

4. The solitaries exhibited a strong sense of *autonomy* by ordering their lives, fixing priorities, and omitting what seemed superfluous or inappropriate with great freedom. The more mature displayed an integrated personality marked by ease, urbanity, and balance, as well as by a fair appraisal of their own talents.

5. Generally, the hermits guarded their *self-sufficiency* jealously, not seeking support, whether material or spiritual, from church or family. It was taken for granted that they earned their own keep.

6. They expressed *simplicity* more in a frugal lifestyle than in outright poverty. Possessions and concerns beyond their present needs were seen as so much distracting baggage. Stockton commonly encountered a disarming unconcern regarding provision for old age or sickness.

7. *Stillness and silence* were the treasures and the discipline found in the hermits' simple, uncluttered life. These often characterized even their movements and posture of quiet listening. Some spoke of "a rich emptiness" which nourished both creativity and transparency to God.

8. *Detachment* freed the solitaries to follow their inclinations toward truthful living. It required letting go of everything except aloneness with God. Hermits had a distinct wariness about being drawn into causes, no matter how worthy. For some, their way of life or location deprived them of the regular reception of the sacraments. It did not matter. Spiritually grounded hermits knew that even these are only a means to an end. God alone is the end.

9. Some found, after an initial radical withdrawal, that they

developed a growing sense of *stewardship and service* to the world through prayer or a ministry not detrimental to their essential solitude. Following the daily news became a spur to intercession, as was being available for spiritual guidance. Loving communion, concern, and compassion characterized their relationships.

Fr. Stockton concludes his reflection on the role of hermits or solitaries by saying, "I was reminded of flag-bearers accompanying an army into battle, unarmed, vulnerable, useless—but expected to show others direction and solidarity."[20]

Not Child's Play: Eremitism as a Mid-life Calling

Many of us can agree with this saying of Abba Isidore of Pelusia: "Living without speaking is better than speaking without living. For a person who lives rightly helps us by silence, while one who talks too much merely annoys us. If, however, words and life go hand in hand, it is the perfection of all philosophy."[21] It is also a hallmark of a mature individual.

The 2001 survey of *Raven's Bread* readers proved that the hermit life is normally a mid-life phenomenon. Of one hundred twenty-two respondents, seventy-seven were in their fifties and sixties, while another eighteen were in their seventies and eighties. Forty-seven percent of these were initially attracted to solitude in their late forties and fifties. Another 8 percent chose hermit life when in their sixties and seventies. Only twenty-four respondents followed a hermit calling while in their twenties or thirties, although many respondents were attracted to solitude earlier in life.

These statistics confirm what intuition tells us, namely, that the eremitic vocation is a calling for the mature. This agrees with the ideal life pattern common in the Orient for centuries. People were expected to devote their earlier years to career and family. Only after these responsibilities were discharged did an individual turn his or her mind toward developing the inner life, by either entering a religious community or withdrawing into a life of study and reflection. Others became pilgrim/hermits, traveling the countryside with their begging bowls and prayer wheels.

Today, with an ever-increasing number of healthy seniors, we are finding a corresponding growth in hermit life. Should we be surprised? If we are aware and honest, we may find that, as the years pass, the world functions quite well without our constant oversight. Yes, the day may come when hours pass without our cell phone breaking into song. The constant hum of electronic voices breathlessly announcing news and weather will begin to bore us. We will have reached a major milestone called *mid-life*.

For some of us, this can also be the moment of conversion. We risk a degree of silence during our day and are surprised to hear voices from within bidding us to assess where we are and where we now wish to go. Many readers of *Raven's Bread* describe this moment as both scary and liberating. Their future suddenly promises something more than just progressing through greater degrees of "assisted living" toward full nursing care. They startle family and friends by downsizing, not only their domicile and belongings but also their social circle and commitments.

One of the attractions of hermit life is that we regain dominion over our personal world, both inner and outer. Instead of looking beyond ourselves for distractions and entertainment, we become aware of the riches available to us within our own spirits. We discover what it is like to live in harmony with the seasons; to experience the marvels of the natural world unfolding "in our face." We may be initially bewildered as things spiritual begin to take on an ascendancy we had not accorded to them earlier. Our friends, our children, even our spouses may question our sanity, and we ourselves may be at a loss to adequately describe what is happening. Fr. W. Paul Jones, now living as a hermit in the Ozark hills, addresses this when he writes:

> "Questioned by friends who are mystified by hermits, I respond: There have always been persons who by temperament or situation are alone in the midst of people, without understanding why. But there are others who, living active and vigorous lives in the world, leave it all behind and go into the desert. Such a hermit vocation is not for the

young, for it dare not spring from either idealism or rebellion. Yet there comes a time when one simply becomes tired of pretenses and games. A thirst for integrity takes over, a passion to undertake the austerity of living in complete honesty, without convenience, support, or distraction. This call into solitude is a pilgrimage into darkness and crucifixion, for it annihilates the self we once knew and fostered.

It is a lonely path, hidden from the eyes of the world that neither knows nor cares—certain that the hermit is a failure. Free from the lure of possessions, power, and status, the contemplative life has no practical use or purpose whatever. Hermits are pilgrims, dependent on a pure faith that this is where God would have them be. To walk into silence is to be stripped of certainty that one has an answer to anything; it is where one patiently waits until the questions that once plagued the mind nestle in the soul as friends.

One would hardly enter such a valley of shadows willingly. Yet amidst all the options one has, strangely, there is no choice. Nothing else matters except to be a person of prayer. And some day, standing in the gentle quietness, amid the ashes of dreams and ambition, one may be blessed with the only certitude likely to be given: that to seek is to be sought, and to find is to have been found.

To be drawn into this dread solitude is really an invitation to keep company, especially in society's growing secularism, with God's loneliness—God emptied in total identification with us—ignored, hidden, forgotten, profoundly poor. Drawn by this Presence, the hermit stands with the rejected ones everywhere, living the joy of simplicity; freed to want nothing more than to grow old loving one's God."[22]

In the far land of solitude, we may find we are spontaneously caught up in a running dialogue with spiritual entities that inhabit all that is, including our own souls. This is where we can encounter demons as well as angels. Only if we have enough well-lived life behind us, can we discern the difference. Among the sayings of the Desert Fathers, we find this: "The devil appeared to a brother, in the disguise of an angel of light, and said to him: I am the angel Gabriel and I have been sent to you. However, the brother said to him: 'See if you are being sent to someone else. I certainly do not deserve to have an angel sent to me.' Immediately, the devil disappeared."[23] Obviously this brother had had enough life experience to know himself well, which is another name for humility!

A reader of *Raven's Bread*, who describes himself as the Yinshih of Mole's End, defined what a "yinshih" is:

> "A yinshih was a scholar-recluse once held in honor in the classical Chinese tradition. Many were poets and writers. Some were mystics. Others were retired scholars who sought a quiet life of spirituality and solitude. But what they all had in common was that they had renounced the "red dust of the world" and were dead to worldly ambition and desire for career success. The fortunate ones who lived in the days of the Empire wrote their farewell poems to the world at the age of forty, hung up their scholar's cap, and took refuge on their estates or their little cottages or huts to devote themselves to contemplation, prayer, study, solitude, literature, and friendship.
>
> In times of great societal corruption, yinshihs withdrew from society and public service in order

to preserve their integrity, no matter the cost to themselves. They were not meant for the big stage but preferred the quiet life in the shadows where it is possible to observe the current flowing quietly beneath the waves. Their ministry through writing and personal friendship was with any individual whom God might send their way. They did not see their way as better but simply as a reasonable alternative to a group-oriented, power-driven way of existence. If they had to scratch a living in the world, they strove to do so with integrity and good will.

They cared about their place within this beautiful and mysterious universe that God created; they cared about worthwhile friendships and good poetry. Once they had earned their living in the world, they felt they had the right to their real life after the working day was over. Yinshihs valued, above all, the inner universe of the individual and the private life within, which they held as most holy."[24]

We find a similar tradition among the followers of the Buddha, where donning the saffron robes of a monk is normally reserved for those who have earned that right only after raising their family and fulfilling the challenges life sets before them during their younger years. They were then freed to roam, to speak little and to spread peace wherever they wandered. Their very silence caught people's attention and reminded them of values they had either lost or not yet discovered.

The little frisson of unease we experience in the presence of a silent elder revered among the First Peoples gently rebukes our anxious striving for success, wealth, prestige, and power. We instinctively appreciate the deference accorded to the "grandmothers" among them, women who quietly wield an authority acquired through years of authentic living. The Lore

Keepers who jealously guard and pass on the wisdom enshrined in the tribal store of myths and legends may have begun their initiation as young people, but they are only accorded status in their later years.

The poustiniks of the Russian hinterlands are another example of the universality of the eremitic call and its inextricable linkage with our later years. These men and women live alone but are available for spiritual counsel as well as practical assistance when extra hands are needed. Even the caricature of the gray-bearded hermit attests to our imbedded and spontaneous belief that the risks of solitude are best undertaken only by those with a fair amount of life experience to sustain them. In the Western monastic tradition, even a monk is not granted permission to retire to a hermitage until he has demonstrated his stability and aptitude to live it healthily by first devoting at least twenty years to the busily ordered life of the cloistered round.

To set off safely for the desert, we need an abundance of inner strength, balance, fidelity, and resourcefulness—qualities developed through years of struggle and experience and seldom found in the young. A nun still recalls her abbess shaking her head over some of her bright young ideas and murmuring with a sigh, "You cannot put a gray head on young shoulders."

We spontaneously expect "gray heads" on hermits and solitaries. One of the few truer conceptions of the hermit is that she or he will have acquired a special gift of wisdom and insight into soul-matters. We also expect them to have the compassion and depth of understanding to accept us as we are without condemnation; without judgment. (How few people ever do! And those who do are not so very young.) The elders we seek out are those who look upon us with serenity and kindness, and quite likely, also with a twinkle in their eye.

No, hermit life is not child's play, but a genuine solitary is often wonderfully childlike. They have learned to live without care. How? Because, having already lost most or all of what they had striven to attain earlier in their life, they care little about losing the rest. This is especially true of their reputation as "holy hermits."

Thomas Merton, no doubt speaking from his own experience, offers this mordant reflection:

> "What if, in the end, our hermit turns out to be not even a contemplative in the ordinary sense of the word? He may not have a high degree of prayer. Worse still, he may not even aspire to one. He may not care to be enlightened. He may have some sardonic, silent, hopeless idea that if there is for him some way to enlightenment, it consists of fleeing as far as possible from every suggestion of professional illumination.
>
> It is true that his life must be a life of prayer and meditation, if he is an authentic hermit. For the hermit in our context is purely and simply a man of God. This should be clear. But what prayer! What meditation! Nothing more like bread and water than this interior prayer of his! Utter poverty! Often an incapacity to pray, to see, to hope. Not the sweet passivity which the books extol, but a bitter, arid struggle to press forward through a blinding sandstorm. The hermit, all day and all night, beats his head against a wall of doubt. That is his contemplation.
>
> Do not mistake my meaning. It is not a question of intellectual doubt, an analytical investigation of theological, philosophical, or some other truths. It is something else, a kind of unknowing of his own self, a kind of doubt that questions the very roots of his existence, a doubt which undermines his very reasons for existing and for doing what he does. It is this doubt which reduces him finally to silence, and in the silence which ceases to ask questions, he receives the only certitude he knows: the presence of God

in the midst of uncertainty and nothingness, as the only reality, but as a reality which cannot be placed or identified. Hence the hermit says nothing. He does his work, and is patient (or perhaps impatient, I don't know) but generally he has peace. It is not the world's kind of peace. He is happy, but he never has a good time. He knows where he is going but he is not sure of his way, he just knows by going there. He does not see the way beforehand, and when he arrives, he arrives. His arrivals are usually departures from anything that resembles a "way." That is his way. But he cannot understand it. Neither can we.

Beyond and in all this, he possesses his solitude, the riches of his emptiness, his interior poverty; but of course, it is not a possession. It is an established fact. It is there. It is assured. In fact, it is inescapable. It is everything—his whole life. It contains God, surrounds him with God, and plunges him in God. So great is his poverty that he does not even see God; so great are his riches that he is lost in God and lost to himself. He is never far enough away from God to see him in perspective, or as an object. He is swallowed up in him, and therefore, so to speak, never sees him at all."[25]

So we may ask of the solitary—are you a sage or a psychotic? The more genuine may respond that it doesn't really matter. Both are beloved of God. For all of us, this is the ground for all else in our lives. Perhaps, then, hermits and solitaries exist to encourage us to befriend solitude and humility as true doors or windows onto a place with no name.

In this kind of hermitage, there is peace, the peace which surpasses understanding. Here, then, is the vocation of the true hermit, the genuine solitary, mediating peace to others while absorbing their pain. She or he may speak some words of wisdom or be humbly silent, willing to admit she or he has no answers. In the words of T.S. Eliot, the hermit prays:

"Suffer us not to mock ourselves with falsehood
Teach us to care and not to care.
Teach us to sit still
Even among these rocks.
Our Peace in his will."[26]

A hesychasterion (hermitage) on sheer cliff
Mt. Athos, Greece

Chapter 2

The Re-awakening of Hermit Life in the Twentieth and Twenty-First Centuries

"The solitary is the bearer of the future, of that which is not yet born, of the mystery which lies beyond the circle of lamplight or the edge of the known world. There are some who make raids into this unknown world of mystery and who come back bearing artifacts. These are the creative artists, the poets, who offer us their vision of the mystery. But there are also those who make solitude their home, who travel further into the inner desert, from which they bring back few proofs of their journey. These are the contemplatives, those who are drawn into the heart of the mystery. Contemplatives have no function and no ministry. They are in the world as a fish is in the sea, to use Catherine of Siena's phrase, as part of the mystery. That they are necessary is proven by the fact that they exist in all religious traditions. Contemplatives are not as a rule called to activity, they are useless people and therefore little understood in a world that measures everything by utility and cash value. Unlike the poet they do not return bearing artifacts but remains in the desert, pointing to the mystery, drawing others in."[1]

Eremitical life is reappearing in Western society at a time when deserts and wildernesses are fast disappearing; when the possibility of a gentle life with a relaxed rhythm hardly exists except in the hearts of dreamers and poets—and when the noun "loner" awakens apprehension. But the impulse to seek solitude is as old as humanity itself, spanning the world and all religious traditions. Initially, seeking hermit life was as simple as packing up and moving into the wilderness. Few people questioned the motivation for such a move, believing implicitly in the Spirit who had always called chosen individuals. Judgment on the validity of the call would be in the fruits. Today, however, skepticism and fear are imposing an incredible number of controls on this essentially simple life, demanding reams of reasons for the revival we are presently witnessing.

Fr. Cornelius Wencel writes:

> "Initially, the desert was a place of refuge, a sanctuary that protected (man) from the corruption of the world. For a hermit, the total uselessness, barrenness, and horror of the desert were its chief values. The desert, strange, inaccessible, and even hostile as it may be, frightened away 'patrons of fairs and markets' and at the same time, it served as a shelter for all those who bent their steps toward finding God and, consequently, finding themselves.
>
> Today, the bare land of steppes and deserts has been conquered; the original place of solitude and silence is now covered with pipes, wires, and roads. At present, the desert gives space for seeking money, power, domination, and prestige, not God. That is why the hermits of today are looking for an

inner desert of their hearts more than for a concrete geographical location. What they are looking for is rather silence, prayer, and contemplation; the art of communing with the mystery shining in the soul of each person."[2]

Hermits appear out of synch with society largely because their goals clash so sharply with the "good life" featured in every ad, from sugar to shampoo. With characteristic droll humor, Thomas Merton expands on the preceding insights:

> "In the eyes of our world, the hermit is nothing but a failure. He has to be a failure—we have absolutely no use for him, no place for him. He is outside all our projects, plans, assemblies, movements. We can countenance him as long as he remains only a fiction, or a dream. As soon as he becomes real, we are revolted by his insignificance, his poverty, his shabbiness, his dirt. Even those who consider themselves contemplatives, often cherish a secret contempt for the hermit ... it is the aimlessness of the hermit that is the great scandal. He is shiftless, insecure, in a sense, idle. He looks too much like (let's face it) a mere bum. ... He seems to have a strange inner need to be a bum. In this, we assume, he is a pathological case, no?"[3]

A reader of *Raven's Bread* offers this variation on the cost of being "different" in a society that has equated sanity with similarity. "My life has been a crazy walk to the hermitage. From an ordinary American middle-class beginning, I wandered down many roads, only to leave most of them in favor of an orientation incomprehensible to almost everyone ... Hermit and Hermitage are two orientations not all that popular or welcome today. A hermit suggests an individual who hides out from ordinary life, perhaps placing him or herself in a superior or condescending position. Reaction to the word 'hermit' is very often negative or dismissing. 'Hermitage' has better press, often suggesting a refuge from which an active, involved, fully socialized individual might meet the world. I think of myself as an 'engaged hermit,' someone involved with ordinary worldly issues and pursuits but finding little personal identity there."[4]

Hermit Life Today?

In one issue of *Raven's Bread*, Wood B. Hermit is pictured standing in front of an office which issues various permits and licenses. His eyes roll wildly as he unwinds a scroll several feet long labeled "Hermit Permit." Today, even choosing to simplify our life, to retire into silence and solitude requires a stamp of approval, a certificate attesting that we have filled out all the necessary papers and met all the requirements.

People are curious about hermits, manifesting the same inquisitiveness which draws people on safari to observe potentially dangerous creatures such as wild boars or tigers. Was not the Unabomber a hermit? Are not those sick individuals who suddenly turn a gun on classmates or fellow workers often described as reclusive types or loners? This general apprehension that hermits are dangerous or deranged is not a modern prejudice. It has existed at least since medieval times when people who lived alone, especially women, were often regarded as witches or demon-possessed. Warnings were passed behind raised hands from mouth to mouth as villagers met at the well or local tavern. Today, we can thank the media for spreading tantalizing misinformation about hermits.

Every so often, *Raven's Bread* is approached by an eager journalist planning to write a feature story about hermits in a particular part of the country. Sadly (for the journalist), *Raven's Bread* keeps its mailing list confidential. Occasionally, the journalist will settle for an interview *about* hermits with the publishers of *Raven's Bread*. Both local and national newspapers, Catholic and secular periodicals have run stories on hermits. We have also been approached by writers preparing programs for radio and TV. One of the most sincere (and intelligent) requests for an interview we have received was from an eighth-grade girl doing research on a topic of her choice—hermits. After asking some astute questions, she observed, "I realize that hermits are often poorly represented in the public eye." Even the very young are aware of cultural biases!

Once the media manages to link "hermit" with religious orientation, it still has a field day, focusing on the more dramatic elements in the hermit's life. A 2005 article about hermits in *Newsweek* begins: "In the photo, Agnes Long looks drop-dead gorgeous ... she wears a zebra-stripe bikini, a floppy hat and sunglasses. The sea breeze has blown her platinum hair across her face, and she is smiling. The 1970s picture says she had it all ... today, Agnes Long is a Roman Catholic hermit. She lives alone in a thickly wooded section of Madeline Island; her beloved husband is dead; she hasn't seen her children in years ..."[5]

In the past twenty years, the media seems to have "discovered" that hermits are good press and enjoys writing up colorful accounts of men or women who have pledged their lives to God as solitaries. Should we be surprised? There is a perennial fascination surrounding individuals who go to the extreme in almost any field. An article in the *National Catholic Reporter* in 1996 started its description of the life of Fr. Bede Jagoe,OP, thus: "Jagoe ... lived twenty-three years in Nigeria in a hermitage by a bayou tree on the banks of the Niger ..." Another article in the November 17, 2001 issue of *Today* was entitled "Man Living in Rowhouse, Named 'Canonical Hermit.'" One is tempted to ask why living in a rowhouse enhances the wonder of being a hermit! Hermits and where they live arouse interest across the spectrum, no matter what a person's religious convictions. The only reason there are not more stories about solitaries is that most genuine hermits firmly close their doors on the inquirer with the notebook, camera, or microphone.

Hermits' Historical R/Evolution

The first writer to interview a hermit was St. Athanasius, who wrote a biography of his friend, Anthony, later known as St. Anthony of the Desert. The story of Anthony's choice of a hermitage, (a tomb); his prayer, (nights spent in noisy conflicts with demons) and his relationship with others, (he was loved by all) became the model of hermit hagiography followed from then on.

If we study eremitical developments, we soon learn that the desert has enjoyed periods of great popularity followed by seasons when it falls out of fashion. Hermit life, as a personal calling, transcends denominations and traditions, but it is profoundly influenced by prevailing social conditions. Society is continually changing. Since the industrial revolution, the pace of change has increased exponentially. Demands on the human person have switched from the mainly physical to the increasingly intellectual. More recently, the psyche has been the focus of much development. Beneath these changes lies the spiritual evolution.

Eremitical life is an expression of spirituality, not religion. When a culture is in a period of profound flux, we spontaneously reach for whatever provides us with a sense of stability. If the religious practices to which we have been accustomed fail to meet our needs, we begin to dig more deeply, bypassing inadequate expressions, usually incarnated in communal formulations, to find our individual roots in the Spirit. Since the end of World War II, there has been a gradual revival of hermit life in Western Christianity. This surprising development is too young yet to be thoroughly analyzed or its fruits fully appraised. At this point, all we have is anecdotal information; experience related by those who are living this lifestyle in a culture that does not understand it. *Consider the Ravens* is a study of a "work in progress," written largely by those personally involved in its revival. This is a rare and dramatic moment, allowing us to witness the rebirth of a rare and (sometimes) dramatic lifestyle.

A brief historical overview will help us see the fluctuation in the desert's popularity. Christian eremitism first flourished during the fourth and fifth centuries when hundreds, even thousands, of men and women fled into the deserts around Egypt and Syria. From what were they fleeing? Not persecution, because that had ceased once Christianity became the state religion of the Roman Empire under Constantine. According to some writers, when martyrdom no longer threatened persons who professed The Way, converts sought other ways to give their lives in testimony to their beliefs. "Red martyrdom" (via sword or wild beast) gave way to "white martyrdom," a lifelong commitment to living solely and silently for Christ in the desert. They "baptized" eremitical life, a phenomena which had already existed for hundreds of years in various cultures and countries. These "first hermits" were first only in the sense that the spirituality on which they based their life was found in the Gospels of Christ.

Although eremitic life has never entirely died out, even in the Western church, it has enjoyed cycles of greater and lesser popularity. The fourth century CE marked only the first great migration of Christians into the desert. As time passed, many of these "first" solitaries began to form themselves into small groups, usually around some revered amma or abba (spiritual mother or father). The total solitude that initially marked the lives of the men and women in the desert gradually gave way to a more communitarian style of life and the "cenobium" (the Greek term for "life lived in common") was born. As time progressed, the cenobium grew so that at one period, more than a thousand monks or nuns could be found living in one of these great establishments.

When new Christian solitaries sought out more experienced men and women for advice and reassurance, the oral advice of some of these "ammas and abbas" was collected by their followers and became the core of what today is termed the Sayings or the Wisdom of the desert.

Amma Syncletica is an example of one of these wise women. After her parents' deaths, this well-educated woman, reputed for her beauty, cut her hair, gave away the family wealth to the poor, and moved with her blind sister to the family tomb outside Alexandria. As others began to gather around her, she reluctantly accepted their requests for guidance. Her teachings demonstrate both the simplicity and wisdom that mark the Desert Sayings.

For example, when instructing a neophyte, she taught: "In the beginning, there are a great many battles and a good deal of suffering for those who are advancing towards God and afterwards, ineffable joy. It is like those who wish to light a fire; at first they are choked by the smoke and cry, and by this means obtain what they desire (as it is said: 'Our God is a consuming fire' Heb. 12:24): so we also must kindle the divine fire in ourselves through tears and hard work."[6]

Syncletica's story illustrates how a movement of essential solitaries gradually changed. Thomas Merton wrote: "They (hermits) were not rebels against society. True, they were in a certain sense 'anarchists' and it will do no harm to think of them in that light. They were men (and women) who did not believe in letting themselves be passively guided and ruled by a decadent state, and who believed that there was a way of getting along without slavish dependence on accepted, conventional values ... The Desert Fathers (and Mothers) declined to be ruled by (others) but had no desire to rule over others themselves. ... The society they sought was one where all were truly equal, where the only authority under God was the charismatic authority of wisdom, experience and love. Of course, they acknowledged the authority of their bishops, but the bishops were far away and said little about what went on in the desert."[7]

Inevitably, the Church began to impose legislation on these primitive forms of religious life. "In the East, the 'Novelles' of Justinian (527–565) were a turning point: it (the church) no longer accepted the eremitical life unless it was linked to a community ... so anchorites and recluses gravitated towards the large monasteries. Eventually the passage to a solitary life was seen as a normal crowning point (if not the habitual one) of the monk's spiritual itinerary."[8] Unregulated hermit life fell into disfavor and the numbers diminished dramatically, except in certain places such as Mount Athos where solitaries continued to congregate in huge "lauras," or hermit groupings.

In the West, invasions by barbarians (who often targeted the large and wealthy monasteries) completed the breakdown of the Roman Empire. In the civil chaos that followed, there was a resurgence of the eremitical life, probably because ecclesiastical influence also waned. St. Benedict began his religious life as a hermit around 500 CE near Mount Subiaco on the Italian peninsula and only reluctantly accepted the leadership of the men who had gathered around his hermitage. The rule he wrote always supposed that some of the monks, after twenty or more years of communal life, would desire to go into solitude. If they had proven their maturity and stability, they were to be granted this grace. Thus hermitages were to be found on the extensive grounds of many Benedictine monasteries, including the most famous one founded by Benedict himself on Monte Cassino.

It should be no surprise that hermits soon dotted Great Britain, Ireland, and other Celtic societies, among them Patrick (a missionary hermit), whose heroic feats of penance appealed to a people with a penchant for extremes. Later, as pilgrims and navigators, these Irish anchorites emigrated to the Continent and played a significant role in the re-evangelization of Europe, which had been decimated by plagues and famines. As the so-called Dark Ages waned and civil order was re-established (approximately 1000 CE), the Roman Church also regained its power and influence.

Naturally, it set about regulating religious communities, both the decadent and the freshly emerging, with enterprising fervor.

From the tenth century on, Mount Athos, situated on a rocky peninsula in northern Greece, became a center for eremitical life, especially for monks and nuns from the Orthodox Churches. As time went on, huge monasteries were built there alongside humble cave dwellings of individual hermits who went to great lengths to protect their solitude on the "holy mountain." They often chose a cave accessible only by rope ladders. A hermitage of the early twentieth century was built of corrugated steel plate and suspended by cables from an overhanging cliff. Another group of cliffside dwellings is at Karoulia at the far end of the peninsula, overlooking the sea. Steel cables and/or rope ladders are often needed for access when weather makes the steep rock trails too dangerous.

In Western Europe, hermits living alone in forests or on the far edge of small villages had, in a sporadic manner, preserved the eremitic tradition during the so-called Dark Ages. The twelfth century saw a revival of hermit life, including the foundation of the Carthusian and Camaldolese Orders, which combined the ideals of solitude and community. The Carthusians, established by St. Bruno in 1084CE near Grenoble, France was a community of hermits who lived solitary lives in large structures made up of connected "cells." The hermit-monks saw one another only at rare intervals, spending the majority of their time secluded in their "suite" of two rooms and a walled-in courtyard. The Camaldoli, founded by St. Romuald in the late tenth century in a remote area high in the Apennines, was distinguished by their beehive-shaped hermitages spread out over the monastic property. New candidates lived in the main building and moved by steps toward complete solitude.

In 1160 in Great Britain, St. Aelred of Rievaulx tried to regulate and re-introduce the style of solitude that the earliest desert dwellers had embraced that emphasized a balanced day of "ora et labora." He composed a rule at the request of his older sister who had become a recluse or solitary. She was not walled into a small building attached to a church (that practice developed later) but lived on her own property, confining herself to her own quarters. There is only passing reference in Aelred's writing about such communitarian devotions such as Mass and reception of Communion, which came into popular religious practice only in the 1300s, thanks in large part to the Franciscan movement. Presumably, Aelred's sister depended on the occasional visits of priests for counsel and the sacraments. Her situation is remarkably like that of many hermits today.

Aelred offered his sister the example of the Desert Fathers and Mothers by enumerating the motives which inspired their journey into solitude. These included: "to avoid ruin, to escape injury, to enjoy greater freedom in expressing their ardent longing for Christ's embrace." The early hermits that Aelred recommended for his sister to emulate lived in total in solitude and supported themselves "by the work of their hands." Aelred, a Benedictine abbot, made selective use of the Rule of St. Benedict in formulating the lifestyle of his sister.

Her solitary life was to depend on subsistence work and alms. "Poor with the poor" is Aelred's recommendation as the ideal for a recluse. She was to avoid the temptation to let her solitary life become one of "aimless wandering" by engaging herself in useful work which, however, would not compromise her essential solitude. In order for the recluse to maintain her separation from the world, she is to have "a good woman with an established reputation for virtue" to take care of household matters, including screening of visitors. Aelred, man of the times that he was, also recommended employing a young maiden for errands.

We are given insight into Aelred's disapproval of how some solitaries conducted themselves at this time when he writes: "How seldom nowadays will you find a recluse alone!" He scolds the behavior of the "typical" recluse who "perches at her window to soak up the scandal of a neighborhood gossip, chattering about the local priest's manner, the young girls' frivolities, the self-justified widow, the cuckolding wife. The recluse is amused and entertained her mind and heart turning over the words and scenes hours later, straight through prayer and reflective reading. And soon the recluse invites the demons into her quarters."[9] Abbot Aelred was obviously a man of experience who did not mince words!

Besides living "by the labor of her hands," Aelred's sister is expected to be silent because "therein lies great peace and abundant fruit." She should limit her communications to expressing her physical needs and providing for her spiritual well-being. "The recluse sits alone, listening and speaking to Christ. She must take care to speak to anyone else but rarely, guard what is said, when and how often. Sit in silence, then, my sister, and if the needs of the body and good of your soul compel you to speak, do so briefly with humility and restraint."

When it comes to keeping herself pure, Aelred is blunt in of his opinion of women solitaries he had heard of, if not dealt with personally: "A recluse today is quite satisfied if she preserves bodily chastity, if she is not drawn forth pregnant from her cell, if no infant betray its birth by wailing!" Enough said.

The focus of the central section of Aelred's rule is solitude, a topic about which he preaches to all recluses, not just his sister. "But now, whoever you may be who have given up the world to choose this life of solitude, desiring to be hidden and unseen, to be dead as it were to the world and buried with Christ in his tomb, listen to my words and understand them. Consider carefully why you should prefer solitude to the company of others." He calls this physical, psychological and emotional independence from others a "free sacrifice, a spontaneous offering." [10]

In the thirteenth century, the mendicant orders (Franciscan and Dominican) emerged, offering the faithful the opportunity to become a religious without joining a monastery—at least the men. These early friars carried their "cell" (their large hoods which they raised to shield their face when in prayer) around with them on the road. The female members, however, were confined to one dwelling place, although Clare, Francis' first feminine and most perceptive follower, wrote a Rule which echoed Aelred of Rievaulx's *Rule for a Solitary* rather than the monastic rule of St. Benedict, which was being urged upon her by cardinals and Popes.

About the year 1222, St. Francis wrote a unique document for his men which allowed them to live as hermits whenever they desired. He, himself, spent a significant portion of each year in solitude. Andre Cirino, OFM, noted a striking similarity between

Clare's way of life and that which Francis legislated for his friars in his *Document on Solitude,* leading Cirino to conclude that the life lived at San Damiano by Clare and her sisters was the direct inspiration for Francis' special rule for hermitages. Instead of a monastery, Clare had established a communal hermitage, although she never used this term. The lifestyle she decreed was one of silence which established a rhythm of solitude. In her Rule, she makes reference to the sisters who "are serving outside the monastery," raising the question that some sisters possibly lived separately from the rest of the community, at least part of the time (like Francis' hermit brothers?)

By 1373, when a young anchoress attached to the church of St. Julian in Norwich was experiencing her "Showings" (spiritual revelations), the eremitic life for women was slowly evolving into a lifestyle where they lived almost entirely on alms given to them in exchange for prayers. It was no longer expected that hermits should have to work for their living. What work they did was to provide a break from the round of Offices and other prayers that took up almost eight hours of their day in many cases. In this, their lifestyle resembled that of the choir monks in the great monasteries of their time. These anchoresses were usually served by at least one "virtuous woman" who did the domestic chores, including going to market and carrying out the refuse.

During the period when plagues and religious wars decimated Western Europe, the numbers who embraced independent eremitical life became so insignificant that the lifestyle fell below the radar of canon lawyers and escaped regulation. Although it thus enjoyed greater freedom, solitary life suffered a certain devaluation in the eyes of the faithful when compared to the glorious abbeys, endowed and inhabited mostly by the wealthy and noble. Those who chose hermit life often did so because they lacked the social standing and/or dowry required to enter a more esteemed form of religious life.

What Goes Around, Comes Around

The hermits of the eleventh and twelfth centuries reclaimed the main traits of the desert fathers and mothers: physical separation from society, poverty, simplicity and manual labor. This latter, which had been mostly abandoned by the choir religious in the large monastic establishments, became the specialty, as it were, of hermits. But in a society where social status depended on whether you labored or, by virtue of owning property, you did not, hermits who (of necessity) worked for their livelihood, slipped further down the religious social ladder. A notable change of emphasis in eremitical life taking place place. Manual labor and poverty were superseding spirituality and contemplative prayer as the distinguishing hallmarks of hermits in the eyes of the faithful.

Hermits became servants of the poor, fulfilling tasks boring or distasteful even to the serfs and peasants. They watched over the flocks pastured on far-ranging monastic holdings; they tended ferries and were toll-keepers at bridges, as well as caretakers of the lighthouses along rough and lonely coasts. When it was time to bring in the harvest, villagers expected the local hermit to pitch in, which she or he gladly did in exchange for a portion of the harvest. The solitary also lent assistance to communal projects such as road repair and maintenance of the local water supply. No villager would dream of approaching a nearby monastery for assistance from the monks, but it was commonly expected of the neighborhood hermit.

Female hermits often served as herbalists and providers of healing remedies, as well as a compassionate ear for those who desired their counsel. Many of these women were anchorites, living entirely within a small room built onto the side of a cathedral, with one window looking into the church permitting participation in the liturgy, and another window opening out to the public through which the "holy woman" received alms and other necessities. Some of these women were penitents who chose this way of life as reparation for scandal they had earlier given through lives of public immorality. Occasionally, the choice was imposed rather than freely chosen. This almost guaranteed that many female hermits and anchoresses were not held in the highest esteem! Even so, the life of prayer to which they were pledged was appreciated by people of the locality, who often prided themselves on having a "holy woman" literally attached to their church.

In the words of J.P. Camus, eremitical life seemed to be especially "the refuge of those who, having lost face in the eyes of the world, could not be admitted to serve God in the monasteries ..." Because these hermits and anchorites had no prestige, the hierarchy continued to disregard them. In time, hermit life fell out of religious law completely. The solitary state was no longer accepted as a valid form of consecrated life—a condition which perdured until after the revision of Canon Law in the 1980s.

Thus, during the Middle Ages, eremitic life was mainly lived by laymen and women outside ecclesiastical jurisdiction.

> "Among these 'ministering' hermits were those who fulfilled important duties in the society of the times. Male hermits, often of the peasant class, were found throughout the country dwelling beside the highways, bridges, and fords. Their duties were those of host, guide, light-bearer, laborer, alms-gatherer, turnpike man or bridge-warden. In the towns, hermits would be found living in crypts and abandoned chapels or among ancient foundations of city walls. Some of these sites were granted to men or women in exchange for performing religious duties on behalf of the local townspeople."[11]

Throughout the Christianized world, numerous forms of hermit life developed, taking shape according to local expectations and/or needs. There were (and are) the monks and recluses of Mount Athos in Greece, the poustiniks and forest dwellers of Russia, the anchorites walled up (by choice) in their little room attached to a church; the recluses and hermits who moved further and deeper into the mountains or deserts or forests. For the most part, they lived alone, unconnected to one another. Not all would pass today's tests for balanced personalities. Some appeared so odd or terrifying they were judged by their contemporaries as possessed by evil spirits. However, the percentage of the unbalanced was probably no higher among hermits than in any other segment of society. Most solitaries were responding to an authentic spiritual call, one that has been heard since the beginning of human spirituality.

After the Reformation began in the sixteenth century, the discredit falling upon religious life also tarred what was left of eremitical life, a life form which had already been benignly ignored by the Church for centuries. At this point, for all practical purposes, eremitism ceased to exist as an independent lifestyle. However, it had found a niche among the mendicant orders, most notably with the Franciscans and Carmelites. Other religious groups also began to allow an individual member to adopt eremitical life, either temporarily or permanently.

Ornamental Eremitism

What hermits were and how they lived, once quite familiar, now became shrouded in a kind of mist that fostered romantic images that persist to this day. Peter France, in his book *Hermits: The Insights of Solitude,* noted a practice, which sprang up in England in the early 1700s and lasted almost to the 1900s, of wealthy families establishing a hermit in their formal gardens as an ornamental fixture for the edification and entertainment of guests. He quotes from an architectural guide published in 1767 which featured detailed suggestions for housing these hermits appropriately, ranging from the simple hut "ten feet, nine inches square made of trees and lined with moss" right up to the top of the line, the "Gothic Grotto, made of six rooms lined with shells." A Miss Cynthia Aldburgham remembered that as a child, visitors to her family home could tour the grounds and "be shown a hermit who sat in a cave fondling a skull." Presumably, he was given advance warning when his presence at the cave entrance would be required!

A Mr. Powys of Marcham advertised for a hermit to live in an underground grotto for seven years. The apartments provided were commodious including a cold bath, a chamber organ (!), and as many books as the hermit desired. If he needed any convenience beyond the food provided daily from Mr. Powys' own table, he was to ring a bell and his needs would be met. Ideal as this might sound, no one lasted more than four years. The most long-lasting of these ornamental hermits appears to have been one who "for fourteen years was Hermit to Lord Hill's father; and sat in a cave in that worthy baronet's grounds with an hourglass in one hand and wearing a beard once belonging to an old goat from sunrise to sunset."[12] The romantic image of the melancholy hermit appeared to have little to do with spiritual motivation, even if provided with an organ, presumably to play religious music to enhance the atmosphere!

In the early decades of the twentieth century, religious life entered upon a period of amazing "popularity," with young Catholic men and women flocking to convents and seminaries in unprecedented numbers. The Anglican and Episcopal communions also experienced a similar explosion of candidates for religious life. But in the 1960s, the tide reversed and religious communities suffered a dramatic drop in membership. Fewer and fewer applicants knocked on the doors of convents and seminaries while an alarming number of professed religious began walking out those same doors. Among the many reasons given for these departures was "too much busy-ness." The maintenance of huge institutions and involvement in a plethora of "good works" left many sincere men and women feeling they were working for a God they did not know; a being they had no time to seek.

In the survey which *Raven's Bread* conducted in 2001, we found that more than one-third of the hermits who responded were formerly religious. Many of these revealed they had been faced with the choice of either giving up their attraction to solitary life or leaving their communities. It takes particular courage to break ties with a group that has supported one for (usually) more than twenty years and to strike out on one's own with almost no material resources. In my autobiographical account, *Where God Begins to Be: A Woman's Journey into Solitude*, I wrote that when I left my "monastery in June 1989 to attempt solitary, contemplative life along that steeper way, I had no financial plan or backing. I had only a bargain I had struck with God. I would put first the requirements of contemplative living—the hours for prayer, reflection, for just 'being.' Whatever time might be left over, I would use to earn my keep. My only skills were sewing, writing, and spiritual direction—none of which is especially remunerative." [13]

Fr. Andre Cirino, who co-authored the book *Franciscan Solitude*, observes: "From the beginning, Francis spent time in caves, in solitude. It seems that Francis spent up to half of his converted life in solitude. Clare joined the movement in these early years. Both of them valued solitude and contemplation. And while Francis preserved his experience for us in his *Document on Solitude*, it seems that Clare had already established this same rhythm as she and her sisters lived as contemplatives in the solitude of San Damiano."[14]

Modern Ammas and Abbas

In our search for the modern hermit in the USA, we need not look under desert palms nor into tombs or caves. Most of the solitaries of the past sixty years live hidden in plain sight and are often found via e-mail or cell phone (two means of contact over which they exercise strict control). In the early sixties, when interest in hermit-hood first revived in the U.S., most of those who felt the call began by gathering in small groups, pooling resources, sharing prayer time, and even living space. However, this cenobitic form of solitary life quickly withered and most of these early "lauras" splintered. Only a few of these original groups still exist, with the number of members hovering between two and five at the most. The individualism which marks American life extends to hermit life as well! The revolution in religious life is mirrored in an evolution of eremitical life.

What sparked interest in hermit life in the mid-twentieth century? Many of today's hermits credit the writings of Thomas Merton with sparking their interest and giving substance to the formless desire for solitude they were experiencing. Merton's "success" in obtaining permission to live in a hermitage on the grounds of Gethsemane Abbey alerted people to the existence and value of eremitical life after a period during which it was simply a footnote to religious life, a form that "no longer existed." Merton had spent most of his twenty-seven years in the monastery agitating to be a hermit but only achieved his goal in the last four years of his life. His journals and other writings, however, are seminal to the resurgence of the eremitic movement and form a sobering handbook for the modern day hermit:

> "The solitary life is an arid, rugged purification of the heart. St. Jerome and St. Eucherius have written rhapsodies about the flowering desert but ... the 'eremi cultores,' the 'farmers of the desert sand,' have had less to say about the experience. They have been washed out by dryness, and their burnt lips are weary of speech ... Physical solitude sometimes takes on the aspect of a bitter defeat. It is an earthly paradise only in the imaginations of those who find their solitude in the crowded city, or who are able to be hermits for a few days or a few hours at a time, no more. But the call to perfect solitude is a call to suffering, to darkness, and to annihilation. Yet when a (person) is called to it, she or he prefers this to any earthly paradise. The solitary who no longer communicates with others except for the bare necessities of life is someone with a special and difficult vocation. She or he soon loses all sense of significance for the rest of the world. And yet that significance is great. The hermit has a very real place in a world like ours that has degraded the human person and lost all respect for solitude. But in such a world, the vocation of the hermit is more terrible than ever. In the eyes of our world, the hermit is nothing but a failure. He has to be a failure—we have absolutely no use for him, no place for him."[15]

45

The loneliness of hermit-hood is a major challenge facing anyone who seeks solitude today. It has always been so. The terror of nightly struggles with demons may be replaced by the specter of "living under a bridge," but the torment is the same. The early Christian hermits had the consolation of knowing others were sharing their vocation ... and that it was an honored calling. The men and women of the nineteen-fifties and sixties who were rediscovering eremitical life experienced an exquisite sense of isolation. Most believed they were utterly alone in reviving this ancient lifestyle. They were unaware that they had any company in that silent resurgence of eremitical life.

Seeking guidance, many approached their local bishops, innocent that the very term "hermit" would strike terror in these episcopal shepherds, who tended to view hermits as wolves prowling uncontrolled among their sheep. The eremitic vocation was an unknown quantity arousing suspicion and uncertainty. In the early nineteen-sixties, bishops and spiritual guides equated encouraging a potential hermit with urging someone to leap off a cliff. It was a foolhardy and dangerous undertaking. Seekers of solitude were solemnly warned away from following their desires.

Even when the hermit seeking official approval could demonstrate years of stability in solitary living, many episcopal advisors still worried. About the hermit? No! Sadly, the concern was about the diocese. What financial responsibilities might the church incur? Would they be held legally responsible for someone who (in their eyes) could easily prove unbalanced? Fear, not faith, dominated the chanceries of many Catholic dioceses. Thus, a large number of earnest solitaries were profoundly disappointed when the hierarchy they approached refused to acknowledge or encourage their vocation. The courageous bishop who did welcome a hermit soon found himself overwhelmed by men and women solitaries who had been advised to "betake yourself elsewhere" by other wary diocesan officials.

One of the few bishops open to hermits was Remi De Roo, Bishop of Vancouver, British Columbia. Before long, he had a small colony of hermits on his hands! The Second Vatican Council was in session, so De Roo took advantage of the discussions about religious life to make a significant "intervention" on behalf of hermits. In 1964, he pointed out that "the Latin Church is experiencing an ever-growing renewal of the life of hermits" (a fact many bishops were valiantly trying to ignore). Eremitical life fills a prophetic role in the church, de Roo reminded his colleagues, adding that "the building of an earthly city is not the final end of all things." As a model for all, the hermit, "fleeing the noisy whirlwind of worldly activities, opens his heart to the Holy Spirit in an atmosphere of calm and interior reflection."

De Roo expanded on the ecumenical value of hermit life: "The solitary life of the hermit seems to have known no decline in the East. Its restoration (in the West) would enhance the vitality and inner integrity of that church," as well as joining it more openly with its Orthodox counterpart, which still holds eremitical life in high regard. As a result of this intervention, the new Code of Canon Law, published in 1983, included a provision for eremitical life that officially recognized it as a valid form of consecrated life.

Canon 603:

§1. Besides institutes of consecrated life, the Church recognizes the eremitic or anchoritic life by which the Christian faithful devote their life to the praise of God and the salvation of the world through a stricter separation from the world, the silence of solitude and assiduous prayer and penance.

§2. A hermit is recognized in the law as one dedicated to God in a consecrated life if he or she publicly professes the three evangelical counsels, confirmed by a vow or other sacred bond, in the hands of the diocesan bishop and observes his or her own plan of life under his direction.[16]

Thus, one of the earliest forms of religious life was once again sanctioned in the Roman Church.

Despite this official recognition, eremitism remains an essentially hidden life with hermits few and far between. Like the proverbial needle in the haystack, we will most likely find one when we are "pricked" by the desire ourselves. Where are these people who embrace a calling which is as visible as a pane of clear glass? A way of life existing only to admit the Light while the hermit disappears? They may be living next door to us, the only thing distinguishing them being their quiet retirement; their serene courage to "just stand still" while the world roars by in a blur.

So we ask, why *now*? Because the world has suddenly become unbearably crazy? In truth, it has seemed that way since civilization developed! Abba Anthony, one of the first of the Desert Fathers (251–356 CE) looked at the world around him and remarked: "The time is coming when people will be insane, and when they see someone who is not insane, they will attack that person, saying: 'You are insane because you are not like us.'"[17]

Who among us can look at today's world, wracked by ear-splitting entertainment, consumer-crazed cultures, and suicide bombers, and pronounce it wholly sane? Can we claim that an attraction to solitude, simplicity, and silence is a sign of an unbalanced psyche? Merton's writings demonstrate how even an intelligent and devout man wrestled to comprehend hermit life. He wryly observed: "It has never been either practical or useful to leave all things and follow Christ. And yet it is spiritually prudent." Merton then touched on the heart of the contradiction found in eremitical life: "For many the solitary life is a 'nothing,' a nonentity. The hermit has all the more of a part to play in our world, because he has no proper place in it ... the presence of the hermit, when it is known at all, is no comfort; it is disturbing. He does not even look good. He produces nothing."[18]

The profound social upheaval of Abba Anthony's day is reflected in today's world on an even larger scale. Merton reminds us that it is in such times that solitude gains in popularity. In our confusion and helplessness, we (like Merton) appreciate those first hermits who spoke with such brevity and paradoxical wisdom. "When a brother asked Abba Bessarion, 'What should I do?', the old man replied, 'Keep silence and do not compare yourself with others.'"[19] The genuine hermit is the one who has forgotten he or she is a hermit and just lives from day to day in simple, hidden circumstances with no concern about what others may think of him or her, or even if they do at all.

The hermits who descended on Bishop Remi De Roo's diocese stemmed from a group originating with a Belgian Benedictine, Dom Jacques Winandy, who met up with Fr. Lionel Pare in Martinique. Fr. Pare discussed his strong calling to a life of solitude with Dom Winandy, and within a year, the two had built hermitages for themselves under the aegis of the local bishop. Word spread and other monks, hungering for solitude, came to join them. Several moves later, Dom Winandy settled with his growing colony of hermits on Vancouver Island in the nineteen-sixties. Before long, the group divided, with several of the monks seeking out even more solitary dwellings in various parts of British Columbia. Dom Jacques eventually returned to Europe and settled in a seventeenth century hermitage. There he remained for more than twenty-five years, praying and studying, giving counsel and becoming the European proponent of hermit life that his friend and correspondent, Thomas Merton, was becoming in the States.

Among the members of the hermit colony which Winandy had led to British Columbia was Charles Brandt, a one-time Anglican priest who had converted to Roman Catholicism. When the group dispersed, Brandt applied for ordination as a hermit-priest in the Catholic Church. Bishop Remy de Roo acceded to his request, and Brandt became the first man to be ordained specifically for eremitical life in two hundred years! He moved to a site on the Oyster River, where he made his living as a book binder and photographer. His passion for saving the environment caused him to spearhead a movement to save the Oyster River from the ravages of "progress" along its banks. Brandt fostered a vision of a "sacramental commons" in which all living things, including humans, have their dignity and place. Such a reverent view of life is a customary fruit of hermit life well-lived.

Among the early revivals of hermit life in the U.S. is the group founded by Carmelite priest Fr. William McNamara, who had been encouraged by a prophetic audience with Pope John XXIII.

In 1960, he established the Spiritual Life Institute, the American Catholic Church's first hermit community. Set up in Arizona's dramatic red-rock country, the hermits developed a simple rhythm of solitude, communal prayer and occasional apostolic work. In 1967, Tessa Bielecki arrived and took over the editorial duties for their periodical, *Desert Call*, one of the first publications focusing on eremitical life.

With inspired foresight, Fr. William quietly initiated a profound shift in the community. The all-male institute began to accept women into its core group. With firm commitments to celibacy and solitary life, the members lived in separate hermitages, copying an ancient form of eremitical life—the hermit laura. "As the community spread to Nova Scotia in 1972, Colorado in 1983 and Ireland in 1995, the witness of celibate men and women living with deep bonds of love has been a hopeful witness to a society embarked on a painful, convulsive search for whole, healthy, mutually affirming relationships between men and women."[20] After the turn of the century, a small lay community, including families, was added to the Spiritual Life Institute. Yurts were built on a forty-acre tract near New Pine Creek, Oregon.

Inspired by these and other examples, various Carmelite sisters began to feel that the cloistered community life the Church had imposed on them over the centuries was a betrayal of the original charism of the Order. The primitive rule, composed by St. Albert, envisioned a hermit group with the prophet Elijah as its spiritual founder. Not surprisingly, most Carmelite superiors were not supportive of this desire to return to the more eremitical form of the Carmelite Order. This view engendered a small exodus as courageous women departed from various priories to begin their Carmelite life anew as hermits.

Among these were Sisters Angela Wyncott and Imelda Knierim. They were from different Carmelite houses but met in an experimental group at Mt. Carmel Hermitage, Amery, Wisconsin in the nineteen-eighties. They developed a mutually agreeable form of life and eventually found a permanent home in the diocese of St. Cloud, Minnesota. Although numerous women have lived with them for varying periods of time, their number has always remained small, a phenomenon true of almost all modern hermit groups.

Even the Amery group, founded in 1980, has had only two permanent members over the years. The evolution that group underwent is not uncommon. When the hermit community was first established, it was modeled on the canonical structure of religious life, having an elected superior, and with new members undergoing a period of initiation before being fully accepted into the group. This proved unworkable with such small numbers, and the sisters went separate ways in 1987. One of the original members, Sr. Kristine Haugen, however, envisioned a different life-form, an association of individual hermits. Each was personally accountable only to the bishop and his or her spiritual guide. They would live in separate dwellings around a chapel and common house, focusing on a life of solitude and intense prayer while collaborating for mutual support. In 1995, Bishop Raphael M. Filiss approved this modern hermit laura as a Public Association of Catholic Women.

Another Carmelite nun desirous of embracing eremitical life in the early days of the movement was Sr. Judith of God. Her calling did not include joining a group of hermits but rather she took the more radical step of living entirely on her own in solitude. Judith's priory permitted her to test her vocation while retaining affiliation with the Carmelite Order. But once the new Canon recognizing eremitism as a genuine form of religious life was promulgated in 1983, Sister Judith was granted the rare privilege of transferring her vows from the Carmelite Order to her bishop, becoming one of the first canonical hermits in the U.S. She lives alone in Star of the Sea Hermitage in Okefenokee, Florida.

About the same time, in the Arkansas Ouchita Mountains, a former opera singer was following a similar course. Sr. Alice Ruth Carr had left secular life for a Carmelite Priory at the age of fifty. After ten years, she too received permission to test the life of solitude. After a period of time had elapsed, the Bishop of Little Rock presided over the ceremony in which she was dispensed from her Carmelite commitment and was received as a canonical hermit in the diocese. She lives in a fixer-upper mobile home next to a monastery, where she follows the Liturgy and attends daily Mass.

Not all hermits were originally members of established religious communities before they turned to the solitary life. Men and women from all walks of life have heard the siren call of solitude and begun to withdraw from their jobs and professional careers. Among these were Joan Sutherland, a teacher; Janice Sehgal, a nurse anesthetist; and a former advertising executive in Arkansas who now (paradoxically!) chooses to remain anonymous.

Among the priests choosing the eremitical life are men such as Fr. Dick Hite, who shared a property with hermit-sister Joan Sutherland in rural West Virginia until her death in 2005. Sister Joan was among the earliest secular women to feel the call to eremitical life. After a brief period in a religious community, Joan packed her earthly goods in her vehicle and headed toward West Virginia with $100 in her wallet. When her car broke down in a small town and repairs wiped out her "nest egg," she took this as a sign from God and stayed put! She eked out a living by doing housework for people who were away from home during the day (a common source of income for many hermits). Another hermit "kept himself" by cemetery maintenance—of course, the "residents" here remained while he worked but did not disturb his solitude!

Sister Joan so impressed Bp. Hodges, the local ordinary of Wheeling, West Virginia, that in 1975, he accepted her profession as a Consecrated Virgin and gave her some land, where she erected a simple hermitage. Numerous people turned to her for advice in discerning their own call to eremitical life, among them a religious priest, Fr. Dick Hite. With permission from his superior, he built himself a hermitage on another section of the same property. The two hermits planted a huge garden and lived off the generous yield they cultivated, picked, and preserved. For cash needs, Fr. Dick would do temp work at a nearby vineyard, while Joan depended on donations, which never failed her.

It is interesting to note that Dick was not required to give up his association with his religious community. The 2001 survey by *Raven's Bread* revealed that while nearly all women religious who became hermits were required to leave their communities, very few male religious or diocesan priests were asked to do so. One priest, a former Trappist, chose to do so when he established himself on a tract of land in east Texas. Over the years, he has built several hermitages on the property, one of which is occupied by a woman who had originally sought out Sr. Joan while in the throes of discernment about her own eremitical call. The most difficult decision she had to make was choosing between her religious community or solitude. Like many others, she took the leap with only God as her "golden parachute." As proves to be the norm, her "financial plan" only deployed *after* she had taken the leap and counted to ten.

Among the earlier female hermits was Sr. Cecilia Wilms, who "accidentally" discovered her solitary calling in 1968, when she took a leave of absence for health reasons from her Cistercian Abbey of Our Lady of the Redwoods in California. As she later wrote, she "discovered a solitary way to live her monastic commitment in the desert of the city in the service of God and the Church." Wilms lived in a poor neighborhood of Spokane, Washington, within walking distance of Gonzaga University, where she earned a small stipend working in the library. At the time, Church law did not yet provide for a public commitment to the hermit way of life, so Cecilia received the Consecration of Virgins (as had Sr. Joan) through the ministry of Bishop Bernard Topel in 1974. She died in 1998 in her apartment hermitage.

In 1982, a Franciscan sister, Carole Marie Kelly, was embarking on a new adventure in the Monterey diocese in California. Although spiritually drawn to solitude, she had to battle both fears and misconceptions when she moved into a small cabin among the redwoods. Her fears ranged from finding a frog in the kitchen sink to worrying that a tree was about to fall on her roof. She collected her experiences and reflections into a book she wrote in solitude, *Symbols of Inner Truth: Uncovering the Spiritual Meaning of Experience*. She, and many others, found writing an occupation that fit well with the eremitical calling.

Maggie Ross, nom de plume for Sister Martha Reeves, an Episcopal nun, agrees wholeheartedly. She found her ideal hermitage in a basement flat of Christ Church, Oxford, after first discovering the beauty of solitude while working in a vineyard. She spent three years in a retreat house, then wandered, experimenting with a wilderness existence. When Sister Martha was formally recognized as a hermit, she did so with the most ecumenical support we have so far discovered. In 1980, New York Episcopal Bishop Paul Moore received her profession as a solitary in the Cathedral of St. John the Divine "with the co-sponsorship of Roman Catholic Cistercians and Anglican Franciscans."

Maggie Ross's writing has benefited from her easy access to the libraries of Oxford and brought her international fame. She quips that no one endows hermits these days but has some hope that author Ross might donate her earnings to local hermit Martha Reeves!

Hermits, as noted, can be found everywhere. Richard Withers, a former bicycle repairman, now lives in a tiny row house he bought for $1 from the city of Philadelphia and renovated into a hermitage. He made national news in 2001 when Cardinal Anthony Bevilacqua formally recognized him as a canonical hermit in the diocese.

Picturesque Gary Robertson, a one-time postal worker, dropped out of society in 1975 to follow a simple tenet common among hermits: *God is in the silence.* When "rediscovered" by society through an article in the *Winnipeg Free Press* in 2001, Robertson more nearly resembled the stereotypical image of a hermit than most, with his long hair and full beard. A journalist described him as looking like a cross between Old Man Winter, Merlin the Magician, and the prophet Elijah! His hermitage, self-constructed from salvaged materials, is a landmark for canoeists on the Whitemouth River in Manitoba. The overall inspiration of his eclectic living space is Byzantine with stained-glass windows, Russian-style icons and a steeple.

Home to another long-time hermit is a two-story yurt along a coastal road in Maine. Sr. Betty Edl, who makes her meager living through weaving, said, "I live the life of a contemplative ... and want a living space open to the elements, a sacred space filled with warmth. The circularness of the yurt gives you a sense of openness and emptiness. It's very peaceful." She was quoted while gratefully watching a group of volunteers, buffeted by cold winds and blowing snow, knock together the framework for her hermitage in November 2000.

Across the country in Arkansas, five hermits live in a variety of dwellings: an A-frame cottage, a mobile home, an apartment, and a cabin built expressly for use as a hermitage. Interestingly, not all hermits are as sedentary as this brief resume of hermitages implies. In the Middle Ages, hermit-pilgrims were not uncommon. These were men and women whose "hermitages" were the roads crisscrossing Europe to various pilgrimage sites.

One *Raven's Bread* reader, a man whose hermitage is in Pennsylvania during the winter months, spends most of the summer weeks walking the roads in a patched blue denim robe with a staff surmounted by a cross. He jingles as his sandals carry him along, a variety of prayer beads and bells swinging from his rope belt. He carefully plans his itinerary so that he will be able to visit monasteries, churches, and holy sites as he travels, but that is not his main purpose. His God-given goal is to carry the Cross and an Icon of Mary along the roads as a visible reminder of God's presence to all who notice him. And he does attract notice! Not surprisingly, he finds that the attention he generates is more accepting of his purpose in Europe and the U.K. than in the U.S. All unaware, he risked more than he realized the year his pilgrimage took him south into the Bible Belt and through areas where the KKK still flourished. He found good angels, however, who directed him onto safe roads.

These verbal snapshots of modern ammas and abbas reveal the paradoxical truth that the only thing all hermits have in common is that each one's lifestyle is completely unique. An oft-quoted saying is that "there are as many ways of living the hermit life as there are people doing it." There is no set rule for a hermit's daily life, dwelling, or spiritual orientation. Hermits can be anything, but mainly they are unconventional and atypical. Some will also label them peculiar and bizarre. Ask hermits themselves and the answer you will get is usually silence.

Counting Spotted Owls

Numbers do not reveal much about individuals but are useful when studying trends. Even a single unexpected number can cause some eyebrows to shoot up. Who would have thought that a simple newsletter like *Raven's Bread*, written specifically for solitaries, would, without any advertising or promotion, attract a thousand subscribers, not to mention the thousands more throughout the world who discover it online? "I had no idea there were that many hermits in the world!" a new reader writes to the editors, implying this strange lifestyle might somehow be contagious. In a sense, it is. The main service that this little bulletin offers is to offer hermits recognition; allowing them to discover the real truth of their lives and that they are neither alone nor particularly odd.

In truth, *Raven's Bread* readers are only the tip of the iceberg when it comes to totaling the religious solitaries in the world, even in just the Western hemisphere. How *do* you count people who have no wish to be found; who are not joiners, who deliberately avoid attention? Would that we could enlist a group of volunteer "hermit-spotters" and turn them loose with notebooks in a likely environment. But hermits, like spotted owls, are skilled at blending into their environment!

Could we treat *Raven's Bread* like bait to draw hermits to one site? In one sense, that is what we do, at least in the U.S. and other English-speaking countries. Certainly not all hermits, even in the English-speaking world, subscribe to *Raven's Bread.* Nor do most of the "lurkers" who secretly read the newsletter online identify themselves. Further, not all hermitages are furnished with computers, although it is apparent that the number of hermits with computers is growing. (A question for the next survey!)

Hermits! How many, and where are they? At best, hermits are un-countable, not mention un-accountable. There is no Bureau of Registered Hermits, nor is there even a single, agreed-upon definition that would fit all those who identify themselves as hermits. It is impossible to even *guess-timate* the true number of individuals who consider themselves hermits. By nature and inclination, hermits are not joiners, so very few form themselves into groups or belong to associations. *Raven's Bread* readers had a lively discussion about "membership" among themselves when this topic was raised by one subscriber. Conclusion? A firm nay!

Those who go into the desert understand this addendum found in a book written by an anonymous Camaldolese monk: "You have sensed the call to disappear, as do all lovers. Hermits themselves are, in fact, lovers who have chosen the shade, a life hidden with Jesus in God ... It ought to be enough for us to be known by God."[21]

A modern-day hermit responded in a similar vein when a *Raven's Bread* reader suggested that all subscribers belong to some loosely formed organization. "We who are exiles from the world live in our alone-ness with the One who called us. We do not need to be recognized by the world; we pray for the world unknown to the world."[22] This topic evoked some other comments, including these: "You mentioned that some readers ask if we are a community or becoming something that persons can join. No way! Those of us who have been in communities know that as soon as you organize people, individual spiritual development goes into cardiac arrest. *Raven's Bread* proves that the Holy Spirit is moving in new and sweeping waves of inspiration today. It is the growth and healing and maturing of the individual that is the feeding ground of the Holy Spirit. There are contemplatives in this world. We know them through this lovely newsletter. Each must walk alone because each has his and her own life-journey. We cannot walk lockstep with swarms of others ..."[23]

Another reader rounded out the idea of spiritual connections thus:

> "You have created a unifier among the diversity of hermits. In this world of individuality and ego dominance, the mystery of humanity as the organically connected Mystical Body is seldom

expressed. Even quantum physics is witness to our spiritual union with each other. Hermits especially need that interconnected concept engraved on their psyche via contemplative experience because it is imperative to realize how our personal search for an intimate love union with God in solitary prayer impacts on all humanity. Otherwise our hermit life would not make sense in the light of the Good News to love both God and others ..."[24]

Survey Surprises

The following data is derived from a survey which *Raven's Bread* circulated in 2001. The newsletter (established in its present form in 1997) has grown into an international publication with subscribers in twenty-seven countries outside of the U.S. Most have found the newsletter through the Web site (www.op.org/ ravensbread) which, thanks to the number of hits it continually receives, stays near the top of search engines when eremitical life is researched.

Of the six-hundred surveys sent out, 22 percent of them were returned, an extraordinary response rate, considering that those surveyed were persons who have chosen a life defined by hiddenness. The information so generously contributed has produced the most comprehensive picture of contemporary hermit life that exists to date—a picture full of surprises no one could have predicted.

Who chooses eremitic life, men or women? At what age? Statistics from the 2001 survey indicate that approximately one-third of present day hermits are men. At least one-third of the *respondents* were men, which was a surprisingly accurate representation. On the full mailing list in 2007, the percentage was the same—three hundred-fifty men and five hundred-ninety women. Of both women and men, the largest number was between fifty and fifty-nine years of age—again about one-third of those represented. Another quarter was between sixty and sixty-nine.

There was about an equal number in their fourth decade and seventh decade. Only six were in their twenties, with eighteen in their thirties.

How long had these individuals lived in solitude? The years seemed fewer than expected until one considers how recent this revival actually is. The earliest dates cited are in the 1950s. We also discovered that this is a lifestyle usually entered upon at mid-life. Eremitism is clearly a "second career" calling.

Hermits with canonical recognition cannot date back further than 1983, when the revised Code of Canon Law, containing the Canon re-establishing eremitism as an official form of Consecrated Life, took effect. Sixteen percent of the respondents surveyed were canonically recognized by 2001. Of these, some had just been recognized; others had lived as canonical hermits for more than twenty years. The other 84 percent who have been "just doing it" informed *Raven's Bread* that they had lived as hermits anywhere from two months to thirty years.

Discussing age naturally leads to questions of mental and physical health. To the degree that self-reporting can be considered reliable, hermits generally enjoy better-than-average health, with 47 percent stating their health is good, while another 38 percent claim excellent health! The bits of humor which consistently turned up in the survey responses are an indirect testimony to robust mental health. On the other hand, a chronic illness or disability has, on occasion, been the impetus behind some individual's choice of hermit life.

Sister Laurel O'Neal, writing from Stillsong Hermitage in 1989, explored eremitism as a call specifically for the chronically ill and disabled:

> "I believe the call to chronic illness itself is, at least for some, an eremitic vocation to 'being sick within the Church' as a solitary whose witness value is potentially more profound because such a person is generally more severely tyrannized by our capitalistic and materialistic world ... Humanity possesses not only great richness,

but an innate poverty as well, which is both ineluctable and inescapable—a poverty in the face of which one must either find that God is enough or despair. The chronically ill witness to the fact that their lives are of infinite value not because of 'who' they are or what they do, but because God himself regards them as precious ... In accepting their situation as a call to solitude, the chronically ill person is freed from the false sense of self provided by society, and in the wilderness of the hermitage assumes that identity which God himself individually bestows. Such a solitary says clearly that every person, at whatever stage in his or her own life, can do the same thing—a task and challenge which eventually eludes none of us."[26]

The predominance of middle-aged solitaries results from the fact, already noted, that most hermits awaken to their calling only after having already lived one cycle of life. Even when there has been a lifelong attraction to solitude, most would-be hermits are not free to follow it in their younger years. For others, it is a gradual recognition: "I slowly came to recognize my call in the restlessness I felt when I was deprived of the solitude my spirit craved,"[27] one respondent admitted. Another wrote: "I began to be drawn toward solitude gradually since my college years."[28] Some experienced a growing attraction to what they called "the prayer of quiet where I encountered God's presence in silence and darkness."[29] Others discovered a sacred presence while "hiking alone in the mountains and forest."[30]

There were those for whom maturing was required: "I knew my call from age nineteen. Over the years, I could see I was not spiritually ready. I knew it would be a disaster if I attempted it. At age sixty-seven, I felt ripe and eager to take the plunge. It has proved a good decision."[31] For others, life's challenges were the catalyst which awakened them to the inner voice heard best in silence. "Through tragedies I became willing to listen to my inner life ..." and "When I became disabled and had to leave my vocation as pastor, I went into total isolation, where I offered prayer for others, following a monastic rhythm. I visited a local hermit monk and became aware God was calling me to hermit life."[32]

Occasionally, the recognition is sudden, almost irresistible. One respondent wrote that it was part of a "profound conversion experience many years ago",[33] an experience which changed his entire life. Another hermit discovered his calling "while making a retreat with the Carmelite hermits in Nova Scotia. I realized 'This is what I long for!'"[34] "My call to eremitic life," wrote another hermit, "came as a shock. I entered into a deep contemplative state and realized I am a natural celibate. This was later clarified as Solitary."[35] One writer could point to the actual date and place: "I recognized my hermit call instantly on December 24, 1976; time has confirmed my original certitude and is the proof of the authenticity of that awakening."[36]

Where do hermits live? Because *Raven's Bread* is published only in English, survey respondents were largely English-language speakers. The questionnaire went to readers in Canada, Australia, New Zealand, Great Britain, Wales, and Scotland, as well as to Ireland, that "Isle of Saints" where hermits have always been found on its misty moors and craggy coasts. One hermit wrote from Iona, an island normally too rugged for year-round residents, but ideal for hermits. The wild winds which scour the Orkney Isles also provide a natural barrier to all but the hardiest of souls, many of these "natural" solitaries.

Islands around the world apparently appeal to hermits, to judge by the mailing list for *Raven's Bread*, which has subscribers in Malaysia and the Philippines, Iceland and Qatar. Copies fly out to larger "islands," including New Zealand and Australia, where hermits are found dwelling in the rugged Outback and craggy peaks of these more sparsely settled lands.

Contrary to the caricature of hermits habitually living in damp caves or inaccessible forests, only two respondents to the survey reported living in an actual wilderness setting. There *are* cave-dwelling hermits in the Himalayan Mountains, as well hermit-monks on that long-famous stronghold of eremitism, Mount Athos in Greece. However, in the contemporary renewal of hermit life that we are exploring, thirty-one percent of solitaries report living in rural rather than wilderness settings. Nearly double that number indicated that they live in urban/ suburban sites. We are continually surprised to receive new subscriptions from denizens in the "canyons" of New York City, proving that genuine solitude can be found in one of the busiest metropolises in the world! In fact, several of our respondents had chosen solitary life in the inner-city areas, where they identified with the poorest of the poor. At the opposite end of the spectrum, we found eremites dwelling on the grounds of a religious community—a seemingly ideal situation, though not one easily available to persons.

Are most hermits Roman Catholic? Perhaps the most truthful response is that the majority of hermits are roaming Catholics! The word "catholic" is defined as "universal" or "broad in sympathies"—a term which ideally describes the genuine religious solitary. In today's world, where many spiritual people have tried a variety of "religions," the question of denominations is extremely complex. Survey respondents fell into at least five declared church denominations: Roman Catholic (69 percent), Anglican (6 percent), Episcopalian (4 percent), and about five individuals came from Baptist, Lutheran, Society of Friends, and Zen Buddhist affiliations. Many of these respondents "sampled" more than one religious group before finding a spirituality which nourished their hearts and supported their eremitical calling.

What proved most interesting was the end result: a majority of hermits live an amalgam of religious practices and beliefs, spirituality more than a religion. Even those most outwardly bonded to a particular church admitted to an inner freedom, a broad spectrum of practices exceeding any single denomination. In other words, hermits have rediscovered what the first Christians wrote about themselves in The Acts of the Apostles: that Christianity was a Way, not a religion. Eremitism, too, is a Way, a spiritual way of life that can be expressed in a variety of religions or none at all, if one defines religion in its strictest terms.

Among Christians, only the Catholic and Episcopal churches offer the possibility of official status to persons living as hermits. As has been noted, the Roman Catholic Church has promulgated a new canon in 1983, attempting to catch up with a work-in-progress. As a result, hermits may now be recognized officially as living a Consecrated Life. Not all Catholic hermits choose to be so recognized and many who wished to, found themselves facing numerous obstacles. Of the eighty-five Roman Catholic respondents, only seventeen (20 percent) have made public profession of eremitic life under Canon 603. Nearly all of the eighty-five others had tried to be officially accepted by their Local Ordinary as canonical hermits but had not completed the process for various reasons—the most predominant of which was refusal by the bishop to accept hermits in his jurisdiction.

Are all hermits considered religious? Should they be? Questions abound, depending on whom you are interrogating. Among the hermits who responded to the survey, sixty-two were single laypersons; thirty-four were members of religious communities; fourteen were ordained ministers; and (most surprisingly) twenty-two were married persons. (If you have just done some rapid math, you have discovered that these numbers add up to one hundred thirty-two instead of the one hundred twenty-two respondents. Why? The survey design allowed people to check off all the categories which applied to them, such as ordained and married, etc.)

Among the ordained hermits were nine Roman Catholic priests, one Anglican priest, one Charismatic Catholic priest, one Lutheran minister, and two deacons—one in the Maronite Rite and one (self-described) Disciple of Christ. Of the thirty-four who were members of religious congregations, the following Orders were represented: Benedictine (nine), Franciscan (seven), Carmelite (four), Augustinian (two), Dominican (two), and one each of the Jesuit, Carthusian, Cistercian, Camaldolese, and Salesian religious families. Most of these, already considered Consecrated Religious by the Church, did not seek further recognition as hermits under Canon 603.

For hermits not affiliated with Catholicism, the religious community which attracted the largest number (still quite small) is the Oblates of Julian of Norwich. Dame Julian was a fourteenth-century anchorite about whom little is known beyond the brief information gleaned from the one book she wrote: *Showings.* Today, an eremitic group with members across the U.K. and North America take her as their patroness and model. These members live their own separate lives, joined by promises made to a "Mother" who keeps the group informed and united. Both men and women can join, married and single. Most of these Oblates are laypeople, not members of the clergy. Many hermits in the Roman Catholic Church are also Oblates, Third Order members, or seculars who are formally associated with established religious Orders.

Lay solitaries who had made a public profession of vows, recognized by ecclesial authority, numbered thirty-six in the survey. Thirty of these have pledged the three Evangelical Counsels of Poverty, Chastity, and Obedience; six more have made profession only of Chastity and Obedience. One hermit has encompassed the vowed life under a public Promise of Simplicity. A larger number of solitaries (thirty-eight) have made private vows or promises witnessed by priests, spiritual guides, or other qualified persons. Six respondents had made their solemn promises or vows to the group of which they were members.

What to conclude? At the time of the survey (2001), the only certainty seemed to be that "many are (being) called" to solitude but "few are chosen" by the church for official recognition. Thus, hermits and solitaries are responding to the invitation from the Spirit to go into the desert with whatever resources available to them. New lifestyles are emerging without significant support from official leadership. This grassroots modality has always been the norm when significant developments were taking place in the Church. Later, the Church would legitimize the movement if it had proven to be "of the Spirit." Time is the ultimate test of the validity of a call. Life on the top of a pillar proved to be a passing attraction, while a hidden life on the edge of society, chosen for spiritual reasons, passed the test of time, having always existed in various forms and places.

When we sent out the survey to hermits in 2001, we had a number of unconscious assumptions about the results, but we tried not to tilt the questions in favor of any particular outcome. Asking what had proven most problematic for the hermit, we listed the following options to check off or not, as the case might be:

- ↑ Finding a suitable (affordable) site?
- ↑ Establishing adequate income from appropriate work?
- ↑ Finding supportive spiritual guidance?
- ↑ Relationships with Church representatives?
- ↑ Physical health?
- ↑ Personal fears and/or insecurities?

Much to our surprise, most of the hermits checked "finding good spiritual guidance" and "equitable relationship with church representatives" as their biggest problem areas. We *had* expected the majority of the potential hermits' troubles to be focused on more material problems. Actually, only 22 percent reported "housing," and 20 percent indicated "adequate income" as their major obstacle. Obviously, most hermits were not as troubled about these more mundane problems as they were with difficulties impinging on their spiritual lives.

The renewal of hermit life has not only surprised Church authorities but seems to have disturbed many of them. Clearly this movement was not mandated by the hierarchy. Perhaps it is lack of control that causes ecclesiastical unease? Twenty-six percent of hermit-respondents named "relationship with the Church" as their major source of distress, while an equal percentage cited the difficulty of finding appropriate spiritual guidance. In other words, 52 percent found ecclesial personnel to be more of a hindrance than a help! When one aspiring hermit, with thirty years in a cloister on her resume, sought permission from the Church to live in solitude, four separate dioceses denied her the right to live within their jurisdiction. In this case, even such evident proof of stability and devotion was not sufficient to gain ecclesiastical approval.

If you are wondering why the bishops in question were unwilling to accept this nun into their diocese as a hermit, the problem was ... yes, money! Bishops appear to be suspicious of a financial plan which begins: *"Consider the lilies..."!* They prefer to have a prospective hermit (if they have one at all) demonstrate that he or she is financially independent. The above-mentioned hermit was not asking for financial support, even for the very modest lifestyle she envisioned, but this fact apparently sailed right past the Episcopal ear, cocked to hear only what was of most concern. Sad. Fortunately, not all hierarchs suffer from (spiritual) hearing loss, and many hermits have been welcomed into dioceses ... though not without undergoing rigorous testing.

Although finding a suitable place to live was initially a problem for 20 percent of the hermits surveyed, all eventually did establish themselves without much assistance from religious authorities. Even the question of finding adequate income proved less troublesome than dealing with the hierarchy! Obviously the saying attributed to the desert father Blessed Macarius still is the "book of life" for most prospective hermits: "This is the truth: if a monk regards contempt as praise, poverty as riches, and hunger as a feast, he will never die."[37]

Since eremitical life is second-half of life vocation, many hermits are recipients of social security or some similar program. However, such governmental provisions only guarantee a life well below the poverty level. Income for the majority (58%) who responded to the survey was less than $20,000 per year. Forty-one hermits got by on $10,000 or less. One admitted that, at times, she scanned the sidewalks for dropped change, which she could use to buy bread at a local food bank.

Recognition, praise, and approval are goals foreign to the genuine hermit. The hidden "farmer of the desert sands" embraces the words of St. Paul: "May I never boast of anything but the cross of our Lord Jesus Christ! Through it the world has been crucified to me and I to the world. It means nothing whether one is circumcised (recognized) or not. All that matters is that one is created anew!"(Gal. 6:14,15.). Newly created desert gardeners of the twenty-first century still cultivate age-old fruits of solitude.

Prayer Mountain Hermitage (of hand-hewn logs)
East Texas, USA

Chapter 3

Don't Just Do Something ...
Be There

Saint Syncletica said: "Just as the bird who abandons the eggs she was sitting on prevents them from hatching, so the monk or nun grows cold and their faith dies when they go from one place to another."[1] The "nest" which this desert mother warmed all her life (she died of cancer in her eighties) was the family tomb, situated outside Alexandria in Macedonia. Laura Swan, commenting on this challenge which Amma Syncletica laid out for those who gathered around her, says, "The desert journey is one inch long and many miles deep. Inward is the only direction of travel."[2] Being is the mode of hermit life, not doing, not achieving.

Stability: At the Still Point

"I sigh at life once set upon
and always moving on.
Once all depended on east or west
Or up and down.
But once my moving began to stop,
'twas then it was
my start began." [3]

An alternate term for hermit is "anchorite," one who is anchored to one site. Recently, a long-time hermit addressed the editors of *Raven's Bread* about the necessity for hermits to "just stay put." "I have always felt the need of exterior stability, of being rooted in one place to nurture and awaken the home of God's Presence within us. Stability is like a sacrament, where the exterior is an outward sign of inward grace somewhat like the finger pointing to the moon. Whoever the wag was who said, 'My favorite place is somewhere else' just didn't get it. Unfortunately, such a guy is very much invested in our always-on-the-move cultural value system. We might call him Mr. Mobile and he's married to Mrs. Delta with two hyperactive kids—daughter, Lexus, and son, GMC."[4]

Present to the Presence

The above writer also identified with Wood B. Hermit, whose hermitage was depicted with the sign, "Harvest Home," in the Thanksgiving 2006 issue of *Raven's Bread*. Not only were seasonal fruits and veggies piled on Wood B.'s rickety porch but a line of hungry banqueters approached, including some ordinarily unwelcome guests such as skunks and mice. The point of this visual parable is that a hermitage is open and home to not only the saintly but also to the unattractive, both without and within one's self. It is impossible to live authentically in solitude without welcoming some less-than-lovely guests at one's banquet table with the Lord.

Wood B. Hermit

"ALL ARE SAFELY GATHERED IN...."

Among these unexpected (and initially unacceptable table-mates) will be personal traits such as selfishness, prejudice, rage, gluttony, lust, duplicity, and other variations on the Seven Capital Sins, familiar to anyone who grew up with Catholic catechism. Many of these ingrained "habits" are not visible to the one in whose company they are found until that person slows down sufficiently to become aware of who is present with him or her when she or he is supposedly alone in the hermitage. As more than one solitary has discovered, life can be quite disconcerting when there is no one around to blame but ...!

Stability, a normal hallmark of hermit life, is profoundly challenging, so much so that, in and of itself, it can weed out the genuine hermit from the merely romantic. It is so easy to dream of living in the ideal hermitage and to believe that our spiritual life will automatically deepen and grow once we find that perfect dwelling. We can spend so much time moving around in search of it that we lose our focus on the God, who is everywhere. A contributor to *Raven's Bread* once wrote: "I have been studying about the eremitical life and planning to live it for years. I was on the point of purchasing some forested acres on which to build a cabin. It was very isolated yet only about five miles to town, which is important since I have given up driving, but the deal fell through. Now I am buying a small cottage only about one mile from town, with close neighbors but in a very quiet area on the bank of a river. It is not my ideal, for I wanted a place that would almost force me to be alone. Nothing like a five-mile 'wall' to discourage frivolous visits! Will I still be a hermit, or am I downgraded to recluse? Such weighty questions!"[5]

This solitary demonstrates the authenticity of his or her eremitical vocation in several unmistakable ways, not least of which is a healthy sense of humor, an indication of mental balance. She or he doesn't permit the search for the ideal to become so all-consuming that it is impossible to settle for the less-than-perfect solution when it is found. Labels are not of the essence. A perceptive spiritual director should congratulate hermit-penitents who know their areas of weakness, their "demons," as the Desert Fathers would say.

What makes *stability* so crucial to the eremitical life is that it nurtures *awareness*, the gift of being alive to the present moment. The longer one lives in a particular place, the more one discovers that it is continually changing. We live on a slope which overlooks a valley with the Great Smoky Mountains not far distant. Only after watching the seasons play over the ridges and mountains across the way for more than twelve years can we say with certainty that the scenes framed by our windows have never been replicated, even once. Shadows shift, revealing clefts and hollows invisible in the dawn light. Mists swirl around peaks like the mythical "smoke" for which these ancient peaks were named. The apple green of April is not the deep emerald of June or the subtle blue-green of August that precedes the golden glow of October slopes. Continually changing ensembles of birds serenade us with new melodies as they follow the ancient fly-ways north and south each year. Peepers in the ditches delight us in the early spring, while cicadas and locusts provide us with the singing nights of early autumn. Would we have noticed these subtle shifts if we were not truly "here" but continually looking for "somewhere else?"

Nature's changes aren't the most significant discoveries the solitary makes as he or she settles into one site. A hermit for more than thirty years uses a wonderful phrase that expresses the essence of hermit life—being "present to the presence." Genuine hermit life is an existence lived deeply within but also beyond time and place. A true solitary is so immersed in the *now* that time and space are no longer the parameters of his or her life. Such "largeness" of life hit Thomas Merton in 1958. Five years earlier, Merton had obtained permission to use an empty woodshed (which he christened St. Anne's) as an occasional hermitage. At the beginning of Lent 1958, he wrote:

> "If I were only here always! The Spirit is alone here with the silence of the world. St. Anne's is like a rampart between two existences. On one side, I know the community to which I must return. And I can return to it with love. But to return seems like a waste. It is a waste I offer to God. On the other side is the great wilderness of silence in which, perhaps, I might never speak to anyone but God again, as long as I live ..."[6]

Attempting to explain the value of, or reason for, eremitical life is somewhat like calling the steps of a dance, the rhythm to which no one but the caller knows. Only the listener can hear the voice of the caller. Being a listener is what hermit life is all about, a listener who believes with his or her whole life that there is a dance to attend to—as T. S. Eliot intuited.

> "At the still point of the turning world, neither flesh, nor fleshless;
> Neither from nor towards; at the still point, there the dance is ...
> Except for the point, the still point,

There would be no dance, and there is only the dance.
I can only say, there we have been: but I cannot say where.
And I cannot say, how long, for that is to place it in time."[7]

At St. Anne's, Merton echoed Eliot's discovery, demonstrating his true stability and the awareness that it fosters:

"It seems to me that this is what I have been waiting for and looking for all my life, and now I have stumbled into it quite by accident. Now, for the first time, I am aware of what happens to a man who has really found his place in the scheme of things. With tremendous relief, I have discovered that I no longer need to pretend. Because, when you have not found what you are looking for, you pretend in your eagerness, to have found it. You act as if you had found it. You spend your time telling yourself what you have found and yet do not want.

I do not have to buy St. Anne's. I do not have to sell myself to myself here. Everything that was ever real in me has come back to life in this doorway wide open to the sky! I no longer have to trample myself down, cut myself in half, throw part of me out the window and keep pushing the rest of myself away.

In the silence of St. Anne's, everything has come together in unity and the unity is not my unity but Yours, O Father of peace. I recognize in myself the child who walked all over Sussex (I did not know I was looking for this shanty, or that I would one day find it.) All the countries of the world are one under this sky; I no longer need to travel. Half a mile away is the monastery with the landscape of hills, which haunted me for eleven years with uncertainty. I knew I had come to stay but never really believed it, and the hills seemed to speak, at all times, of some other country. The quiet landscape of St. Anne's speaks of no other country. It speaks the word 'longanimity', going on and on and on; and having nothing."[8]

Doing or Being (With Dishes and Things)

Thich Nhat Hanh, Buddhist monk and writer, is revered for his teachings on mindfulness, teachings which have been concretized in a wonderful story he told about a guest at his table, Jim Forest.

> "Last winter, Jim came to visit. I usually wash the dishes after we've finished the evening meal, before sitting down and drinking tea with everyone else. One night, he asked if he might do the dishes. I said, 'Go ahead, but if you wash the dishes, you must know the way to wash them.' Jim replied, 'Come on, you think I don't know how to wash the dishes?'
>
> I answered, 'There are two ways to wash the dishes. The first is to wash the dishes in order to have clean dishes, and the second is to wash the dishes in order to wash the dishes.' Jim was delighted and said, 'I choose the second way—to wash the dishes to wash the dishes.' From then on, he knew how to wash the dishes. I transferred the 'responsibility' to him for an entire week.
>
> If while washing dishes, we think only of the cup of tea that awaits us, thus hurrying to get the dishes out of the way as if they were a nuisance, then we

are not 'washing the dishes to wash the dishes'. What's more, we are not alive during the time we are washing the dishes. In fact, we are completely incapable of realizing the miracle of life while standing at the sink. If we can't wash the dishes, the chances are we won't be able to drink our tea either. While drinking the cup of tea, we will only be thinking of other things, barely aware of the cup in our hands. Thus we are sucked away into the future—and we are incapable of actually living one minute of life."[9]

To do what one is doing with full awareness is the great virtue of Mindfulness. Hanh's personal definition reads: "Mindfulness: the energy to be *here* and to witness deeply everything that happens in the present moment, aware of what is going on within and without."[10] If one is struggling to find a practical reason, a purpose or value, for eremitical life, this "dishwashing parable" comes perilously close to exposing our utter failure to comprehend the hidden heart of desert living.

We are hermits in order to be hermits. If we are seeking the desert to find silence and tranquility of heart, or in order to become holy, or even because we believe we can praise God more perfectly in solitude, we will never become a true hermit. Genuine eremitical life is, as we have already noted, an exercise in transparency. Merton often wrote that he wished to "disappear." Ironically, his last word on the day he was found electrocuted in his room in Bangkok was, "And now I will disappear." For many, they were a prophetic statement by a man who went into the desert "not to find Christ but because he believed that was where Christ wanted to find him."[11]

W. Paul Jones looks at the desert calling this way:
"What do I do now?
I listen to water
Falling
Into the
Gentleness
Of being.

Nothing
More
Than liquid sound.
And I, at last,
Want nothing
More."[1]

With Open Eyes

A "famous hermit" is a contradiction in terms and arouses serious questions about the validity of that particular hermit's call. Thomas Merton is a case in point. Many people, including his best friends, questioned how Tom could honestly call himself a hermit. Not only did he engage in a vast correspondence and entertain well-known persons at the monastery with extraordinary frequency, but he had a habit of slipping off into nearby Bardstown to catch jazz bands he admired when they were playing in the local bars.

But Merton did not try to kid himself, nor did he hold up *his* lifestyle as a model for others. What was carefully buried beneath these occasionally "scandalous" breaks in his solitude was a life of continuous searching for God, a search he eventually realized was initiated by God, the relentless Hound of Heaven. Prominent in the mindfulness which Merton cultivated, particularly through his journaling, was a brutal honesty. "The great thing is to go on, miserably, honestly, recognizing one's dishonesty and one's cowardice, not covering it with any kind of sham, betraying nothing and faithful to one's search for the real truth that does not need any kind of declaration."[13]

Surprisingly, one of the best known "mystical" incidents recorded in Merton's journals did not take place in his hermitage but in downtown Louisville.

> "Yesterday (March 18, 1958) at the corner of Fourth and Walnut, in the center of the shopping district, I was suddenly overwhelmed with the realization that I loved all those people, that they were mine and I theirs, that we could not be alien to one

another even though we were total strangers. It was like waking from a dream of separateness, of spurious self-isolation in a special world, the world of renunciation and supposed holiness. The whole illusion of a separate holy existence is a dream.

This sense of liberation from an illusory difference was such a relief and such a joy to me that I almost laughed out loud. And I suppose my happiness could have taken form in the words: Thank God! Thank God! That I *am* like other men, that I am only a man among others. It is a glorious destiny to be a member of the human race, though it is a race dedicated to many absurdities and one which makes many terrible mistakes: yet, with all that, God Himself gloried in becoming a member of the human race. Such a commonplace realization suddenly seemed like news that one holds the winning ticket in a cosmic sweepstake. How can the sorrows and stupidities of the human condition overwhelm me? Now I realize what we all are. And if only everybody could realize this! But it cannot be explained. There is no way of telling people that they are all walking around shining like the sun."[14]

Why can we not tell everyone this glorious truth? Because too few of us love ourselves sufficiently to believe it. The true hermit loves himself in God so purely and so passionately that he can see and embrace himself and others as wondrous works of a Great Lover, even when he clearly sees himself and his companions daubed with all the "sorrows and stupidities" of the human condition.

Also a true hermit has slipped the trap of considering him or herself as different from the rest of humanity. I venture to state that the more genuine the recluse is, the less distinctive she or he will appear. Hermits do not need manners or garb that will cause people to give them any particular notice at the rare times when they must be "out and about" doing the normal round of shopping, banking, dropping off the trash, or going to church. An authentic hermit knows him or herself too well to wish to be pointed out from across the street with the exclamation: "Oh, there goes that hermit ..."

Loving the Unlovely

At the heart of genuine eremitism lie two virtues that the desert abbas and ammas traditionally emphasized—compassion and hospitality. "What? Why?" I exclaimed to myself when I first heard this. It didn't fit my initial image of the hermit I hoped to become. Had you asked *me*, I would have listed virtues like humility, prayer and penance, etc. rather than such principles of basic humanity. It didn't take me many months in the hermitage to discover that the spiritual practices I associated with eremitism honed and challenged my compassion ... and after a few more months, people seeking God started out by seeking the hermit. Sheesh! Where is my peaceful solitude? My hours of uninterrupted prayer and contemplation? The sweet silence filled only with bird song and the wind sighing in the trees? In truth, I did have all of the above, but intertwined with them was the Spirit's plan for my eremitical life.

The "Plan of Life" over which so many aspiring hermits labor before ever moving into their first hermitage is normally tried and tossed to the winds only weeks after literal practice is attempted. As the pages flutter away, many find themselves holding a book they hadn't written and, quite possibly, had not read very intensively up to that time. The Bible ... brimming over with all the wisdom and guidance that a serious hermit needs.

It is true that prayer and penance, silence and solitude are essential to eremitical life, but the "problem" with these virtues is that they cannot be easily measured. We all know that once a person stands up and declares he or she is humble ... well, suddenly that is questionable! The desert ammas and abbas used many stories to impress on those who came to them for a "word" of guidance, the difficulty (and uselessness) of gauging progress in virtue. "A brother asked Abba Tithoes, 'Which way leads to humility?' The old man said, 'The way of humility is this: self-control, prayer, and thinking yourself inferior to all creatures.'"[15]

"Theophilus of holy memory, Bishop of Alexandria, journeyed to Scete, and the brethren coming together said to Abba Pambo: 'Say a word or two to the bishop, that his soul may be edified in this place. The elder replied: 'If he is not edified by my silence, there is no hope that he will be edified by my words.'"[16] The same Abba Pambo had learned his lessons from Abba Anthony, the earliest of known Desert Fathers: "Abba Pambo questioned Abba Anthony, saying: 'What ought I to do?' And the elder replied: 'Have no confidence in your own virtuousness. Do not worry about a thing once it has been done. Control your tongue and your belly.'"[17] To confuse matters further for those sincere disciples who needed to know if they were good hermits or not, a friend of Abba Anthony, Abba Nisteros the Great, was asked: "What good work shall I do?" And he replied: "Not all works are alike. For Scripture says that Abraham was hospitable and God was with him. Elias loved solitary prayer, and God was with him. And David was humble, and God was with him. Therefore, whatever you see your soul to desire according to God, do that thing, and you shall keep your heart safe."[18] Safe from what? Any certitude about one's holiness, it would seem!

The paradoxical replies which the abbas and ammas passed on to their disciples appear to be deliberately designed to squelch the kind of pride that wishes to measure our state of soul. None of us can know for sure how genuine our prayer is or how helpful to ourselves or others our penitential practices may be. But compassion, the inevitable fruit of humble prayer and honest penance, is more easily recognized. Thus, many of the stories about the holy abbas and ammas show them breaking their fast in order to eat with a guest who might be embarrassed dining alone or washing the feet of visitors who were known "sinners." Or welcoming intruders who have obviously come to steal what little these desert dwellers might have had. Everyone loves the story of how "some bandits came to the hermitage of an old man and said: 'We have come to take away everything in your cell.' And he said: 'Take whatever you see, my sons.' Then they took whatever they found in the cell and went away. But they left behind a little bag that was out of sight. The old man picked it up, and ran after them, shouting, 'My sons, take this! You forgot it!'"[19]

Why did the desert fathers and mothers continually focus their followers on compassion and hospitality? Every genuine solitary has one major goal: to become more and more transparent to the Holy, and in so doing, lose sight of him or herself. Those parts of our less-than-holy self (which any serious hermit meets all too soon!) have to be embraced like a wandering Magdalene. Instead of being horrified that there is room in our hermitage for such a disgraceful bedfellow, we must learn to spread clean sheets for this embarrassing companion who has stumbled into the desert along with us. If we try to drive away this shadow self, we will only hear a voice crying out in the night, like the lonely coyotes, disturbingly beautiful as they howl at the unreachable moon.

In truth, these unwanted parts of ourselves can be compared to the familiar Zen warning about the finger pointing toward the moon. We should not make the mistake of focusing on the finger and missing the glory of Sister Moon. These scruffy creatures can lead us toward the moon only when we give up trying to drive them away and simply love them. Yes, *love* them! The mindfulness which grows over years of cultivating our soul-garden in the desert sands should make us increasingly compassionate—with others as well as with ourselves.

How best can a hermit practice hospitality? One of the better-known mandates for hermits, passed down from the earliest desert fathers and mothers is: "Receive all visitors with hospitality, and let them go in peace."[20] The secret wisdom of this saying lies in the lack of possessiveness which characterizes the authentic hermit. Even a beginning solitary knows that we can become possessive of our reputation as a holy hermit. We can err by safe-guarding our solitude so resolutely that we refuse to receive a genuine seeker. Or we can carry on displaying our "wisdom" long after our guest should have been on their way in peace!

A *Raven's Bread* contributor offered this bit of modern day desert wisdom: "The beginning hermit must extend hospitality with wary prudence, especially to members of the opposite sex. If someone 'must' unburden themselves to you, don't let them squat in your living room while they tell their life story for hours. Tell them you can only listen to their troubles while you both go for a walk, or while they help you work in your garden in the hot sun! It helps to keep only minimal and uncomfortable stools or benches on your hermitage porch when you must sit with someone. Remember that most people don't want your advice, they just want someone to listen to them and offer encouragement. Extend this charity without damaging your own soul, for the devil loves to subvert your charity by luring you into imprudence. The hermit must learn when to say no to spiritual and emotional leeches eager to take advantage of our patient courtesy."[21]

There is a kind of harmful hospitality that a solitary may stumble into, due to lack of self-knowledge. We are familiar with the saying about entertaining angels unaware. We sometimes entertain the opposite when we cling to faults and failings which blind us to our true motivation. They are a familiar part of our personality, identifying us as us. "I am just not a patient person. Blowing my top is simply a natural response for someone like me." Or "Perfection is not my thing—good enough will do." These attitudes are so easy to believe, and they justify all kinds of spiritual weakness. We wouldn't consistently welcome someone who always arrived at mealtime and left before the dishes were washed. Why then should we allow selfishness or self-indulgence to continue in residence in our hermitage? On the other hand, we shouldn't insist that we will only open our door to a potential guest if they arrive with halo aglow! We practice true hospitality when we not only welcome the unlovely at inconvenient times but when we also see that they leave with their peace enhanced (even if our own is in temporary disarray!)

Such manifestations of unselfish love can and do happen in every hermitage where a solitary acknowledges all those parts of him or herself which might once have been classed with the Untouchables (the lowest class of people in the now abolished caste system in India). When we see ourselves honestly, warts and all, we are in a much better position to be compassionately open to all sincere seekers. We have wiped out a class system we unconsciously carry around within us and, by doing so, have allowed one of the finer virtues of eremitic life to blossom. Compassion, as we soon learn, is not an isolated virtue, but a way of life. Our eyes are opened; we are awakened; and all beings are welcomed unconditionally.

We fold our hands and bow before the beauty which we suddenly discover surrounds us.

In Eastern traditions, this recognition is called enlightenment. The monk or hermit who achieves enlightenment is wakened to love, a discovery which once experienced, leaves one indelibly changed. Love is the heart of hermit life—all else is merely window dressing. A Wood B. Hermit sketch from *Raven's Bread* shows the patched and scruffy "hermit" standing at a gate, puzzling over a sign. Behind him, placards reading "Keep Out" and "No Trespassing" are nailed to trees, but on the gate itself, the sign has been altered. "Trespassers Will Be Prosecuted" now reads: "Trespassers Will Be Forgiven." Beneath Wood B., stopped dead in his barefoot tracks, are the words from John 14,3: "That where I am, you also may be ..." Wood B. is no longer an unwanted bum, warned away and threatened, but a welcome guest. It no longer matters what he looks like or who he is or what he may have done. He is invited in!

Wood B. Hermit

"That where I am, you also may be ..." Jn. 14.3

Welcome is the word we all long to hear. Once we walk through that invisible gate of compassion/welcome, also known as forgiveness, our craving to be known for anything beyond our simple humanity diminishes. Even the need to be recognized (by oneself or others) as a hermit ceases to matter. Accomplishing anything that others might admire (even writing a book!) loses the value it once had. We agree completely with an "elder who was asked by a certain soldier if God would forgive a sinner, and he said to him: 'Tell me, beloved, if your cloak is torn, will you throw it away?' The soldier replied and said: 'No, I will mend it and put it back on.' The elder said to him: 'If you take care of your cloak, will God not be merciful to his own image?'"[22]

Skipping to the fourteenth century, we encounter the anchoress Julian of Norwich, writing: "So I saw how Christ has compassion on us because of sin, and just as I was before filled full of pain and compassion on account of Christ's Passion, so I was now in part filled with compassion of all my fellow Christians, because he loves very dearly the people who will be saved, that is to say, God's servants."[23]

Julian's writings languished, largely unappreciated, in monastic libraries for centuries, in part because her insight into God's pity and love clashed so strongly with the "death and doom" motif dominating popular preaching in her day. Few medieval Christians dared accept a God that Julian described thus: "I saw that he is to us everything which is good and comforting for our help. He is our clothing, who wraps and enfolds us for love, embraces us and shelters us, surrounds us for his love, which is so tender that he may never desert us. And so in this sight, I saw that he is everything which is good."[24]

If Julian had been writing with an eye toward fame, she would have had to take a very long view of it since it would be six centuries before her words were "discovered." The comfort and optimism which permeates *Showings* are as desperately needed in the twenty-first century as they were in the fourteenth when the Black Death, the Hundred Years' War, famine, and civil chaos ravaged western Europe. Who of us does not need to hear: "I may make all things well, and I can make all things well, and I shall make all things well, and I will make all things well; and you will see yourself that every kind of thing will be well."[25] Julian lived tranquilly, knowing that hers was a God who wishes us to be enclosed in rest and in peace.[26]

Commenting on the stories of some Cistercian hermits, Merton observed:

"The hermits never seemed to get anywhere. Their stories were inconclusive. They seemed to have died before finding out what they were supposed to achieve. Now I understand there is something important about the very incompleteness of Blessed Conrad, hermit in Palestine, by St. Bernard's permission. Starts home for Clairvaux when he hears St. Bernard is dying. Gets to Italy and hears St. Bernard is dead. Settles in a wayside chapel outside Bari and dies there. What an untidily unplanned life! No order, no sense, no system, no climax. Like a book without punctuation that suddenly ends in the middle of a sentence. Yet I know that those are the books I really like!

Blessed Conrad cannot possibly be solidified or ossified in history. He can perhaps be caught and held in a picture, but he is like a photograph of a bird in flight—too accurate to look the way a flying bird seems to appear to us. We never saw the wings in that position. Such is the solitary vocation. For of all men, the solitary knows least where he is going, and yet is more sure, for there is one thing he cannot doubt; he travels where God is leading him. That is precisely why he doesn't know the way. And that too is why, to most other men, the way is something of a scandal."[27]

Merton's own life seems to have ended "in the middle of a sentence!" He was planning to give another talk later that day discussing all that the contemplatives, or mystics, of the world have in common. Instead, he demonstrated their most common of all human traits—their mortality. He shared the water of his own hard-won wisdom, not in a little pitcher of an hour's conference but in the flood of his life, poured out for many.

Hermitage of St. Francis, a two-story yurt
Stockton Springs, Maine, USA

Chapter 4

A Solitary Canon

Marvel of marvels, the Catholic Church decided, due to a groundbreaking "intervention" during Vatican Council II, that hermits exist! And in sufficient numbers that they should not be allowed to run around unregulated. They deserved to be recognized in canon law. So canonists were appointed to devise some directives for this growing number of people. They did so, and second marvel, wrote everything necessary into *one* canon! This solitary canon for solitaries and its brevity are both welcome.

This dry but most complete definition of a hermit that is imbedded in Canon 603 was written into the 1983 revision of Roman Catholic Church law. What it says and what it doesn't say is remarkable.

> §1. "The church recognizes the eremitic or anchoritic life by which the Christian faithful devote their life to the praise of God and salvation of the world through a stricter separation from the world, the silence of solitude, and assiduous prayer and penance.
>
> §2. A hermit is recognized in the law as one dedicated to God in a consecrated life if he or she

publicly professes the three evangelical counsels, confirmed by a vow or other sacred bond, in the hands of the diocesan bishop and observes his or her own plan of life under his direction."

Part 1: Wild Dogma for the Desert

Although this definition is tailored for members of the Church of Rome, its marvelous simplicity is helpful in defining the basics of hermit life anywhere. The other remarkable point about this definition is the lack of specificity in regard to how these various elements are to be practiced. For once, church law assumes that the subjects of the law are capable of thinking on their own! Hermits are allowed to define how they will live the three distinct elements mentioned: a) stricter separation from the world; b) the silence of solitude; and c) assiduous prayer and penance, in the Plan of Life which they themselves develop.

I sometimes envision canon lawyers, charged by their bishops to provide them with a clear definition of how the genuine hermit should live, ripping out their hair in frustration. They may either feel overwhelmed or empowered, depending on their own nature when faced with such a task. Some canon lawyers comb the law looking for a precise and irrefutable statement; others rub hands gleefully, contemplating an opportunity to write their own bit of "law." Rarely do they consider asking the hermit who has applied for public recognition how they are, in fact, living their eremitical life. They might have more hair left if they recognized the wisdom of the Roman canonists who so deftly drafted this bit of legalese.

There is a wondrous latitude here, permitting the hermit or anchorite to meet the intent of the canon in a broad spectrum of lifestyles. One commentary on Canon 603 notes that these "terms are centuries old and describe the solitaries of the fourth century as much as they do those of the twenty-first."[1]

An important fact to be noted is that the Canon uses the terms "eremitic" and "anchoritic" interchangeably, something with which many people will take issue. Originally, these terms were synonymous. It was only in the late Middle Ages that the term "anchorite" came to mean someone who lived in "deeper reclusion" than most hermits. It was also applied to the solitary who was "anchored" to one place in a very obvious manner, such as those who lived walled in a room attached to a church.

One of the better known anchorites is Julian of Norwich, whom we have cited earlier. Actually, she was such an extremely hidden hermit that even her real name has been lost. She is simply known by the name of the church building to which she was (literally) attached in the city of Norwich. Very few details of her life have been preserved beyond the date of the most important event that ever touched her—the series of revelations she received on May 13, 1373, when she was "thirty and a half years old." The next twenty-some years of her life were spent pondering the meaning of what she had been "shown" and writing down her reflections. Thus, she was anchored, not only in place but also in spirit.

Today, an anchorite is recognized as living the vow of stability more rigorously than the eremite. The majority of solitaries accept this distinction. Thomas Merton clarified the issue a bit more when he wrote that a recluse and a hermit are two separate animals, the recluse being equated with the anchorite.

Separation from the World

For once, church law and popular imagination are in agreement. "The characteristic element of the eremitical life is 'stricter separation from the world' in its most literal sense, and the canon places this first among the three essential elements of this state."[2] The first way to identify a hermit is to take note of his or her separation from society. But many people live alone, so we may legitimately ask what makes a hermit so different from, say, a lonely old person whose family has died off and friends have likewise disappeared.

The "difference" is brought out in the following sentence in the same commentary: "At the inspiration of the Holy Spirit, the hermit goes apart from society in order to live with God alone, thus having little contact with others except for reasons of charity or necessity."[3] The hermit is different from one who lives alone because of circumstances over which he or she has no control, because the decision to live apart from others is a freely made. The genuine desert dweller perceives his or her lifestyle as a calling, one with a profoundly spiritual motivation. There is a goal to his or her separation from society—a purpose which may be known to him or her alone, secret, holy, world-affecting. These are the hermits who do not seek public recognition of their vocation. Other eremites may choose to give witness to their calling by making their choice known through a ceremonial acceptance by church authorities. The requirements for this are treated in the second paragraph of Canon 603.

In a periodical devoted to canonical studies, researcher Helen Macdonald elaborated on the critical sine qua non that makes a hermit a hermit:

> "The characteristic element of the eremitical life is 'stricter separation from the world' in its most literal sense, and the canon places this first among the three essential elements of this state. The hermit is separated externally from society, but in fact lives a life which is in profound communion with the whole Church and, in deed, with all humankind; living apart from society is an expression of the solitary dimension of all. The solitary, though she or he may spend much time alone, is never alone in the sense of being alienated from humanity, unaware of its sorrows and agonies and unmindful of his or her responsibility to bring persons, known and unknown, to the mercy of God through prayer. As 'watchmen upon the walls,' the solitaries are at the point where the forces of evil and the redemptive power of God meet. The life of the hermit is an icon of the solitude of all Christians in their solitude before God. This separation from the world is the hallmark of the hermit."[4]

Another commentator offers examples of sites he considers ideal for the eremitic life—"far from urban habitations, on the shore of the sea, on an island, in the mountains, or in the forest."[5] This certainly fits the romantic picture that most people cherish about the hermit ... but does it describe where most contemporary hermits are actually living?

In the 2001 *Raven's Bread* survey, the majority of respondents reported living in urban and suburban settings. Only two reported living in a wilderness setting. (Sorry, Fr. Beyer!) However, there were some quite creative sites mentioned, including a houseboat, an apartment above a group home for recovering crack addicts, and a remodeled building bought from a city after it had been condemned. One enterprising hermit literally picked up his hermitage and walked it to a new site, board by board!

Canon 603 is refreshing in the flexibility it gives the hermit to define his or her separation from the world. Rome usually placed strict controls on religious, particularly nuns. For example, until the 1983 revision of Canon Law, the only times that nuns were permitted to leave their monastery without first obtaining permission were fire, flood, and invasion by soldiers! Even under such extreme conditions, it was implied that the nuns *should* apply for Episcopal leave. (Was it assumed that each monastery housed a nun with prophetic gifts?) Regarding anchorites, I vividly recall an etching depicting a veiled figure behind a small barred window supposedly dispensing wise counsel in exchange for the basket of bread at a petitioner's feet. The bread would be sent into the anchorhold by way of the "squint," a small opening in the wall next to the sealed doorway. Today (at last), hermits may use the "law of common sense and charity" in determining how their separation from the world will be lived out.

The foremost reason for a hermit today to modify his or her separation from the world is simply financial. Some eremites are more able than others to live for extended periods without dealing with the outside world. Others have to leave their hermitage daily in order to earn a living. Hermits we have dealt with are quite ingenious in finding occupations where they can work alone for limited periods of time. Some manage to find part-time jobs which generate sufficient income that permits them to have several days of the week full-time in their hermitage. Common sense, wise frugality, and creative use of time all help the hermit garner as much solitude as is possible in their particular circumstances.

The Plan of Life which those who apply for official recognition will submit to their bishop will detail how the hermit plans to provide for adequate income. In addition to the usual errands of shopping, seeing to medical needs, servicing vehicles, etc., the main reason for a hermit's interaction with the world has always been charity—which could be receiving a guest, caring for an ailing family member, or providing a special service to someone. If the eremite is canonically recognized, she would be expected to inform the bishop whenever she must either leave her hermitage or have someone living with her for an extended period.

Considering forms of withdrawal from the world, new ones are being developed while older ones drop from sight. No one who responded to the *Raven's Bread* survey claimed to be living as an anchorite. This does not mean there are none in the twenty-first century but that, as one might expect, they are deeply hidden. We received one reflection from Grace (a pseudonym), who desired the anchoritic life and lived it for two years until permission to continue was withdrawn. She recounted for us her tale:

> "There was a time in my eremitical journey when, after having lived for some years in a small experimental group of hermits located on bustling Abbey grounds, a discernment was made in collaboration with the abbot and my spiritual advisor. So that I could be freer to live my vocational response in greater hiddenness, and in deeper silence and solitude, I would request of our neighboring Archbishop the permission to be permanently ensconced as an anchorite attached to a certain Church located in his Archdiocese.
>
> Suffice it to say that all the preparations were in order, and the agreed-upon procedural norms

were in place. The pastor and people of his parish, the abbot, my spiritual advisor, and I all concurred that the situation was ideal and desirable. The Archbishop was amazed to see the openness, acceptance, support, and encouragement being given by those who were eager to see his granting of my request

He, himself, was understandably uncertain as how to proceed. There was no precedent to justify it in his Archdiocese, and no reference point in Church law to which he might turn for supportive guidance in the midst of his uncertainties. (This was prior to promulgation of Canon 603.) In his discussion with me, the archbishop even wondered aloud if such a vocation wasn't outdated, antisocial, and too extreme for our times.

Nevertheless, after some cajoling from all the parties involved, the archbishop very kindly agreed to grant me a two-year experimental period to live in the anchorage, as requested. He also solemnly added that if all went well, if final discernments proved favorable, and if I still wanted to continue at the close of the experimentation, then he would give his permission for permanency.

The two years seemed to pass quickly and uneventfully. Only God knows the extent of his invisible work of love taking place interiorly during this time. As the experimental period came to an end, and the discernments were made, the results were happily unanimous! We would now request of the archbishop that I be allowed to remain in the anchorage on a permanent basis.

When the archbishop heard the positive unanimity of our discernment and saw the joy on my face in repeating my request, he shook his head in consternation and disbelief! He haltingly confessed that when he had given his permission for the two-year experimental period, he had felt certain that I would have come to realize beyond the shadow of a doubt that this would *not* be the way I would want to live for the rest of my life! He simply could not imagine it as an ongoing commitment. I found this to be very disconcerting, to say the least!

In the midst of this sudden impasse with the archbishop, a letter arrived from a dear friend whom I had met a few years previously. She, too, had been looking for a stable eremitical situation. Her present letter was to inform me that if my current situation did not work out, she sincerely hoped that I would consider joining her in a promising eremitic endeavor. She and a few others were part of a newly forming monastic-eremitic group which, in her estimation, held much hope for a favorable outcome for all of us.

When the archbishop heard of this invitation, he was overjoyed! He thought it to be a providential solution to his fears of enclosing me or 'anyone' in an anchorage for life! There was no doubt in my mind that the archbishop meant well, but his words felt like daggers of betrayal and abandonment. My trust and confidence in his word had been shattered, even though it was obvious that his intentions were good. There was nothing left for me to do but accept it."[6]

One of the newer forms of eremitic life that surfaced out of the 2001 survey is that shared by married couples. Ideally, both spouses embrace withdrawal from all unnecessary interaction with society and allow their partner to experience as much solitude during their daily lives as desired. Another arrangement exists where only one spouse is drawn to solitude. If his partner understands and supports this desire, a loving, workable lifestyle can be developed which allows the solitary spouse to devote the majority of his or her time to prayer and silence while the other takes care of the necessary activities which modern life requires. Once we recover from the surprise that the possibility of married hermits evokes, we can begin to see there are some unique advantages.

The survey revealed that out of the one hundred thirty-two respondents, twenty-two were married men or women. Some couples share their home in a harmonious division of space and labor; others such as this couple in North Carolina have chosen a different arrangement. "My husband and I joined forces in 1987. I acquired sixteen acres on my own, and he acquired half an acre, where he built his own house. Then we built another house together on my property. We separated, and he is living on my property and I am living on his to further our eremitic lives. It was quite an accomplishment for two hermits to live together and build an environmentally sound house on my land. It is much easier now that we can both live in peace 'waiting on the Lord' at different locations."[7]

We find this arrangement not so very different from the ancient hermit "laura," where a small number of hermits live in separate hermitages on a shared piece of land. This form of eremitic community is being revived in the years since the early 1960s, often open to both men and women in the same laura. These hermit clusters are usually small, with a stable core of only two or three. The degree of interaction among the members varies with some who seldom gather at all, to others who meet daily for celebration of the Liturgy and sharing of meals.

Reading between the lines of the many letters to *Raven's Bread*, it appears that the highest degree of satisfaction with daily life seems to be among the laymen and women who live their hermit life independently—well over half of the respondents to the survey are in this category. Could this be linked to the fact that the largest number of respondents were from the U.S., where "give me freedom or give me death" is still the underlying "modus vivendi" of the majority? However one looks at it, "successful" hermits are individuals who can "go it alone," gracefully riding the waves of loneliness and contentment, as these successively wash over the shores of their lives.

The Silence of Solitude

During a phone interview with a journalist about my ideas on eremitical life, I was asked if I thought hermits should have telephones. After all, since they keep strict silence, of what use would a phone be? I was tempted to hang up and let the interviewer decide for himself whether a phone could be considered necessary! However, I plugged in my patience and pointed out, not for the first time, that hermits do talk to people when necessary. I suspect, from personal experience, that a fair number also talk to themselves or to their cat. As always, it is pleasant to discuss thoughts with someone who agrees with you!

We learn from the earliest traditions that the desert dwellers visited one another when in need of guidance, as the Sayings of the Desert Fathers and Mothers clearly reveals. Some hermits, still new to desert life, appeared to have the same concern about speech as my recent interviewer. Abba Theodore of Pherme asked Abba Pambo, "Give me a word." With much difficulty, he said to him, "Theodore, go and have pity on all, for through pity, one finds freedom of speech before God."[8] Once again, we are confronted with the major role that compassion plays in the spiritual life of the solitary.

In *The Forgotten Desert Mothers* by Laura Swan, we read about a holy woman anchoress who had shut herself up in a mausoleum, where she received food and supplies through a curtained window. However, she apparently had no qualms about speaking when she judged it necessary. "Despite her strict privacy, Alexandra developed a reputation among Christians for her wise advice and spiritual direction."[9]

Canon 603 uses an unusual phrase: "the silence of solitude." Obviously, this choice was intentional and refers to something more than just speech. Fr. Jean Beyer, SJ, informs us that the expression "silence of solitude" is borrowed from Carthusian terminology and carries a richer meaning than either silence or solitude alone convey. "It unites these values ... referring not merely to the external silence of the desert but to a profound inner solitude found in communion with God, who is the fullness of life and of love. It implies a lifetime striving toward union with God, a state which causes the one who becomes silent in this divine solitude to be alone with God alone. Such silence of solitude requires the other silences—of place, of surroundings, of action—all that furthers solitude and distances one from anything which could disturb it, from all which does not enhance the solitary mode of life."[10]

Helen Macdonald expanded on this spiritual quality of silence when she wrote: "Solitude and silence do not mean that the hermit must live absolutely alone, never speaking to another human being, for this has never been the eremitical tradition. Thus, for instance, the Fathers of the Desert, receiving any visitor as though it was Christ who was present, practiced a carefully discerned hospitality."[11]

The "careful discernment" implies that the desert solitaries learned (the hard way, most likely) to distinguish between those who came to see them out of a desire to know more about solitude and those who came out of mere curiosity. In other words, wise hermits develop the sensitivity and common sense to recognize the varying motivations of their visitors.

A *Raven's Bread* contributor offered this thoughtful advice to a beginning hermit: "Try as long as possible to be 'invisible' to society ... Eventually you will be 'discovered' to be a hermit. A hermit attracts the idly curious and admirers who will want to turn you into a guru. This is a trap of the devil, and you must put them off by being as politely dull and un-fascinating as possible. How can a beginner lecture others except by silent example? Tell people who want to 'talk about spiritual things' that your 'thing' is silent prayer, that you will pray for them, and then be on your way. If they beg for counseling, say you are not a counselor, and send them to one who is. This is not to forget that hermits (mature ones) are hospitable and sometimes are spiritual directors, but they do not take this on by their own will. It is a charism granted by God and validated by others who have the authority for this."[12]

Assiduous Prayer

When God is after you, there is no peace, nor any place to run except into his presence, which is overwhelmingly everywhere. What distinguishes hermits from others who live alone is their focus on seeking God ... or more pointedly, waking up to God's search for them, as the author of *The Hound of Heaven* poetically portrays. The hermit hears those relentless footfalls and decides to stop running. What happens next is unique to each individual, although every hermit soon makes a common discovery—the cultivation of an ever-deepening prayer life, like the planting and nurturing of a garden in desert sands, is shockingly simple but definitely not easy.

Fr. William McNamara (farsighted founder of the earliest hermit lauras in the U.S.) often employs a symbol for God that C. S. Lewis developed in his series *The Lion, the Witch and the Wardrobe.* Throughout the stories, a great golden lion, Aslan, appears, and the children are repeatedly warned: "Remember, Aslan is good. But he is not *safe!*" In other words, our solitary search can be dangerous! Even the hermit who lives a hidden life of prayer in the midst of the city realizes she or he is dealing with a Wild God, appropriately found in the desert. How found? Through *assiduous prayer*—that challenging and easily misconstrued term suggesting intense work and concentration.

In a letter addressed to other *Raven's Bread* readers, a beginning hermit asked, "I have had a number of amazing experiences where I was used by God to allow his peace and forgiveness to flow into the world. Now I want to live more for God and for the world that is so much in need of being held in prayer and love. How do I do this without sitting in prayer all day?"[13]

Another reader with a few more years of experience offered this response: "I personally find it close to impossible to separate the spiritual life from the secular life. God is in me and I am in God, so everything I do or think or say is done or taught or said, not only in God's presence but by our mutual consent and agreement. Of course, often I read the signals wrong and do the opposite of what is intended ... so I make amends and begin again. The 'doing and thinking and saying' is my constant prayer, whether doing laundry or reading a good book or on my knees in intercession and adoration. So 'sitting in prayer all day' is only part of the hermit life. Recognizing that every aspect of your life is a prayer will go a long way in knowing where God is leading."[14]

This hermit has made an essential discovery: *assiduous prayer* is a form of contemplation overflowing set times or specific exercises, causing the whole day to be awash with awareness of God's presence and activity. Another interpretation for this phrase may be the mindfulness that we have already considered. Many Christian solitaries begin their hermit life with a daily schedule modeled on monastic life which includes recitation of the Liturgy of the Hours and, for Catholics, attendance at daily Mass if possible. Most set aside periods for meditation and Lectio Divina (prayerful reading of Scripture), as well as perusing other edifying material. Many earnest hermits also add devotional practices such as recitation of the rosary and/or the Jesus Prayer, as well as running through a list of people and world situations which are in need of prayerful remembrance. No wonder they find themselves "sitting in prayer all day!" And soon, our beginning hermit is exhausted, especially if he or she has included "vigils" during the night, an admirable practice also borrowed from monastic life.

More than once, we have received letters or e-mails or phone calls from desperate individuals who, after six months or so of this intense schedule, are asking some serious questions about whether they are suited for the solitary life after all. This is the crucial time when discernment and guidance are required. The first question a good director asks is which of these many practices most nourishes the hermit and which feel like burdens and/or distractions. This is an excellent guideline to apply when discerning which prayer practices should be retained and which either curtailed or eliminated altogether.

One well-meaning solitary had read that rising early for mental prayer was helpful if one wished to pray without the distraction of the busy world intruding. She set her alarm for 2:30 a.m. and grimly dragged herself out of bed morning after morning. Instead of growing used to praying while the world slept, she found herself continually longing for sleep while the rest of the world was awake!

When her guide asked if she was a "morning or night" person, she admitted that she was "draggy" during the early part of the day and was at her best and most alert in the late evening. It was suggested that she experiment by changing her mental prayer period to 10:00 p.m., allowing her body its natural rhythm. Although it was initially hard to give up the idyllic vision of praying as the sun rose, our hermit soon learned that, for her, praying as the sun set was much more beneficial to herself and her prayer life. She was being respectful of the way her body was designed rather than trying to fit herself into a model developed when people rose and retired with the sun, regardless of their personal needs.

The point is that "assiduous prayer" is not possible if it isn't in synch with our natural biorhythms. In addition, attaining a state of continual attentiveness to God requires different supports in a hermitage than in a monastery. Many beginning hermits fail to make that distinction and unwittingly set up a daily horarium intended for a group rather than a single individual. Praying the Liturgy of the Hours is one example of taking a form of prayer designed for choral recitation and trying to make it serve an individual without allowing for some adjustments. Some of us are gifted with a singing voice and can easily chant psalmody, as well as sing the recommended hymns that commence each of the seven "Hours" spread throughout the day. We hear from hermits who, not too surprisingly, begin to find the full recitation of the daily Office a burden which disturbs rather than enhances their interior quiet.

This is the moment when a solitary needs to look more closely at the purpose of the Liturgy of the Hours. It is designed to sanctify the various times of the day by praying Morning Prayer (Lauds), Evening Prayer (Vespers), and Night Prayer (Compline). There are also Midday Prayer, Mid-afternoon Prayer, and Office of Readings

Vigils, the latter prayed at a convenient time during the day, unless the monks rose to pray it during the night. All serious hermits will want to pray at special moments of the day, but they may find it more helpful to modify, shorten, or change parts of the daily liturgy than to grimly "get in" every word of the breviary. What we hear, via the eremitic grapevine, is that many solitaries stop for a period of prayerful focus at the recommended times but use the psalms and Scripture readings of the breviary as a springboard for meditation. On a "dry" day, praying all the prescribed prayers may be helpful; on most days, a few verses of a psalm may be all that is needed to prime the pump and allow the water of contemplation to flow freely.

When the Liturgy of the Hours is prayed in common, the monks or nuns can easily slip into a contemplative mode, carried by their singing brothers and sisters. But when a solitary pray-er attempts to focus on all that is prescribed for each time of the day, it can be overwhelming—much like sitting down to a banquet served up for twenty. Just sampling each dish may leave one surfeited rather than hungry for more! A wise hermit dips into whatever is most appealing, grateful for the liberty that being solitary grants him or her.

Freedom? Yes! Hermits, more than most, enjoy the liberty of the children of God when it comes to prayer. They know there are dozens of ways to cultivate their prayer garden. It is their privilege to nurture whichever perennials and annuals they wish, designing a landscape with plants and flowers drawn from numerous traditions. The desired result is a state of continual prayer that refreshes and delights the hermit even when he or she has to contend with stubborn weeds and deeply rooted habits. The rule of thumb for determining whether one's prayer life is well-balanced is, naturally, the fruits produced. Is one growing more patient? Developing deeper compassion? Enjoying more enduring periods of peace and contentment? Spontaneously simplifying the prayer that sustains one's daily round? Eremitical life, like every other lifestyle, continually evolves, sometimes in quite unexpected ways.

One "shocker" encountered by many Catholic hermits after a few years in solitude is the realization that daily Mass, which at one time had felt essential to their routine, is now becoming a major source of distraction! Anxious solitaries have asked us if there is something seriously awry when this happens. Why should they now be glad when, for some reason, attendance at Mass isn't possible? Nothing is "wrong." On the contrary, something is very right and quite normal.

A genuine lover of solitude experiences such delight in the quiet peace of his hermitage, a quietness that profoundly frees his spirit, that leaving that lovely space is not only uncomfortable but profoundly disturbing. It can even be counterproductive to the goal of "assiduous prayer." This is not to say that a Catholic should give up Sunday Mass prayed with the local community— that has a particular grace of its own. It is merely a recognition that when attendance at Mass during the week has become distracting rather than helpful, this particular practice may be lovingly surrendered.

Abba Anthony said: "Just as fish die if they remain on dry land so monks (hermits), remaining away from their cells, or dwelling with men of the world, lose their determination to persevere in solitary prayer. Therefore, just as the fish should go back to the sea, so we must return to our cells, lest remaining outside we forget to watch over ourselves interiorly."[15]

St. Teresa of Avila was once approached by a nun who complained of her great difficulty in focusing on the points for meditation which were read out to the nuns each morning. She kept getting carried off into a peaceful silence and had to wrench her mind back to what had been offered to the community. Teresa, recognizing the degree of prayer which this nun had attained, comforted her with the observation that she was like a person who left the second or third floor of a house in order to start climbing the stairs again!

Once a person is launched upon the vast ocean of contemplative prayer, it is usually better to raise the sail, throw the map and oars overboard, and allow the wind of the Spirit to carry one where it will. It feels like the skill developed by Malaysian sailors who guide their little skiffs between distant, unseen islands literally by the seat of their pants. Seated in their fragile craft, they develop such familiarity with the subtle currents beneath the surface of the sea, that they steer their craft into these unseen streams which carry them safely to harbor with little or no interference on their part.

Similarly, the experienced pray-ers sense the movements of the Spirit within their hearts and entrust their spiritual life to this delicate guidance, knowing that their main "work" at this point is to not interfere, no matter how rough the seas may be. There will be periods when it is better to lower all sails, batten down the hatches, and like the sailing masters of old, turn the ship into the waves where, astonishingly, the ship no longer pitches and rolls but is rocked as gently as if it were a cradle by the hearth. The gift to know when to do this is learned by devout people only after a long and arduous period of initiation.

Among the Sayings of the Desert Fathers, we find this: "A brother asked an old man: 'What shall I do? For many thoughts are bothering me, and I don't know how to fight back.' The old man said: 'Do not fight against all of them, but against one. In fact, all thoughts of monks have a single head. Therefore, you have to figure out which and what kind it is, and fight against it. By doing so, you can defeat the rest of those thoughts.'"[16]

Assiduous Penance

Occasionally, we meet solitaries who equate degree of difficulty with a higher call, almost as if a hermit was in preparation for some kind of spiritual marathon. "No pain, no gain!" The more demanding the penitential practice is, the better it is, especially when it is corporal and more easily measured. This mindset was common in earlier centuries, but most prudent spiritual guides discourage their directees from placing undue emphasis on this aspect of their spiritual life. Asceticism is a support for prayer and virtue, not an end in itself. The focus can profitably be shifted to self-control; Abba Agatho would say: "Even if an angry man were to revive the dead, he would not be pleasing to God because of his anger."[17]

In plain words, penitential practices are not to be limited to merely corporal forms but should begin within the heart, calming turbulent responses and inordinate cravings commonly known as temptations. Even someone living in total solitude has his or her share of drives and desires which impinge on the interior peace that is both the atmosphere necessary for deep prayer and its fruit.

In *The Wisdom of the Desert,* we find the question posed to Abba Agatho: "Which is greater? Bodily asceticism, or watchfulness over the interior man?" The elder said: "A man is like a tree. His bodily works are like the leaves of the tree, but interior self-custody is like the fruits. Since, then, it is written that every tree not bearing good fruit shall be cut down and cast into the fire, we must take all care to bear this fruit, which is custody of the mind. But we also need leaves to cover and adorn us; and that means good works done with the aid of the body." This Abba Agatho was wise in understanding and tireless in his work and ready for everything. He applied himself energetically to manual labor and was sparing in his food and clothing.[18]

This bit of wisdom from the earliest years of eremitical life alludes to several forms of penance, interior and exterior: control over the passions; moderation in food, drink, clothing, and shelter; and manual labor. All the traditional practices of penance such as the discipline (self-flagellation), vigils (breaking one's sleep to spend time in prayer), and fasting have the goal of gaining self-control so that one is less troubled by temptations and able to maintain a tranquil state of prayer.

Some earnest beginners in eremitical life unconsciously merge assiduous prayer with assiduous penance, so that their meditation period becomes equivalent to time spent on a rack! However, stories of early Celtic hermits who spent nights standing in freezing water or kneeling on nails are not intended as a manual of eremitical practice! Even the incredible feats of penance attributed to St. Patrick are recorded more for admiration than imitation. No one knows for certain the truth of the tale that the beloved bishop of Ireland rid the island of reptiles but that he introduced Christianity into a pagan culture is undeniable. Some of the druidic practices eventually resurfaced in baptized form among the Celtic monks and hermits and were often copied by the layfolk when they were in need of a special favor from God. This persisted even into the twentieth century.

As a young nun, I listened in astonishment as one of our elders, originally Brigit Burke of County Cork, recounted with great satisfaction how she had endured the rugged retreat known as St. Patrick's Purgatory twice in order to "save the soul" of someone she feared was living "in sin." This retreat began when the penitents removed their shoes and boarded a small boat that transported them to an island in an Irish lake, where for two days and a night, they engaged in a continuous round of prayers and penitential practices, always barefoot on the rocky ground. When one's feet were too bruised and bloody, the retreatant was allowed to continue circling the little church on his or her knees, rosary in hand.

Water was provided but no food, nor were the retreatants expected to spend much time, if any, on the unpadded pallets provided for those so weak that they needed an hour's rest. Sr. Brigit proudly told us that when the boat returned her and the other weary penitents to shore, she was greeted with a telegram that the person for whom she was praying had suffered a bout of double pneumonia, inducing him to make a full confession which, it was presumed, included a promise of amendment of his wayward conduct. Intrepid Brigit boarded the next boat back to the island for another round of prayer and penance, this time in thanksgiving! I was secretly glad that St. Patrick's Purgatory was no where near Ohio! Even when I, many years later, became a hermit, I was cautious about the penitential practices I chose.

The Commentary on Canon 603, which governs eremitical life in the Catholic Church, offers this somewhat ambiguous reflection: "The traditional forms of penance for hermits include vigils, fasting, abstinence, and mortification of the body. The hermit can be expected not only to follow the penitential practices suggested for all the faithful but also to go beyond the norms of fasting and abstinence as well."[19] This strong statement is qualified by an interesting footnote: "The ascetical practices of the hermit must be discerned with the help of the spiritual director and the bishop's delegate. Obedience to them in this matter may constitute an act of ascesis in itself. In the time of medieval solitaries, the life itself was to be considered penitential and all extreme forms of penance or fasting were eschewed."[20]

In other words, a balanced approach to penance is sine qua non for the solitary. Every hermit should carefully discern the results of his or her chosen ascetical practices. Do they promote his or her growth in humility and self-forgetfulness? Or do they so focus the mind on the misery of the body that the true goals of eremitical life are lost sight of? Anything which threatens to destroy one's health or peace is highly suspect. Things fall into right order in the eremitical life if the primary goal is kept in focus—union with God in prayer and solitude. Therefore, the most important "ascetic practice" is solitude itself and sitting alone in the silence of the cell.

One must patiently accept loneliness, emptiness, and exile from the world of others, which means listening to a "different drummer." We will have to accept that many, often those we most love, will not understand us at all. Added to this painful situation is our inner confusion as we confront the baffling mystery of God himself. The God we meet in solitude is different from the one met in the pews, and this "difference" sets the tone for all our actions and decisions as a solitary. Once we come to a clear-sighted acceptance of the exigencies of solitude itself, all the other practices—fasting, work, vigils, psalmody, and so on, will fall into place. We will know their need and their efficacy in relation to the whole of our eremitical life, as well as their value for the world which we love all the more, despite its failure to appreciate the gift we are making to it by our lives of silence and solitude.

A word often found in eremitical literature is "ascesis." It is a broad term encompassing the practices which under-gird a solitary's life, particularly the assiduous prayer and penance we have been exploring. In an article entitled *The Dangers of Solitude*, Kenneth C. Russell addresses the crucial importance of keeping one's focus and balance when the going gets tough. He says bluntly that "more awaits the novice hermit than the beauties of nature and the spiritual delights which ancient and contemporary enthusiasts of the eremitical life tend to emphasize."[21] The most difficult penance that a solitary faces is simply … being solitary. That means living the daily routine unseen, without the encouragement that a little praise might provide. In medieval times, the hermit was referred to as buried with Christ, and some anchoresses actually went through a form of funeral rites when they formally entered into their hermitage. However, once inside the hermitage, the eremite discovers—not surprisingly—that he or she is quite alive!

Russell goes on to observe: "Hermits also soon discover, as the Carthusian Guigo II puts it, that they are a crowd unto themselves … For all the images of being cut off and buried, the reality is that a living human being goes into the desert. She or he wants to be there, of course, but the spiritual and especially the psychological conditioning to solitude is not achieved by a mere act of will. The hermit, in fact, begins with some interior dividedness. Part of the self has no interest in disappearing. Inevitably, the life force will rise up against the isolation and denial of achievement that the solitary life demands."[22] And this is where ascesis has its role to play.

As already alluded to, the penance most necessary to eremitical life is fidelity to the life itself. Accepting the tedium of a simple, unseen life, enduring the ups and downs of emotional states, and keeping one's focus on the task of the moment, refusing to be enticed by visions of future successes or depressed by memories of past failures … this is the true discipline of the hermit. As Russell puts it: "The solitary's fundamental temptation, it seems, is to focus on something other than God."[23] And the most enticing object is, of course, one's own self! Even spiritual housecleaning, when we focus on every dust mite of envy or streak of selfishness or mess of pride, keeps our focus on *me*! The hermit must not only disappear from the world but also from him or herself. The mirror on the wall should proclaim who is fairest of them all—the God whose radiance outshines the image of the solitary.

Part 2: Norms for Consecration

The second paragraph of Canon 603 delineates four conditions to be met if a Catholic man or woman wishes to have his or her dedication as a hermit recognized publicly by the Church. First, "the three evangelical counsels, confirmed by a vow or other sacred Bond, in the hands of the diocesan bishop" must be professed. This is done in a public ceremony in which the Church, in the person of the bishop of the diocese where the hermit resides, accepts the person's intention to dedicate his or her life to God in the eremitical state. The "evangelical counsels" are the three traditional vows which all religious make: poverty, chastity, and obedience. Because a hermit is not a member of a religious community, the manner in which these will be lived out day to day is unique to each hermit. The Plan of Life which the hermit has submitted to the bishop for his approval describes the details as simply as possible.

Vow of Poverty

For example, how does a hermit live the vow of poverty? "Holy" poverty is different from destitution. Although both imply material limitations, there is a radical difference in one's attitude toward the situation. Dependence on God is the heart of the vow of poverty. Worry is its antithesis. A hermit may not know where the rent or grocery money for next week will come from. But, as a vowed solitary, she or he makes a crucial choice at this point— she or he chooses not to fret over a situation about which, at that moment, nothing can be done. The God who has called him or her into a life of solitude and prayer is as aware of the looming crisis, as the hermit is, and has deeper pockets.

The spiritual person puts the problem in God's hands and waits … waits until something changes or God shows him or her what to do. I clearly remember sitting in my prayer space in a cabin in West Virginia, hugging my knees and fighting panic. I had no steady income, and winter was approaching. The prospect of obtaining food and heat looked grim. I had managed to find a roof (of sorts)— an abandoned cabin the owner offered to me rent-free. It was late September, and not only did I not have a stick of firewood, I didn't even have a stove in which to burn it. There were only a few pieces of chimney pipe rusting in what passed for a front yard. As I felt terror close in on me, I glanced at the wall across the room and noticed how daylight (and a breeze) was seeping through cracks only visible in the late afternoon. "Jesus! What am I going to do?" My cry was more expletive than prayer, but someone responded anyway.

"Are you cold today?" No, actually the weather still felt quite summery.
"Do you have enough food in the house for this evening?" Well, er, yes.
"For Merton?" My kitten wasn't going without supper either.
"How about for tomorrow?" I admitted there was food on the shelf to cover several days.
"What more do you need to get through tonight?" In truth, nothing.
"Then can we say you have enough for the moment, the only moment you have, by the way?"

Chided, I bowed my head and admitted I was borrowing unnecessary burdens. I didn't need tomorrow's food today ... couldn't eat it anyway. What I *did* need was *trust* for the morrow. I needed to believe that the hand which had provided for me this past summer would not abandon me this fall and winter. It didn't! A stove was found, plus a pickup truck and volunteer labor to move it in and hook it up. (Only a year later did I learn that the damper didn't work ... but at that time, I did not know how to use it anyway.)

Enough firewood was found to get me as far as Christmas and a major snowstorm. Just as I was moving the last of my wood pile into the house to dry out and warm up, a truck loaded with split logs came trundling down my drive. My provider had come through—at the last minute, of course, but then, I hadn't needed that wood until today. Ditto with food and clothing. Family and friends collected and delivered boxes of tinned goods and warm garments—even enough to share with others.

One cousin insulated the "thin" wall, and another cousin came through with carpet remnants to cover the sagging floorboards. In late November, I picked up my mail and noticed an envelope from an unfamiliar bank. When I opened it, a cashier's check for three hundred dollars fell out! Only the line for the sender was left blank. Similar envelopes arrived monthly during the six years I lived in West Virginia. No matter how I tried, I could never trace the donor to thank him or her. So I thanked the ultimate source and trusted that my mysterious benefactor would be rewarded as generously as she or he deserved. My other task was to exercise careful stewardship over all the riches poured into my lap.

Two attitudes which must be avoided if vowed poverty is to be "holy" are worry and hoarding. Without confidence in God's providence, we are living in a state of anxious indigence where there is no joy and no generosity. I grew up, as it were, in the school of Franciscan spirituality where Lady Poverty, whom St. Francis had courted all his life, was our benign but demanding teacher. She taught me that worry and joy cannot coexist. She also insisted that good stewardship was not the same as hoarding for future catastrophes which may never occur. Our American lifestyle is based on the opposite premise. First, we must have insurance to cover every eventuality, including death. This insurance is marketed as though having thorough coverage will *prevent* illness, accident, or death!

The other attitude fostered in our society is to always have more than just what you need—who knows when the total loss our insurance is supposed to prevent will happen? Better have a storage unit filled with all those things which we can't bear to part with, even though it is unlikely that we truly need them or would use them under ordinary circumstances. The hermit vows to live with only the barest of necessities, witnessing to the joy of having little and desiring less.

Lest we begin to believe that hermits shall always have ravens with no other purpose in this world but to carry bread to them, we have this tale about John the Little: It was said about John the Little that one day, he said to his older brother: "I want to be free from care and not to work but to worship God without interruption."

110

And he took his robe off and went into the desert. After staying there one week, he returned to his brother. And when he knocked at the door, his brother asked without opening it: "Who is it?" He replied: "It's John, your brother." The brother said: "John has become an angel and is not among people anymore." Then he begged and said: "It's me!" But his brother did not open the door and left him there in distress until the next morning. And he finally opened the door and said: "If you are a human being, you have to work again in order to live." Then John repented, saying: "Forgive me, brother, for I was wrong."[24]

Many bishops, it seems, fear that a John the Little may turn up at their chancery. So, when faced with accepting the vows of a hermit, they require the future solitary to sign an Intent of Financial Independence, freeing the diocese of any fiscal responsibility in their regard. This insures that the hermit "has the responsibility to provide for one's own living, health care, ongoing formation and educational experiences, retirement, etc. The bishop or diocese has no obligation to provide for the hermit's temporal needs."[25]

The diocese also presents the applicant for hermit life with a form for a budget and a chart of accounts, as well as recommendations for financial stewardship. The recommendations begin: "The individual hermit is responsible for his or her financial independence. All forms of income can be accepted in one's personal name or the name of one's incorporated hermitage title. Appropriate records must be kept. Excess available funds should be invested rather than being held in the personal checking account. The Diocese cannot be held liable for an individual hermit's financial independence or actions."[26]

1. Where is Lady Poverty with her joy and freedom? The parable of the ravens and the lilies of the field is not a piece of pretty fiction that our poetic Savior spouted one lovely afternoon. It was a solemn warning: *"This is why I warn you.* Do not be concerned for your life, what you are to eat, or for your body, what you are to wear. Life is more important than food and the body more than clothing ... *stop worrying.* The unbelievers of this world are always running after these things. Your Father knows that you need such things.

Seek out instead his kingship over you and the rest will follow in turn. *Do not live in fear,* little flock." (Lk 12: 22,23;30-32.)

The genuine hermit takes this warning to heart and does his or her best to *stop worrying* and to *live without fear.* The vow of poverty is a more a matter of the heart than of the checkbook. *Our Father knows we have need of these things* (even insurance!), and our challenge is to believe and trust, to share what we have when we can, and to be grateful for the goods of the earth which are entrusted to us, be it a box of chocolates or a bag of spinach!

Vow of Chastity

The vow of chastity is a much less complex matter—at least on the surface. Basically, the solitary who chooses to make a public consecration as a hermit is obliged to live in perfect continence observed in celibacy. "Perfect continence" is distinct from the chastity required of all Christians because it is lived out in celibacy and because it is chosen in order to give one's total love to God in Christ. The goal is an undivided heart focused on living "alone with the Alone," as the Carmelites phrase it. The major obstacle to living chastely is selfishness, which focuses on the self rather than on fruitful love, a love which pours out good works in generous measure.

The chaste lover who takes God as his or her life partner forgoes fruitfulness of body in order to parent spiritual children, directly or indirectly. It is not just fanciful terminology to refer to a spiritual father or mother—the abba and amma of desert lore. However, not everyone who "goes into the desert" is given the charism to be able to advise others and nurture their spiritual growth. As St. Paul points out, there are a variety of gifts and "the same God who accomplishes all of them in everyone. To each person the manifestation of the Spirit is given for the common good." (1 Cor.12,6-7)

The chaste soul humbly offers her or his gifts to the service of others with a pure intention and prefers those which are appropriate to the hidden life of prayer and sacrifice. The major "good work" of the hermit is prayer. In a treatise on the hiddenness of the Camaldolese monk, an anonymous writer quoted Silouan: "To pray for men is to give of one's heart's blood." The celibate becomes a giver of life through the mysterious channels of grace which link all human beings together.

In addition to selfishness, pride is the enemy of the truly chaste. Some might name sexual offenses the major failure against the vow of chastity, and no one can deny how essential it is to live a modest, continent life. But it is even more important to have a pure heart that is humble, generous, and self-controlled. During the period when the Jansenist sect dominated portions of the church in France, there was a cliché regarding the nuns of Port Royale, a center of the movement: "pure as angels; proud as demons." Not the most flattering of epithets, but sadly true.

Speaking of demons, we read a lot about them in the Sayings of the Desert Fathers and Mothers, and frequently, they are presented as tempting the hermit to commit fornication. In the Life of St. Anthony, St. Athanasius wrote that the Enemy's choice snare against the solitaries was sexual temptation:

> "He advanced to attack the young man (Anthony) troubling him so by night and harassing him by day, that even those who saw Anthony could perceive the struggle going on between the two. The Enemy would suggest filthy thoughts but the other would dissipate them by his prayers; he would try to incite him to lust, but Anthony, sensing shame, would gird his body with his faith, with his prayers, and his fasting. The wretched Devil even dared to masquerade as a woman by night and to impersonate such in every possible way, merely in order to deceive Anthony. But he filled his thoughts with Christ and reflected upon the nobility of the soul that comes from him and its spirituality and thus quenched the glowing coal of temptation. And again the Enemy suggested pleasure's seductive charm. But Anthony, angered, of course, and grieved, kept his thoughts upon the threat of fire

and the pain of the worm. Holding these up as his shield, he came through unscathed."[29]

Today, most of those called to the hermit vocation are in their middle years and may be divorced or widowed. Although one can be sexually disturbed at any time in life, it is more often loneliness, rather then celibacy, which causes the most serious struggles for the aspiring hermit undertaking his or her second "career." One contributor to *Raven's Bread* shared her struggle with grief while living in solitude:

> "Death is a numbing experience, and the ensuing grief is proportionate to the depths of love. How does a hermit deal with the death of a loved one? There is no comfort to be found anywhere when the tidal waves of grief crash over. A hermit is one who loves God passionately and whose life is hidden with Christ in God. Such a one has to believe that all voids, darkness, numbing pain, and brokenness are the hand of God carving a deeper space for himself within us. The poet William Blake wrote: 'We are placed on this earth for a space of time to learn to bear the beams of love.' The death of a loved one is surely one of the heaviest to bear. Being a hermit is its own comfort. The willingness to bear what is unbearable—in silence, solitude, aloneness, difficult as it may be, brings deep healing. In this self-abandonment, in being alone with an infinite, living, loving transcendent Presence, one does not necessarily feel comforted but rather experiences an unearthly peace which imperceptibly spirals into the great mystery of communion with the loved one, and the One Beloved."[30]

This hermit has found the true grace of chastity—that there is no lasting loneliness when one has ceased looking for comfort and companionship except in the Presence which permeates the hermitage (and the hermit's heart). Instead of selfishly demanding that one be understood, the solitary learns to understand; instead of seeking to receive, the desert dweller finds ways to give; instead of striving to be loved, the solitary learns how to love unconditionally ... and discovers that everything he or she needs is poured into his or her heart in abundance beyond measure. We may feel like we are being broken, but then we realize that we are merely being enlarged so that we can continue to give and receive in greater measure.

Vow of Obedience

Chastity is about abundance even as is the vow of poverty. Can we say the same for obedience? The first question to arise regarding obedience is: to whom does the hermit give his or her submission? God, first and foremost, is the one the hermit seeks to obey ... but God's responses to the concrete questions that arise can be somewhat nebulous, so the Church appoints a representative "with skin on" (and some impressive robes) in the person of the bishop.

Usually the bishop, in turn, chooses a delegate who has more frequent contact with the hermit and deals with matters in the "external forum" of the hermit's life. This delegate makes certain that the hermit has a spiritual director who oversees the "internal forum" or spiritual development the solitary may need. Once this "chain of command" is in place, the goal of all of the above is to make certain that the hermit is faithful to his or her Plan of Life which has already been approved by the bishop. Does this answer the first question?

If so, it raises another: where is the freedom that characterizes the life of the genuine solitary if he or she is subject to so much oversight? It dwells in the heart of the hermit who has freely chosen to offer his or her independence to the Lord. The essence of freedom is the ability to give one's most cherished gifts to the Loved One as a pledge of deepest love. No one is forced to become a canonically recognized hermit, a choice which includes vowing the three evangelical counsels. Often, it is quite the opposite!

The potential hermit has had to fight long and hard for this privilege, often moving from one place to another in search of a bishop who is open to receiving the vows of a hermit. We receive many letters from women and men who have achieved this goal only after twenty or more years of patient waiting and asking; of praying and searching. The joy expressed in these letters of literal triumph is palpable. Clearly, the hermit who is pledging to live the solitary life in a canonically recognized manner is answering a deeply felt call in the most radical expression of obedience possible. Like Samuel, he or she has heard the Lord's voice and answered, "Speak Lord, your servant is listening (1 Sam.3,9)

The liberty of the children of God is a freedom *from* as well as a freedom *for*. One of the gifts which obedience bestows is a "freedom *from* excessive self-love." It is difficult to be enthralled with one's own plans and ideas when someone else makes the final decision regarding his or her fulfillment. Being subject in obedience reminds us that we are not independent beings and that our dependence extends to all aspects of our lives. We are basically and totally dependent on God for every breath we draw. The vow of obedience could determine whether or not it is sweet-smelling. Oh no! Oh yes! Although the bishop may not decree what kind of toothpaste we may buy, he has approved our budget, which limits what we can spend on "personal care items." Gulp.

Many people who explore what the vow of obedience entails may initially grow red under their collars. It can sound like an insult to one's common sense as well as a distinctly distasteful control over the most personal aspects of our lives. Why would anyone freely subject him or herself to a relationship which could potentially place one in a very childish situation? Would even God ask the sacrifice of one his most marvelous gifts—our free will? What are we being freed *from*? What are we being freed *for*? We are being freed from our pride, excessive self-will, and from endless uncertainty about what is the will of God for us. If observed authentically, obedience will set us free, free to be our truest selves.

While this book was in process, I shared this section on obedience with a hermit who was not among those who chose canonical recognition. She observed that, even without vows, all hermits find their choices limited. We don't need a bishop. Life itself will do that for us! If we overdo anything, we will pay the price. Just by virtue of being human, by having a human body, we are restricted by what our nature requires. Ergo, our vaunted freedom is not without its limitations, boundaries which we find we must obey if we are to live fully.

Instead of kicking and screaming, we should just get down to the business of doing the best we can and submitting to the laws of humanity. Life itself can be our ultimate bishop and the Law of Consequences our most demanding teacher. So whether or not we make public profession of living the hermit life with all that the Church requires, we are always bound by limitations on our free will. Ultimately, it is to our Creator that we tender our obedience in love.

The advantage of making the vow of obedience, with its built-in structure, is that we are freed from consequences we might never have anticipated. In a perfectly honest moment, we must admit that we do not always see the whole picture in a given situation, nor do we possess a perfectly balanced judgment. True, the bishop is not omniscient either, but when the hermit and his or her superiors together seek God's good pleasure, it is more likely to be found in all its fullness. It is humbling but also liberating to give up to some degree our treasured right of self-determination.

We do so in order to be assured that the inspirations and ideas which arise in prayer are truly from the Holy Spirit and not from some negative spirit. Have we never been "seduced" by an excessive confidence in our own dazzling insights? It is often a matter of temperance. We want our prayer to lead us to a truthful, honest, and open communication with our God, to become a pristine channel. The Lakota shaman, Fool's Crow, speaks of our becoming a hollow bone uncluttered by our own ego, and so, pure and clear, Creator's voice can be clearly heard.

There are definitely limits on what our superiors can ask of us—their main task is to assist us in observing the Plan of Life which we ourselves have developed. Beyond that, most bishops or their delegates are more than pleased that "their" hermit conducts his or her life as quietly and unobtrusively as possible. The spiritual guide, which the vowed solitary is expected to choose, helps to interpret the daily calls of God, the inner directives which draw us even more closely to the holiness that is everyone's goal.

As a novice, I was told the classic stories of the nun who was commanded to plant the cabbages upside down and of the good sister who was required to water a dry stick every day. Of course these paragons of obedience were rewarded by an amazing crop of cabbage and a flourishing tree. I must admit that I was not particularly inspired to "go and do likewise," even if I happened to *like* cabbage (which I do not). It took me many years to fully appreciate the value of obedience ... and many more to put it into practice in a genuinely grace-filled manner. The Desert Fathers told similar stories to their disciples, trying to instill appreciation for the virtue of obedience. Abba Nilus said: "Do not want things to turn out as they seem best to you, but as God pleases. Then you will be free of confusion and thankful in your prayer."[32] More often than not, when I refused to grow cabbages upside down, I only grew confusion! Only after many years did my efforts to walk the road of obedience lead me to profound peace, a sense of being in harmony with the laws of the universe, as well as with the desires of my superiors and the consequences of life's events.

The author of the *Book of Wisdom* puts it well: "The first step toward discipline is a very earnest desire for her; then, care for discipline is love of her; love means the keeping of her laws; to observe her laws is the basis for incorruptibility; and incorruptibility makes one close to God." (Wisdom 6,17-19) The hermit chooses to give over his or her independence in order to gain something even greater—the joy of living close to God and at the service of others rather than focused on one's own needs and desires.

Public Profession

"A hermit is recognized in the law as one dedicated to God ... if he or she publicly professes the three evangelical counsels, *confirmed by a vow or other sacred bond ...*"[34] For the sake of simplicity, we have used the word "vow" when talking of the three evangelical counsels. In truth, they are precisely that—counsels or words of advice. Taken together, they establish a lifestyle which fulfills the Gospel in all its dimensions. Most religious communities require their members to pledge themselves by making a vow, although some substitute another form of binding promise, such as an oath, a pledge, or other expression of consecration that is binding in conscience. The hermit also has the option of choosing what form his or her sacred promise will take. Most bishops will require that the first profession of hermit life be taken only for a specified number of years. Once the consecrated solitary has demonstrated his or her ability to live the eremitical life and flourish in solitude, he or she will be permitted to make consecration for life.

"The vows are made publicly to underscore the fact that hermits, like members of an institute, should endeavor to be associated with the work of redemption and to spread the kingdom of God. In seeking solitude, they also, in a hidden way, help the Church more effectively in its task."[35]

From a canonical point of view, making consecration in a public manner confirms the status of the professed hermit in the eyes of the Church. Now the hermit "belongs" to the Church in a unique manner declared for all to see. There is no single written format which all hermits must use when making their public profession. Each one is free to devise whatever kind of ceremony he believes will most adequately express his understanding of the sacred promises he is making, as well as declaring the meaning of eremitical life. We have seen "vow formulas" consisting of two sentences, as well as those which run two lengthy paragraphs! As long as the essential promises are clearly expressed, Church law is satisfied.

Conducting a public ceremony doesn't necessarily involve a church full of curious people, although that has happened. The public nature of the profession is satisfied when a representative of the bishop, if not the bishop himself, receives the vows or promises of the hermit and at least one other person witnesses the event. Most hermits prefer to avoid much hoopla, but sometimes that desire is set aside in favor of giving public witness to a unique and valuable vocation.

Such was the case when Cardinal Anthony J. Bevilacqua, archbishop of Philadelphia, presided at the lifetime profession of Richard Withers in November 2001. Brother Richard accepted the situation good-naturedly, knowing his five minutes of fame (thanks to the wire service) would change nothing essential. He hoped he might help clarify some of the mystery which surrounds the hermit life. "People often equate being a hermit with living in a cave. They'll say to me, 'Do you have electricity? Do you have a phone?' To cut that short, I tell them I have e-mail ..." and then he added, "It's nothing extraordinary ... like I'm not hanging from my toes anywhere or anything like that."[36]

One hermit stumbled on a summary of the three vows which suited her exactly and became the centerpiece of her future Plan of Life. During prayer one day, she asked: "How shall I live true poverty?" The answer: Live without worry. "How shall I live true chastity?" Love without fear. "How shall I live true obedience?" Live continually attentive to the Spirit.[37]

Plan of Life

No, hermits do not pledge to hang by their toes ... or fingernails. If such a promise were found in a hermit's Plan of Life, the aspiring solitary would be promptly referred to a mental health professional. The Plan of Life can be as brief and succinct as a single page or run to a small tome of thirty-six pages, filled with quotations from Scripture and the saints expanding on the theology of eremitism.

The Plan of Life is best formulated only after a person has lived in solitude for religious reasons for a significant period of time. Only then can someone sort the ideal from the real. In ancient times, hermits learned their way of life by imitating an experienced hermit. A non-hermit, no matter how holy, cannot speak with the same authenticity as a real one. Today, however, trial and error may be the only way for most hermits to learn. It was a favorite saying of the desert that the cell would teach the neophyte all that was necessary. This is still true today; eremitical life is learned only day by day in the hermitage itself, where most surprising things are discovered. This is where what is central is separated from what is peripheral. The hermitage itself will either nourish the truly called or drive the unsuitable back into the world, hopefully wiser for the experience.

Many aspiring hermits initially devise a very detailed rule and enter into hermit life with every minute of the day mapped out. It does not take long to discover that life continually intrudes on the horarium (daily schedule) and the carefully planned day is shot to pieces. I remember the day when I had just settled down for my morning meditation and caught a glitter out of the corner of my eye. Looking more closely, I found to my horror that water was creeping out from under the bathroom door and had obviously been doing so for some time! The "creep" was gradually turning into a creek, soaking the carpet and the boxes stored nearby. My prayer time suddenly transformed into a series of exclamations, alternating between *"Oh my God!"* and *"Oh, s——,"* while I mopped, danced on squishy carpet, searched for, and fixed the cause of the interior stream.

True, I admired Frank Lloyd Wright's architectural gem *Living Waters*, but my old Jenny-Lind-style cabin was not designed to accommodate an indoor waterfall (though running water was ordinarily appreciated)! By the time I could return to prayer, several hours had passed, including my period for spiritual reading, praying the Liturgy, and eating breakfast. What to do? There was no way of salvaging my morning routine; besides, by this time, I was "powerfully hungry," as they say here. So I stirred up a quick brunch, which further wrecked my schedule but definitely improved the state of my tummy as well calmed my shattered nerves. Rigidity has no place in a hermitage ... but a sense of humor definitely does!

A commentator on canon law, Helen Macdonald, observes: "Hermits must take their vocation very seriously, but it helps if they do not take themselves too seriously."[38] Time and the Holy Spirit will bring about a balanced Plan of Life which, helpful though it may be, must neither become an idol nor an end in itself. The hermit does not live to observe a rule; the rule exists to assist the hermit on his or her journey toward God.

Continuing solitude will infallibly unmask aspects of the false self we have unconsciously retained. There is no way to avoid seeing our pretensions and illusions when the only face in the bathroom mirror is our own. If our vocation is genuine, we will survive repeated revelations about our true selves, e.g., our inability to control our temper, our distressing bouts with doubt, our repeated infidelities to our daily routine, our love of comfort, etc.—all the dark sides of our good gifts.

We will be humbled to discover that our God is more forgiving of our failures than we ourselves are! The great miracle that perseverance in solitude brings about is the merging of our views with that of our God. Our values shift and it becomes more important to have a daily routine that is in synch with our God-given nature than to have a Rule that impresses all who read it ... but which is impossible for us to keep without a major "makeover" of our true selves.

All this and more leads us to listen humbly to the Spirit, who may suggest modifications to that ideal rule we had developed for ourselves. We accept (with a bit of chagrin) that we may need more sleep or at different times than we had allowed. For instance, a siesta at midday could make a world of difference, not just in our health but in our prayer life as well. Most people pray better when not battling the urge to find a pillow! Or we may discover that we are not physically fit for all the manual work we had assumed a hermit must do (growing our own food or heating with wood are real killers for our back), or the deep studies we had planned to plunge into utterly bore us ... all this and more teaches us to listen to our own rhythms and needs, our true nature, as we refine our daily routine and rewrite (once again) our ideal Plan of Life.

Alone in our hermitage, we begin to realize that no one is watching us, noting our every slip. No one is judging us. No one cares if we wear burlap and fast on mustard greens and berries. One of the most liberating moments I experienced during my early years as a nun occurred when my novice directress quoted an old saying: "We will worry much less about what others think of us when we realize how seldom they do!"

This wry comment sent floods of illumination through my soul. I discovered that my deepest fear was *not* what others thought of me (they *were* more concerned with themselves) but what that critical voice within *me* was liable to say about my every move. I learned that the magic words are: "Shut up!" I gave up the practice of picking over my every action, looking for each imperfection and began focusing my eye instead on the God who was beholding me with love each day. The desert amma is right: If you sit in your "cell" long enough, it (and the Holy Spirit) will teach you all you need to know.

A most influential element in a hermit's Plan of Life is not explicitly mentioned in Canon 603. That is the spirituality to which the hermit is drawn. This will permeate the hermit's plan in numerous ways, dictating what is emphasized and the sources chosen for inspiration. A hermit who is deeply attracted to the monastic style of the Benedictines will draw much guidance for his or her daily life from the Carthusian or Camaldolese Orders. For instance, this hermit's rule will place much emphasis on the recitation of the Liturgical Hours and on practices adapted from a monastic lifestyle.

Another hermit may favor the simplicity and joyful poverty that characterizes the followers of St. Francis of Assisi. Others may draw inspiration directly from the writings of the Desert Fathers and Mothers, while still others may be influenced by the strongly eremitical Carmelite tradition. There is no one "right school" for a hermit to follow—all can flavor the basic soup that is eremitical life. How do we know which one is right for us?

We will find we are spontaneously attracted by one or another; the Franciscan spirit excites us; the Benedictine looks too rigid. Or vice-versa. Additionally, Christians can be particularly inspired by one incident or virtue in the lives of Jesus or Mary. For instance, one is drawn to the hidden life of Jesus, naming her hermitage Nazareth or Bethlehem. Another may be struck by an incident such as the Transfiguration or the Agony in the Garden. For those with a strong Marian attraction, the Visitation or the Annunciation may provide a deep well of inspiration. We are not talking about what is most "correct" but what most fits our personality; about which spirituality most nourishes and challenges us.

Whatever moves our spirit or stirs our heart is a valuable gift from the Holy Spirit, guiding us, uplifting us, and renewing our hearts when the going gets rough. A scene from the life of Jesus, for instance, is like a secret talisman, a touchstone that stabilizes us and reminds us of where we are going. It is always there for us to "mine" for further inspiration. Many of us will sample various traditions and schools, slowly developing a unique spiritual mix which is purely our own. Some ancient eremitic rules exist to this day and can serve as the basic inspiration for our Plan of Life, such as the Ancrene Rule, written for the anchoresses of Great Britain in the fourteenth century. Another is The Little Rule of Master Romuald, which is a short collection of pithy statements, not unlike the sayings of the desert ammas and abbas.

Nearly all of us discover that it is necessary to "walk the walk" before we can "talk the talk," learning by living how to compose a viable Plan of Life. Those who write it out beforehand and then try to fit themselves into this preconceived notion usually discover that their perfect rule is soon "red-inked" with numerous modifications that life in solitude has taught them. Even if we copy the Rule of a more experienced solitary, the tried and true text of another does not guarantee personal satisfaction. No two people can live the same daily schedule, nor do they express their ideals in exactly the same fashion. When *Raven's Bread* asked readers to share their Plan of Life, we met with a resounding silence! Apparently, our hermits felt that their Rules were much too personal to be shared. A few sent us outlines of the essential elements they incorporated into their Plan of Life or offered a Table of Contents such as the following.

A Hermit's Plan of Life:

Prologue
I. Goals of the Eremitical Life
> *Praise of God*
> *Salvation of the World*

The above outline is impressive in its completeness and would meet the standards for a Plan of Life that could be submitted for canonical approval. For hermits who do not need to have everything spelled out in such detail, the following Plan, simple as it is, provides a profoundly inspirational means for keeping a solitary focused on his or her goals.

COVENANT OF HOPE

I seek union with God in the spirit of Carmel through silence, solitude, simplicity, solidarity, obedience, and prayer so that I may love properly.

SILENCE: To choose communion with God over my own voices.

SOLITUDE: To choose solitude as a dwelling place for God over my own desire for society.

SIMPLICITY: To choose to give rather than receive.

SOLIDARITY: To choose oneness with the poor and dispossessed by becoming poor and dispossessed in spirit.

OBEDIENCE: To honor the obligations of my life over my own preferences.

PRAYER: To be in God's presence always.

I enter freely into this covenant on *(date)* with the desire to live it for the remainder of my life.

Fr. William McNamara has recently circulated a statement covering the development of his Spiritual Life Institute:

"Since 1950, I have had a dream. In 1960, Pope John XXIII urged me to embody it. Done, by the grace of God, in Sedona, Arizona; Crestone, Colorado; Yarmouth Country, Nova Scotia; Sligo County, Ireland, and now underway in New Pine Creek, Oregon, where I just completed two years of total solitude in a lusciously beautiful wilderness. This will be my final hermitage/retreat house with individual yurts and cabins built for a core community that will be

- lay, composed of individuals and families;
- contemplative, overflowing into discreet action;
- ecological, taking good care of the earth;
- ecumenical, various religions or none at all;
- eremitical, located in the wilderness and infused with the wildness of God;
- and mystical, the direct and immediate experience of God born of love.

Today's lackadaisical acceptance of subverted Christianity makes it very difficult for Christians to become distinctively human. Mark Twain said: 'There was only one Christian and he died.' J.D. Salinger shoots another arrow: 'See Christ and you are a Christian; all else is talk.'

The first thing Jesus said to the apostles was 'Come and see.' See things as they really are; see how everything is related, how others reveal the mysterious, ultimate Other, the Beyond in our midst, how history is charged with significance. See how the cat is the feline nature of God, the dog the canine aspect of the creator, the rhino the rhinoserosity of Yahweh, of Allah, of Love.

Without this kind of vision, we perish. But something is required of us: stillness and attention. We need to live each day deliberately. So the American native people say, 'Listen to the chickadee.' What will we hear? 'Be still and see that I am God.' Their song is not pantheism but panentheism.

God longs for our undivided attention, for our fullness of life. When that happens, there will be peace. For this purpose, Corpus Christi Hermitage exists. The guests and retreatants who come seek the same peace—not a placid peace, a private contentment but unity, integrity and freedom to be, to love, to be intimately touched by God and therefore transformed by God and therefore transformed into a Christ-man or Christ-woman for the life of the world."[39]

We are reminded of the famous saying of the Russian poustinick and mystic, St. Seraphim of Sarov: "Seek peace and thousands around you will be saved." Such is the goal of every hermit, the purpose toward which their Plan of Life must tend. How is this accomplished?

By keeping our eyes focused on God and knowing that the Gods we worship write their names on our faces, be sure of that. And a person will worship something, have no doubt of that either. One may think that tribute is paid in secret, in the dark recesses of his or her heart, but it is not. That which dominates imagination and thoughts will determine life and character. Therefore it behooves us to be careful what we are worshiping, for what we are worshipping, we are becoming.[40]

The genuine hermit is always becoming. So his or her Plan of Life will always be in a state of mild flux, as well. This is a healthy sign. As we become more at home in our solitary state, our need for words diminishes until the Silent Word himself governs us within and without. We find we have less need of a written life plan (except to satisfy our ecclesiastical overseers). Over time, we may find ourselves simplifying it to the essentials and consigning the rest to footnotes. At its best, our Plan of Life serves as a reminder, a means to keep us focused whenever we stray or stumble over unseen obstacles. But gradually, we become so accustomed to our life in solitude that we no longer need the feeble flashlight that a Rule provides. We learn to walk in the dark without fear—a fortunate development, for gradually our God will grow dark as well. But it will not matter. Seeing isn't the essence; being is.

The genuine hermit lives for the most part unseen and unknown, but through his or her hidden life of prayer, the world is being profoundly influenced for good. The best Plan of Life will be only as good as the hermit who lives it—wholeheartedly and joyously.

Windbourne Hermitage, Mulgoa
New South Wales, Australia

Chapter 5

Helps and Hazards

Disciple to Master: "Is there anything I can do to make myself enlightened?"

Master: "As little as you can do to make the sun rise in the morning."

Disciple: "Then of what use are the spiritual exercises you prescribe?"

Master: "To make sure you are not asleep when the sun begins to rise!"[1]

Spiritual Guidance

When the Christian eremitical movement began in the fourth century, the first thing that a man or woman aspiring to become a hermit did was to find an experienced elder from whom they could learn the elements of the life, be warned of its pitfalls, and be advised about the helps and hindrances they would meet. Experienced abbas and ammas offered this service as part of their ministry of hospitality. Even today, this conception of hermit as wisdom figure persists. The Solitary is someone with direct access to the will of God; someone who can infallibly guide us on our spiritual journey, if we are fortunate enough to unearth this reclusive figure.

We admit we grinned at a nineteenth-century drawing of a woman in a dun-colored traveling dress, seated with reticule in hand, listening raptly to the bearded hermit at the window of his humble shack. The recluse serenely offers advice about whatever urgent problem has prompted her arduous journey to his off-the-beaten-track abode. Such faith persists and people still make pilgrimages into the forests of the Russian hinterland to find a holy staretz or, as in the Native American tradition, young people transitioning to adulthood seek out a renowned elder or grandmother. Similarly, when people in mid-life face an unexpected call to the eremitical vocation, they also search for an understanding and experienced guide.

Over the years, one matter causing hermits and wannabe's anguish is their own often fruitless search for competent spiritual guidance. One commentary on Canon 603 airily assumes that the bishop who decides to give a hermit a chance will delegate a priest or religious (or even, in some instances, a committee!) to oversee the spiritual and material preparation of the person who has applied for hermit status. Spiritual guidance by committee?

The old fable of five blind men standing around an elephant and describing what it looks like according to which part each is handling, comes to mind. The lawyer interprets the requirements of Canon 603; the medical and psychological gurus weigh in with their assessments; the confessor supplies his recommendation (or not, as the case may be) regarding this person's suitability; and the spiritual guide offers yet another appraisal of the hopeful applicant discerning the Spirit's voice. Each professional offers advice from his or her area of expertise. Difficulties can arise, and they often do, because these individuals usually possess only a hazy idea of what a hermit truly is.

More than one *Raven's Bread* reader has written to us in great distress as they struggle to meet requirements generated by a chancery, requirements at odds with what the aspiring hermit senses as God's call. "Wannabe" hermits are asked to prove their financial security, including having a burial trust and costly forms of insurance, when they are aspiring to live the vow of poverty with its implicit insecurities. Others who seek only to be hidden from the eyes of the world are told they must wear a habit, which will insure that they will be instantly noticed wherever they go. As we read these cries for help, we suspect that the root of the problem may be the *image* of a hermit that governs the religious imaginations of these various professionals.

The hopeful hermit must be clear enough within his or her own mind what being a hermit entails so as not to become confused by what these "authorities" are trying to impose on him or her. It is fascinating to read or hear how differently each aspiring hermit conceives of his calling. No two cherish the same image. Serious discernment is required to sort out what characteristics the aspiring hermit/solitary/recluse is meant to incorporate into his future lifestyle. At this point, finding a gifted and disinterested spiritual guide becomes crucial.

Discernment

What exactly does an aspiring hermit need in terms of spiritual guidance? The initial priority is to determine the authenticity of the call to solitude and the source from which it springs. Is the individual running away from a difficult life situation? Is he or she seeking paranormal manifestations of the Holy more likely to be experienced in a hermitage? Is the aspiring hermit someone who feels inadequate to meet life on life's terms in the world of work and relationships? Even with the best motives and the most powerful yearnings for solitude, a hopeful hermit will be plagued by questions and self-doubt. They should be. Someone with absolute certitude that "God has spoken" is suspect.

Who would be an ideal spiritual guide for someone on the verge of making the life-changing decision to become a hermit? Another hermit? Yes, if this person has successfully lived the eremitic life for a sufficient number of years and possesses a special charism for spiritual direction. Alas, hermits are, by definition, not easy to find! There is no directory of local hermits, nor should there be. Yet it is amazing how they become known via word of mouth. Many aspiring hermits find their way to an experienced solitary through the mysterious workings of the Spirit. As has been said, when the student is ready, the teacher will appear.

If you are not fortunate enough to make contact with an experienced hermit gifted in the guidance of souls, you may find someone trained to lead you through a discernment process based on the Spiritual Exercises of St. Ignatius of Loyola. As far as I know, no one has developed a better instrument for true discernment than this Basque saint. When I was discerning the validity of my attraction to solitude, I was blessed to have an experienced Jesuit who led me through the process that Ignatius had developed. Our agreed-upon goals were to discern from whence came this compelling desire I had for solitude; to weed through all the various reasons and their value; as well as to rule out any possibility that the devil might be involved, tempting me to leave my cloistered community where I had lived fruitfully for thirty years. We also discussed whether my personality was suited for living the eremitic life healthily. The length of time that I had felt this desire was also examined. In my case, the yearning for solitude had governed my thoughts for more than a year.

The final analysis my director gave after I had completed an eight-day retreat was hardly earth-shaking ... except to me. He confirmed that I had fulfilled all the steps for a valid discernment and concluded that positive motives outweighed negative ones. This assurance that I was not self-deceived—something I had feared from the beginning—lifted me up like a helium-filled balloon. I will never forget how beautiful the world appeared to me that June day ... until my good director informed me of the next step in the process.

I was to live solitary life for a trial period of three months. During this time, I would have the opportunity to assess how I reacted to being entirely alone ... and on my own. I might also meet some of my own particular "demons" which would follow me into my hermitage—wherever that might be. It suddenly hit me that simply *finding* a hermitage was part of the test. Ads announcing hermitages for rent were not easily found. The few rentals I did find far exceeded my limited resources.

I finally learned of an unused house on church property in West Virginia where I could live during the bleakest season of the year, January through March! Bleak also described my spirits during much of this time. Not far from my dwelling, a "bold" creek tumbled into the New River. Its turbulent waters, which were never the same two days in a row, became a mirror of the emotional and spiritual tempests that scoured my spirit during those fateful days. I journaled, prayed, and "met my maker" more intimately than I had ever done. The self I thought I knew so thoroughly presented me with many unwanted revelations. However, when my three-month experiment was completed, I returned to the monastery, convinced that solitude was my calling. The actual experience of living hermit life had itself effected the final "sorting out."

With the help of my Jesuit guide, I made the literally life-changing decision to apply for exclaustration, a permission from Rome allowing me to live outside the walls of the monastery which had been my home for thirty years. Of course I had changed during those three decades, but by 1989, the American landscape I had left in 1959 was barely recognizable. Hermit though I planned to be, I would be living it in a very different world from the one I had left at age seventeen.

This anecdotal account of one person's discernment process may help point out how important spiritual guidance is when you are trying to untangle the Gordian knot of conflicting emotions, needs, and desires tumbling around in your heart. An even-handed, objective, and experienced director, preferably personally acquainted with eremitic life, is the ideal. But a skilled guide who knows the art of listening for the voice of the Spirit, even when not living as a hermit him or herself, can prove adequate. It is crucial for the aspiring hermit to have some competent assistance as she or he struggles to interpret the reality of the Call and seeks to avoid some of the many spiritual, psychological, or physical traps that could ensnare the inexperienced seeker. But, as has been said, such skilled guides are extremely hard to come by.

If one cannot find a hermit gifted and willing to offer guidance, it may be possible to find someone skilled in guiding one through the Spiritual Exercises as I did. Such a person may well be a monk or nun with at least ten or more years of life experience in a monastery. Alas, monasteries are also few and far between. Diocesan priests are usually easier to find but are not considered the best choice because few of them are trained to be spiritual guides, particularly for someone considering a lifestyle many of them regard with little favor. Sisters and priests in religious communities may be marginally better guides. Lay spiritual directors, well-trained, and hopefully blessed with the charism of spiritual direction, are increasing in number. But here we may have to beware of the overeager. Instead of our having to beat the bushes in search of them, they may leap out into our path eager to help. We could be very lucky in who approaches us, but the old adage is still true: Having no spiritual guide is better than having an unskilled one.

According to the letters which *Raven's Bread* receives, many hermits had to learn about hermit life and discern their calling mainly in the school of hard knocks, profiting by their mistakes and learning to listen ever more honestly to that *still, small voice* within. Self-discipline and integrity of heart can assist us to acknowledge the "warts and all" which appear when we intently study the mirror of our inmost reactions and responses. This is not to say that being without assistance as we discern our eremitical vocation is ideal, or even desirable. However, when we have prayed and searched and have still not found that uniquely qualified spiritual director we seek, then it is safe to say that our Inner Guide will be there for us. God will never leave us without his Holy Spirit.

Accountability

What is the value of having a spiritual guide beyond the initial stage of discernment? Accountability! Even the desert dwellers of many years' experience knew the value of opening their soul to another. Abba Pambo came to Abba Anthony and said: "Give me a word, Father," and he said, "Do not trust in your own righteousness; do not grieve about a sin that is past and gone; and keep your tongue and your belly under control ..."[2]

Because of our innate tendency to gloss over our weaknesses and ignore how our ideals may be on the slippery slope to outright sloth, we can all benefit by having someone to whom we must make an honest accounting at established intervals. A story written in the Native American tradition highlights the value of accountability:

> "When you need to look into darkness, the owl will come. When you need to peer deep into your own fear and hesitation, this great bird of the night will somehow find its way into your life. The owl is about exploring the shadow of your life, the part you might not want to see, the dark side of our moon. The owl is about emotional honesty, self-knowledge, and especially, self-examination.
>
> How do you do personal self-examination? How do you look into the darkness of your own resistance and your own fear? Some write down a systematic inventory and share it with a friend. Looking deep into your own shadow, you uncover your dishonesties and your dark places. Then you are checked and humbled by sharing your list with another who knows you well. Discover the inner hermit in a natural setting and owl medicine will come to you. Watch the discursive mind jerk nervously from place to place in its monkey-like hijinks. You'll meet the owl of self-examination in retreat. The inner hermit lives on the land and she will help you. In league with the owl, she'll show *you* to *you*."[3]

During the early years of evaluating our experiences as a hermit, weighing what works and what does not, giving a spiritual account to another, should be as frequent as once a month. After we are more firmly established in our life and are bumping along at a reasonable rate, these meetings may become less frequent. This is desirable for what was required in the beginning—a close scrutiny of all one's experiences in the desert—may, at a later stage, prove a distraction.

The goal of eremitic life is to become more and more hidden, unseen not only by others, but even by our own self. As has been said earlier, the mature hermit is the one who no longer thinks of him or herself as a hermit. Instead, as Thomas Merton wrote, he is just a man (or woman) who lives in the woods. Giving a spiritual account of oneself too frequently may result in focusing our thoughts on our self overmuch, when our goal is to focus ever more continually on the One who beholds us at every turn of our way. Some minor spiritual ills heal better when ignored than when picked over too often. If we find ourselves depressed by the necessity of preparing for yet another session of spiritual mentoring, it may be a sign that we no longer need such close supervision. If, when the question is raised, both you and your guide concur that frequent meetings are no longer necessary, then one may safely step out into the unknown alone with the Alone.

Bumps in the Night

"Acedia" is not a word frequently bandied about these days. Not so when hermits were filling the Egyptian desert. Then it was regarded as the Noonday Devil, a listlessness that fills the hermit with an unholy sadness, robbing him or her of the joy of his or her vocation. Thomas Aquinas described how this kind of depression in the failure of the victim to make the necessary effort to embrace totally one's commitment to the Divine Good. A person becomes susceptible to acedia when he or she does not wholeheartedly give the "yes" to his or her eremitical life. Kenneth Russell keenly sums up the effects of acedia:

> "That (not given) 'yes' seems to threaten individuals with a negation of all their potentiality and to promise a lifetime of misery. They choose, therefore, to swim no further. What they really opt for is some measure of control over their own comfort in front of the incalculable risk of relatedness. Not wanting to push any further upstream and not wanting to lose face by turning back altogether, the victims of

acedia tread water, as it were, and either console
their anxieties with sleep or attempt to dissipate
them in one distraction after another."[4]

Acedia is a failure to give oneself wholeheartedly to all the
demands of solitude—a dismal hanging on to control over one's
life and keeping the back door open. As such, it is a virus virulent
enough to destroy one's hermit life. Is there a cure?

Acedia is a deceptive condition and when not recognized for
what it is, we may apply precisely the wrong remedy. Accurate
diagnosis is crucial at this point. If our condition is the result of
too intense an application to prayer, reading, and study, we may
well need relaxation and a better balance to our daily life. This
makes sense if the "better balance" keeps us firmly in our solitude.
We need to keep on keeping on but with some healthy variety in
terms of physical exercise, interesting occupations which break up
our day, and simple enjoyments to which we can look forward with
pleasure. If we are so inclined and gifted, various forms of craft
work can perk up one's daily routine. So can quiet entertainments
such as puzzles, solitary games, or carefully chosen light reading.
At this time, having a TV in the hermitage might prove to be the
equivalent of the first-century "demon in the corner." Media, for
the hermit, requires special handling and strength of character, lest
it take over one's day and dominate one's imagination.

Few people realize how defenseless a hermit may become
against the impact of electronic media, especially visual forms.
When one has lived in solitude for a considerable period of time,
hearing only the natural world, closely observing all the subtle
shifts nature presents, and keenly registering one's own inner
states, one becomes both physiologically and psychologically
transparent. So much so that one can be incredibly vulnerable
to the assault of electronic visuals and noise. People who always
function with background music, have the TV running continually,
wear earphones while jogging, and flick on the radio when the car
keys are inserted seem to build up a protective wall that filters what
one really hears or absorbs.

Those of us who have abstained from the continual assault of media lose that type of armor. Media, especially the electronic form, can be the equivalent of an invading army. When continual waves of sight and sound assault us, we are unable to maintain the delicate alertness to spiritual realities that would ordinarily color our days.

When I mentioned my difficulty in even watching the evening news, someone suggested that perhaps I needed *more* exposure so I could be desensitized and less distressed by the horrors others routinely watch. To what end? So that I could now spend *more* time watching TV or movies? I had spent years cultivating a special sensitivity to things of the spirit. Why would I want to destroy this hard-won gift? And pray tell, when would I find *time* for both? As was said earlier, a hermit must learn the difference between healthy enjoyments and distractions that destroy the heart of the contemplative life.

Hermits also need to be wary of those who advise a change of scenery, a pilgrimage, or a bit more interaction with "the world." Too many vocational crises these days are handled by prescribing sabbaticals, extended vacations, or a period of psychological treatment when the heart of the problem is spiritual. The end result of these "cures" is frequently even more restlessness, disgust, and boredom with our calling. We are not talking here about serious problems such as alcohol abuse or other chemical dependencies which can, conceivably, creep into a hermitage. These ills clearly need radical treatment and may be indicators that the person is not suited to the solitary life. However, when the problem is acedia, the prescribed cure is deeper commitment to silence, solitude, and contemplative practice.

Hanging tough through sadness or mild depression strengthens one's trust in God's care. Not all bouts of depression are symptoms of acedia. We may discover that we are suffering from some mild physiological affliction such as Seasonal Affective Disorder (SAD) when our body is deprived of needed sunlight during the short days of winter. Our spirits droop despite our best efforts. Instead of booking a flight to the Riviera, new light fixtures may resolve the problem ... and keep one in the hermitage!

Another cause of distress for hermits arises from too frequent or prolonged absences from their accustomed solitude. Some hermits have found, after having had to spend a prolonged period outside the hermitage, that shortly after they gladly return to their solitude, they are hit with profound ennui. They feel stranded on the surface of the world that was once so rich for them and are unable to return to the depths they had enjoyed. Here the solution is time and patience. Before long, we will find ourselves gradually recovering the deep peace that was the atmosphere of our life before the interruption.

Many hermits have remarked on this experience when writing to *Raven's Bread*. As one said, she felt as if she had to enter an elevator which slowly descended to her accustomed level. Such experiences are a warning that constant effort is required to maintain a quality prayer life. Even if our outings are brief, we should be careful about their frequency. Elder hermits, advising individuals new to the life, often suggest that they "bundle" their errands so that they don't have to leave the quiet of their hermitage more than once or twice a week.

Balancing what has just been said, we have this invaluable bit of wisdom from the Desert Fathers: "A hunter in the desert saw Abba Anthony enjoying himself with the brethren and he was shocked. Wanting to show him that it was necessary sometimes to meet the needs of the brethren, the old man said to him, 'Put an arrow in your bow and shoot it.' So he did. The old man then said, 'Shoot another,' and he did so. Then the old man said, 'Shoot yet again,' and the hunter replied, 'If I bend the bow so much, I will break it.' Then the old man said to him, 'It is the same with the work of God. If we stretch the brethren beyond measure, they will soon break. Sometimes it is necessary to come down to meet their needs.'"[5]

Balance is the secret to a healthy and enduring eremitical life. Each hermit finds his or her own means of "relaxing the bow." Even media in measured doses can have its place. When we discussed the subject in an issue of *Raven's Bread*, some hermits remarked how helpful it was to listen to daily news on the radio. Interest in the world outside the hermitage can be advantageous. It helps to keep one grounded in the real world, gives one needed perspective on one's own trials, and provides incentives for prayer.

Normally, the hermit can maintain control over how much of "the world" enters the hermitage. However, this can be a particular challenge during the inevitable periods of loneliness which crop up. God's presence doesn't erase the need for human companionship, even for the most committed of solitaries. Loneliness is never "cured," because it isn't an illness but a simple result of the human condition. What is needed is a *reason* to embrace the personal emptiness that is part of solitary living. One *Raven's Bread* reader put it this way:

> "I would hope that I am not the only hermit who is alone but not because they desire aloneness per se. I am called to it even though it conflicts with my extrovert personality. I have no desire to chuck the world but to bring it with me. I see it as part of the calling to be informed about the world on a deeper level. I hope to reject the mentality of our environment but engage its suffering in a way different from before. And while I know the 'aching void' deep inside, I am unlike a mystic who might hope to fill it with an experiential sense of God. All I have is the gift of courage to depend on something more, a pure faith deprived of supportive consolations. It is like being lured, as was Moses, to see from afar but not be able to enter the promised land. Contemplation for me is a difficult discipline that must be engaged, promising an inner conflict with my penchant for doing. All I hope for is little more than a balanced peace. Although I did not choose this life but have somehow been chosen for it, I would not want it any other way."[6]

Thus speaks an experienced hermit who accepts loneliness for what it is—an ever-present reality—but who can live with it fruitfully because he has found a purpose for its presence in his life. Viktor Frankl's *Psychology of Meaning*, developed during his years as a prisoner of the Nazis, can be instructive for hermits. Although the hermitage is not exactly a concentration camp, the element of survival under often difficult conditions exists there also. Frankl had observed that those who survived in the camps were the ones who kept their hope alive, who did not give into despair but continued to believe, against all odds, that they would make it. What kept these prisoners' hope alive? They had something or someone to live for. For Frankl, he desperately wanted to be reunited to his beloved wife. Tragically, she died before the camps were liberated. But by then, Frankl had discovered how meaning or purpose could determine whether a person would choose to live or die. Sharing his new insights with his colleagues and testing his theories on clients gradually gave Frankl's own life needed goals.

As hermits, our goals are spiritual in nature. Although we have freely chosen the limitations of our lifestyle, we can still be surprised by the demands of fidelity. We may bump into some grueling struggles, but they normally won't have much drama. Actually, it is this very lack of drama which often proves to be the hair shirt that makes some days feel unendurable. Crucial questions arise: *Why am I here? Does this matter to anyone? Wouldn't I be doing more good somewhere else? Anywhere else?*

Suddenly, we are desperately groping for a reason to stick it out … anything to keep us afloat. Sometimes, we may simply have to let ourselves sink. There is no reason, no worldly reason, for our life in solitude. We must accept the fact of our life as it is and let that itself become our meaning. "Accept life on life's terms," as a nearby hermit often says. We must choose to consecrate the everyday-ness of our life for the sake of our sisters and brothers who are stuck with no choices in meaningless situations or in jobs which pay a pittance and leave them wholly unfulfilled.

While living in my little cabin in West Virginia, there were days when I had to haul jugs of water from my neighbor's house up the road. Amidst the heat and dust, I suddenly had the mental image of a long line of women encircling the earth, all with jars balanced on their heads or buckets hanging from shoulder yokes. My daily task became a moment of blessed communion with the millions of women throughout the world who, that very day, were walking miles to fetch water for family needs. Drawing water has been "women's work" since time immemorial, and now I was among them. Their daily drudgery was now mine as well. We walked together, them and me. Their presence gave meaning to my task, and (I hoped) my orientation to the Holy blessed and eased their steps.

Another challenge to eremitical life is that this life is usually lived for an extended period, if not a lifetime, within one rather small dwelling. Although few hermits these days are consecrated as anchorites, committed to living entirely within a single cell, those hermits who are city dwellers face unusual demands on their fidelity. Their hermitage, often a studio flat or small apartment, could, on occasion, feel like a prison where the hermit is trapped within four walls. These city hermits normally do not have the pleasant vistas and soothing quiet that those solitaries enjoy who have a certain amount of "green space" or picturesque vistas to entertain the eye and rest the mind. Enlarging their inner vision is essential if city hermits are to find contentment within their small but consecrated space.

More will be said later about the ideal placement of hermitages. At this point, we are looking at the troubles a hermit may have who doesn't take his or her own needs into account. More than one hermit has freely admitted that life without trees would be unbearable. But there are others who have felt the call to be a praying presence in the inner city. They believe they can limit the violence and crime that surrounds them by living a specialized form of eremitic life. These find it possible not only to survive but to thrive in a very restricted environment because of their strong belief in the meaning and value of their choice.

With the call, comes the grace ... and the call is suited to the nature of the one called. I, who had been a city girl, once chose a rural cabin provided with only "natural plumbing" and heated only by wood. I didn't even know how to light a camp fire, much less manage to keep a wood stove going twenty-four/ seven. My foolishness was only outweighed by God's mercy. He sent the instructors and provided the necessary strength to meet the trials my choice entailed. When others asked why I had made such a choice, I ruefully replied, "because I was too stupid to know better!"

The Big D's

Solitude has its inherent dangers, though in this more sophisticated age, we would not normally label them demons or devils. But the "Big D's" still lurk among us: despair, doubt, deception, and discouragement, to name four obvious ones. By our choice of solitude, we have renounced always having sympathetic help at hand. It is up to us to wrestle with these emotional imps. By now, it is obvious that a person needs to have developed some "Big C's" to overcome the temptations common to eremitical life. Prominent among these are character, confidence, and creativity, as well as a contemplative spirit.

Speaking of temptations, many people would love to ask a hermit about sex, but seldom get the opportunity or summon the courage. "Do you miss it?" "How do you deal with desires for sexual relations?" "Doesn't solitude make you an even easier prey to sexual temptations?" It would be simple (and also true) to just reply that God gives each of us the grace necessary for our state in life. However, this is dodging the issue. What do you *do* when these issues surface? It is naïve to assume they won't, at least for the majority.

Ideally, the wise solitary takes some preemptive steps by limiting his or her exposure to the subtle, as well as blatant, messages carried in the media. Ads, news stories, music, as well as most entertainment, intentionally create images to which we react, even without our consent. We are told that life without sexual activity is nearly impossible and definitely abnormal. Books and Web sites tell both men and women how to maintain their health and vigor by indulging in sexual pleasure frequently, with or without a partner. How individual hermits deal with their needs depends on their age, the urgency of their passions, and their personal beliefs about chastity. Some hold that masturbation is always and everywhere sinful; others have a more moderate view. Sexual activity for some can be like imbibing alcoholic beverages—the more one indulges, the more one craves. In this situation, abstinence may be the road to peace. Most people who have chosen solitary life have also assessed their ability to live without sexual activity.

When we consider married hermits (and these are not unheard of), the propriety of sexual relations is open to discussion and depends upon the desires of the couple. Conjugal love is normally expressed sexually, so it is not unthinkable that a hermit couple may wish to continue this dimension of their marriage as one aspect of their eremitical life. Admittedly, this is rare, but it can be a very beautiful state of life where physical affection and spiritual love sustain one another. Each couple will have their own path to walk, and the decision whether or not to include sexual activity within their hermit calling requires honest and respectful discernment.

Most hermits are solitaries, so the resolution of sexual temptations is dealt with knowing that interpersonal sex is not part of their vocation. Knowing this and living this, of course, are two different things. Many hermits who say they have problems with sex are often talking about loneliness—a desire for companionship and love. Once again, if someone has found a convincing reason to sacrifice the fulfillment of this desire, it is possible to overcome its urgency.

As we spend more and more time in our hermitage, these cravings normally diminish though they may never go away forever and always. There shall always be the gray days when loneliness and/or sexual needs impinge on our contentment. This is the time to take a page from The Big Book for Alcoholics Anonymous and endure the struggle one hour at a time. We may also have a friend on whom we can call when we feel the need for a helping hand. Experience and patience will help us live through the tough times, and gradually, if we guard against undue exposure to suggestive situations, sexual temptations will be no more than a passing distress.

Doubt and discouragement, though not the same thing, often arrive at our door hand in hand. For some reason, we begin to doubt the validity of our call. How can we be *sure* that eremitical life is God's will for us? We can't. Certitude is not one of the gifts that God gives to hermits ... nor to anyone else, as a rule. In this regard, I was impressed by an incident in the autobiography of a young woman who was bedfast due to severe rheumatoid arthritis. She was talking to her priest-confessor about her desire to know God's will as well as her envy of his calling, so clearly confirmed by the hands of the bishop.

He gently reminded her that many priests and religious, once convinced they had found God's will for themselves, later left the calling they had so sincerely embraced. Even the most fervent among the vowed or ordained will have periods of doubt about their choice. She was one of the very few, he said, who could be totally certain about God's will for them. Her calling to be chronically ill was undeniable; she could embrace this fact or fight against it, but it still remained an absolute certainty. Hermits, then, will always have questions about their choice popping up from time to time. Often, the only assurance that a solitary may have about their vocation is what I call "negative certitude." That is, as long as they have no clear indication that they should be living another lifestyle, they may trust they are doing what God wants of them at this time.

As someone who has lived four lifestyles, all of which are "seamed" together by the single thread of my desire to follow God's call, I have concluded that our deepest vocation is to continually seek God's will as it unfolds through life circumstances and our own evolution. If this sounds lacking in certitude and possibly subject to whim, it is! All I can do is earnestly use the tools of discernment, should a major change suggest itself. My hope is that God, in his mercy, will guide my stumbling feet and forgive my mistakes, right my wrongs and bring good out of my failures. As for certitude, I trust that the peace and contentment I feel are indicators I am doing what the Spirit is asking. If I am on the wrong track, I trust God will administer what my beloved Daddy occasionally threatened—a swift kick in the seat of my pants!

The old men used to say: "When we are tested, we are more humbled, for God knows our weakness and protects us. Yet when we boast, God takes his protection away from us. Then we are really lost."[7]

While we are wrestling with doubt, we are usually also engaged in a struggle with discouragement. For hermits, one of the greatest sources of discouragement is the sheer nothingness that their life appears to produce. It is not easy or pleasant to look back on years with nothing to show for them except survival. This is the temptation that really cuts to the chase and cross-examines our reasons for becoming a hermit. If our purpose in choosing eremitical life is to allow God to use us for his saving purposes, we should not expect tangible fruits. We are engaged in spiritual work, and the results will be in the same realm.

Among the sayings of the Desert Fathers, we find: "Abba Isidore of Pelusia said: 'Living without speaking is better than speaking without living. For a person who lives rightly helps us by silence, while one who talks too much merely annoys us. If, however, words and life go hand in hand, it is the perfection of all philosophy.'"[8]

This kind of silence is the equivalent of the "nothingness" which plagues the hermit raised in a culture where "the product" is the measure of a person's life. Nothing to say? Nothing to show for all those years? What a shame! Still worse, what a *waste*—particularly when the hermit is a gifted and/or well-trained person with "so much" to offer the world. The solitary must disregard questions for which the interrogator has obviously found a ready answer. All that a hermit need do is guard against allowing such intrusions to become doubts which disturb his or her peace.

Occasionally, we wonder about a person's intentions when we receive a letter full of excitement over the details of becoming a hermit but with very little said about the why. Perhaps this is because the "why" is extremely hard to express in words and is also deeply personal. Matters of appropriate food, clothing, and shelter are much easier to discuss and do have their value since, in becoming hermits, we do not automatically become angels. A bout of discouragement is proof of that!

Another "Big D" that angels need not contend with is self-deception. Initially, one might think that self-deception would be easy to get away with when living in solitude, since the normal "corrections" of rubbing elbows with others just doesn't happen. Actually, except in the case of mental illness, it is very difficult to persist in lying to oneself when living alone. Why? Because, with so little to distract us, we become acutely aware of the contradictions between the truth our heart knows and the lies our head would like us to believe. We cannot long ignore the increasing unease we experience, similar to a thorn or splinter which slips under our skin and begins to fester. The day arrives when we waken to find a pus-filled infection threatening the loss of a toe or finger. The moment of decision is upon us. Live in the truth or lose it! Self-deception is not an option!

Laura Swan, in her book *The Forgotten Desert Mothers*, offers this story that Amma Theodora told: "There was an ascetic who, because of the great number of personal temptations, said, 'I will go away from here.' While putting on sandals, she saw another ascetic who was also putting on sandals. This other ascetic said, 'Is it on my account that you are going away? Spare yourself, because I go before you wherever you are going.'"9 In other words, wherever we flee, we will always meet ourselves. It is pointless to run from difficult situations—they simply run with us since we ourselves are our greatest difficulty!

Life without Care

By the time a person has made the decision to follow a call to eremitical life, he or she has also pondered the injunction: "Consider the ravens; they do not sow; they do not reap; they have neither cellar nor barn—yet God feeds them. How much more important you are than one of these! If the smallest things are beyond your power, why be anxious about the rest?" (Lk.12,24–26)

Thomas Merton defined the essence of monasticism as a life without care. In a recorded talk to his novices, he evoked much laughter by wryly pointing out how easily the monks manufactured things to worry about—from how to feed the rabbits (creatures notorious for nibbling on everything in sight!) to what would happen if the choir leader for the week came down with a cold (when there were at least ten trained alternates). All this worry existed in a community where a monk's every physical need had guaranteed coverage.

Hermits also must learn how to lead a life without care. In fact, unless a hermit masters this art, he or she will not last long in a lifestyle where security is not on the list of guarantees. A genuine hermit finds a certain thrill in living on the edge and discovering how amazingly God provides for him or her, if we but give the Almighty a chance. The secret to "funding" a life without care is refusing to buy into the myth that material goods guarantee security. Actually, stocks and bonds, houses and lands, titles and jobs generate more insecurity than anything else on earth.

The scriptural passage which immediately precedes the admonition to consider the ravens is the parable of the farmer whose harvest had been so abundant that he had torn down his old barns in order to build larger ones in which to store up goods for years to come. The decision had hardly been implemented when God said to the self-satisfied landowner: "You fool. This very night your life shall be required of you. To whom will all this piled-up wealth of yours go?" (Lk.12:20)

This farmer had failed to consider two major items that head up God's "to-do" list: He had overlooked the needy with empty barns just beyond his property and had forgotten that security meant more than barns filled with goods. Hermits learning to live a life without care must take the risk of turning all their concerns over to God, who has proverbially deep pockets. As long as we are satisfied with a sufficiency, as St. Paul put it, we will always have enough. The "enough" that God provides may not match what the ad writers want us to believe is necessary, but it will be more than adequate for our peace (and joy).

Most hermits are able to find a hermitage within their means because their expectations are modest. That does not mean they are looking for a broken-down hut in the wilderness or a damp cave on a mountainside. Many live hidden lives in a government housing complex or in a single-wide off the beaten track. On occasion, a gifted hermit may build his own hermitage from parts of discarded buildings he can obtain for the price of hauling them away. Another may find a place available to her rent-free in exchange for upkeep because the owner is unable to live there or take care of it.

Among solitaries, we find many talented crafts persons—a gift which affords them much pleasure but little income. But for many, profit is a bonus. Their artistic abilities help them share God's delight in creating a world he pronounced "very good." They, too, find joy in the work of their hands and would agree with Abba Elias, who said: "Unless the mind sings with the body, the labor is in vain."[12]

The contemporary revival of one of the earliest forms of spiritual living still draws from the timeless wisdom of the desert abbas and ammas of the third and fourth centuries CE. As he was dying, Abba Benjamin taught his sons this: "Do this and you'll be saved: Rejoice always, pray constantly, and in all circumstances give thanks."[13] And how does one learn to "rejoice always"? Abba Nilus said: "Do not want things to turn out as they seem best to you, but as God pleases. Then you will be free of confusion and thankful in your prayer."[14]

More than one potential hermit has written to us in distress. The only valid economic system they wish to embrace is one that was taught more than twenty centuries ago and begins: "Consider the ravens. They neither sow nor reap ..." What most impressed them was the comforting consideration that "Your Father knows you need all these things ..." In other words, holy poverty is not meant to be destitution. Hermits do not normally live under bridges or in cardboard boxes over sidewalk vents. Our divine Parent does not want any of his children to lack basic necessities. Neither does he want us to worry over how he will provide for us. The other Scriptural injunction crucial to living a life without care is the reminder that no one can serve two masters. We are meant to live in trusting simplicity, focused on only one master, one goal, and one purpose.

Amma Syncletica understood this when she advised her followers: "There are many who live in the mountains and behave as if they were in the town, and they are wasting their time. It is possible to be a solitary in one's mind while living in a crowd, and it is possible for one who is a solitary to live in the crowd of personal thoughts."[15]

As we know, the most enticing "crowd" is composed of worries over our welfare, spiritual and physical. But once we set our focus on the one thing necessary, the ideal rhythm for "ora et labora" is automatically revealed. The sure-fire plan is to put our spiritual obligations in first place, relegating work to whatever time is left. By keeping first things first, we are prepared by our prayer life to find the work that will not only be compatible with our eremitic aspirations but which will supply us with the necessary income … not too little, not too much, but that golden mean of sufficiency with which God's servants are supposed to be content.

A simple caveat may be helpful for persons who tend toward scrupulosity. Although our prayer life is our primary "task," it usually does not take up the most time in an ordinary day. Work of some form or another normally fills the majority of our hours. For many hermits, after a few years in solitude, work and prayer are no longer separate entities but flow seamlessly into a gentle pattern—our prayer continues as we work, and our work becomes an expression of our communion with God.

It is possible that an individual hermit may be able to earn his or her sufficiency by weaving baskets as the desert fathers did … possible, but not likely. However, the hermit will always be adequately provided for if he or she learns how to weave trust in Divine Providence into a life a without care—always open to receive whatever is given and always ready to give away what has been received. Hermits are not hoarders, so when someone in need knocks on our door, we should be ready to share what we have. The following episode from the Desert Fathers demonstrates that living a life without care is a lifelong project, one we must always begin anew. God provides for those who are willing to risk personal loss when caring for a brother or sister.

It was said of Abba Moses at Scetis that after he had arranged to go to Petra, he grew tired in the course of the journey and fretted to himself, "How can I find the water I need there?" Then a voice said to him, "Go, and do not be anxious about anything." So he went. Some Fathers came to see him and he had only a small bottle of water. He used it all up in cooking lentils for them. The old man grew more worried, pacing in and out of his cell, praying to God. Before long, a cloud of rain came to Petra and filled all the cisterns. After this, the visitors said to the old man, "Tell us why you went in and out of your cell?" The old man said to them, "I was arguing with God, saying, 'You brought me here and now I have no water for your servants.' This is why I was going in and out; I was going on at God till he sent us some water."[16]

Even the most experienced hermits have moments when their trust is tried to the limit. Apparently, arguing with the God who appeared to ask more than the hermit had to give is an approved form of prayer under such circumstances!

Underground hermitage on the Wallowa River
Eastern Oregon, USA

Chapter 6

Practical Points

A brother questioned Abba Motius, saying, "If I go to dwell somewhere, how do you want me to live?" The old man said to him, "If you live somewhere, do not seek to be known for anything special." The brother said to him, "What shall I do then?" The old man said, "Wherever you live, follow the same manner of life as everyone else and if you see devout men whom you trust doing something, do the same and you will be at peace. For this is humility: to see yourself to be the same as the rest. When men see you, do not go beyond the limits, they will consider you to be the same as everyone else and no one will trouble you."[1]

The practical realities involved in setting out to live a solitary vocation are similar to those encountered when moving to a foreign country. One must consider "when?" (is now the time?); "where?" (is there a place available and affordable where I can set up housekeeping as a hermit?); "how?" (what is my first step?); and inevitably, "why?" (for which there is no entirely "reasonable" response).

What *am* I setting out to do? Basically, nothing. Nothing unusual, that is. Hermits live ordinary lives but with an extraordinary motivation. Something, or rather some*one*, has caught our "scent" and will not give us up. It is a game of hide and seek, a game where we are by turns both the hider and the seeker. Initially, we are the one who hides from those Following Footfalls that Francis Thompson describes so vividly in *The Hound of Heaven*. We flee "those strong Feet that follow, follow after … with unhurrying chase, and unperturbed pace, (that) beat with deliberate speed and majestic instancy …"[2]

The "when" of our hermit vocation is answered the moment we give up our futile flight, when we admit we don't wish to "win" and finally let ourselves be caught. The flare of joy we experience astounds us and we wonder why we struggled so long against accepting this gift which has been repeatedly offered despite our apparent rejection; despite our suspicion and fears. The "where" is also answered in that moment for we discover that we have come home—our hermitage is wherever we are together with our Relentless Lover.

Eremitic life, however, is more than just a matter of poetry and ecstasy. We must still live this life "in the flesh," so dealing with down-to-earth details is part of eremitical life. Modern-day hermits can no more live like angels than did Brother John the Dwarf in the fourth century, as was noted earlier.

Another story from the era of the desert fathers emphasizes that hermit lauras also must work. "A brother came to visit Abba Silvanus at Mount Sinai. When he saw the brothers working hard, he said to the old man: Do not work for the food that perishes. For Mary has chosen the good part. Then the old man called to his disciple. Zachary, give this brother a book and put him in an empty cell. Now, when it was three o'clock, the brother kept looking out the door, to see whether someone would come to call him for the meal. But nobody called him, so he got up, went to see the old man, and asked: Abba, didn't the brothers eat today? The old man said, Of course we did. Then he said: Why didn't you call me? The old man replied: You are a spiritual person and so do not need that kind of food, but since we are earthly, we want to eat, and that's why we work.[3]

The Hermitage: Caves to Condos

Most aspiring hermits have an idea of how and where they want to live and what degree of solitude is desirable and possible. Are they drawn to solitary life amid natural surroundings or in an urban setting? Are they attracted to the countryside or a mountain slope? To life deep in a forest or far out in the desert? Perhaps they long to be sequestered on an island. When choosing a hermitage site, it is prudent for aspiring hermits to take into account not only their attractions but also their needs and abilities. There is no "model" hermitage nor any set requirements regarding an appropriate site. Some hermits are drawn to live in natural solitude far from the sights and sounds of human activities. Others find such physical isolation frightening and prefer to look for a hermitage where there are people relatively close at hand. Some choose to live as "hidden hermits" in an apartment building or suburban neighborhood, the neighbors unaware of the intense prayer life being pursued so near at hand. A "hidden hermit" does not stand out from others but melds into his or her surroundings, modest in attire and activity.

There are hermits who have felt drawn to live in another country with the social isolation that this entails. Occasionally, a man or woman from Western society joins an ashram in India or lives some time among Tibetan monks. Normally, these adventurous souls spend only a few years in such intense transcultural solitude and then return to their country of origin enriched and ready to live the fullness of what they have experienced. Wherever a would-be hermit finally settles, it should be with the intention of a long-term commitment, since stability is essential to living eremitical life to the full. Aspiring hermits who are continually relocating seldom reap the benefits of "settled depth" where their roots can entwine the Rock that will hold them steady through any and all storms.

Ownership, too, is a question potential hermits must consider. For members of a religious community who intend to remain so, this matter is taken care of by the Order. The vow of poverty precludes private ownership. However, the majority of hermits are not monks or nuns. In modern culture, the most secure guarantee of stability is to hold a deed to the hermitage, whether it is on a tract in the woods or a condo in the city. More than once, hermits have contacted us in dismay after being informed that the apartment or rental they had lived in for years is either being torn down or the lease is increased beyond their means. One small group of hermits were profoundly distressed when told that the property for which they held a lifetime lease was to be timbered by the owners, thus destroying the privacy and seclusion they so valued.

Hermits who have made profession to a bishop have their options determined by the diocesan guidelines. Most bishops prefer that the hermit own his or her own property, although they may be required to cede the administration of it to some other designated person. A few bishops have provided a hermit under their authority with land and, occasionally, suitable housing, but this is rare.

Hermits living in a group (laura) may own property in common, but this can create serious problems should one of the members decide to leave. Eremitical life, even where hermits live in proximity and share certain buildings, is not meant to be a quasi-community life. Each hermit should be responsible for his or her own living arrangements and financial affairs. All too often, the one who controls the purse strings exercises undue control over the life of the group.

In one situation, a sister had been permitted by her community to use her inheritance to purchase property for herself and another woman under private vows in order to live there and provide hermitages for others. Eventually the differences between the two women proved irreconcilable, and it became clear that one would have to leave. Because the original purchaser was a religious, the property had been bought in the name of her companion, and it remained so when the other asked her to leave. This is one example of how an injustice can occur when common use of privately owned property is abused.

Yet another question needing attention in addition to site and ownership of a hermitage is the *type* of dwelling place that is possible and practical. No longer do religious solitaries perch on pillars or dwell in anchorholds attached to cathedrals. Nor do many lurk in caves, unseen for years at a time! Modern solitaries can be found anywhere, living in mobile homes, apartments, wilderness cabins, or urban townhouses. We have already noted the ingenuity that some hermits have exercised in building or finding their hermitages. Environment profoundly influences the quality of daily life, and some questions answered in advance can make a major difference as the years go by. Is the hermitage spacious enough to allow the solitary to live and work and pray comfortably? For those who crave intimacy with nature, does their dwelling place provide satisfactory access to the "green world?" If one chooses the more confined space of an apartment, is the hermit able to meet the challenge of devising strategies to introduce needful variety where the living situation is deprived of much external stimuli?

Some readers of *Raven's Bread* are men and women who are currently guests of this country's vast system of correctional institutions. It is amazing to read how ingeniously these "anchorites" turn a prison cell into a prayerful refuge. God calls people to be hermits in all conditions and circumstances. These incarcerated ones have taken their situations and infused them with meaning and purpose by turning them into a search for God. They may not be able to exercise much control over their outer life, but they have transformed their inner worlds.

A final point about the hermitage itself is that it should be stable. We are not talking about solid construction but the hermit's solid intention to stay put. Under ordinary circumstances, once a solitary has found satisfactory living conditions, he or she should not move. The desert fathers had this saying: "Just as a tree cannot bear fruit if it is often transplanted, so neither can a monk bear fruit if he frequently changes his abode."[4]

The type of eremitical life one plans to live determines what will be included and excluded from the hermitage. People who are not hermits often imagine heroic recluses in one-room cabins, roughing it without any modern conveniences. Some beginning eremites are "seduced" by these romantic images and determine to live as "simply" as possible; i.e., without indoor plumbing, electricity, or other "concessions" to the twenty-first century. However, they soon learn that such a choice makes their daily life far from simple.

Water must be obtained (and heated) several times daily; wood cut, stacked, dried and, then, when burning, tended continuously; oil lamps must be cleaned and refilled regularly to obtain even a meager light which strains the eyes and occasionally, the sinuses. Cooking, cleaning, and laundry become Herculean challenges. Even a hardy hermit may come to the realization that an inordinate amount of time and energy is absorbed by everyday chores. Where is the time for resting in contemplative prayer? How can one attend to Lectio Divina when there is not sufficient light to read by? Self-maintenance becomes all-consuming. A primitive lifestyle and a contemplative rhythm can prove to be mutually exclusive, even if one is physically able to meet the demands of such a rigorous routine. The simple life and a primitive life are not synonymous.

When I lived as a hermit, I was surprised to learn that most people assumed I grew my own food. Many of my neighbors in the rural community did. I had observed them working ceaselessly in their impressive gardens. I also noted that in addition to being time-consuming, gardening was also costly. The gardeners had sheds full of tools, some of which required gas and oil as well as maintenance. Seeds and starter plants were purchased in the early spring and tended in "hothouses" or "cold frames" until hardy enough to be transplanted. Then came various fertilizers, mulches, and pest controls to protect the growing plants. I witnessed one neighbor erecting a fence (nine feet high!) in order to protect her garden from foraging deer and hungry creatures. At harvest time, kitchens and root cellars yielded an impressive array of canning and drying equipment required to preserve a hard-earned crop of fruits and vegetables.

People who grow their own food often do so for the satisfaction it gives them, not for the money it saves them. Few hermits have the income and time for such an undertaking. Most, like myself, learn to stock their larder with the best they can afford and survive with their health intact, if not their image!

Anyone who has carefully viewed the starkly beautiful documentary of life at the Grand Chartreuse, *Into Great Silence,* may have noted that while there were monks who lived as total recluses, there were also lay brothers who daily delivered hot meals and clean laundry to the quarters of their enclosed brethren. Electricity and running water were available to the monks, and useful tools such as laptops were employed where needed. True, many of the monks got healthy exercise by cutting wood for the small stoves in their cells, but those whose age or disabilities made this impractical had the benefit of radiators.

It was clear to the viewers that the primary reason these monks lived in almost total solitude was to have time for prayer, hours and hours of prayer, undisturbed by the many household tasks attended to by the lay brothers. Hermits who live on their own ordinarily don't have the benefit of such personal service. Thus, most gladly make use of modern conveniences which allow them to have a quiet daily rhythm with prayer holding primacy of place.

Once the questions about the site and type of hermitage have been resolved, one is faced with furnishing it appropriately. Household appointments, normally modest, need not be uncomfortable or ugly. Most hermits are into their middle years and relish the comfort of at least one upholstered chair or rocker when reading or relaxing. A kitchen supplied with a variety of pots and pans is essential and could also include items such as a microwave, electric mixer, bread machine, and whatever else contributes to easier food preparation. Other household appliances such as a washer, dryer, and vacuum cleaner are welcome aids that minimize time spent on daily tasks, freeing up the solitary for prayer and reflection.

One may wonder why such mundane and obvious things are mentioned here, but for many, such modern appliances don't fit the image of a "real" hermit. More often than not, visitors expressed surprise to see a microwave on my kitchen counter and a computer on my desk. As recently as 2007, a radio interviewer was explaining the life of a hermit while introducing me to her listeners and tossed off the comment that hermits live such secluded lives they wouldn't know what a cappuccino machine was, much less have one. I laughed softly in the background but chose not to shoot down her storyline.

Many hermits agree that it is ideal if a religious solitary can earn a living working from her or his hermitage. This requires that it have a studio or work room with adequate space for equipment and supplies. If the hermit is a crafter, tools can run the gamut from a potter's wheel to a digital camera, from a loom to a skill saw. Quilting machines and computers turn up in many hermitages. Once a hermit has developed his or her skills, the vexing problem of selling one's crafts or products raises its head. Fortunately, we live in an age when sale via the World Wide Web is now possible. The one caveat that should be observed is that the hermit stock his or her hermitage modestly, having only those items and supplies she or he really needs and uses. Hoarding can become a serious temptation when the source of provisions is not stable or secure.

A valuable piece of advice concerning the daily rhythm of work and prayer saved me considerable anguish. I had heard the notion that the amount of time one devoted to something indicated how much one valued it; i.e., if prayer is one's highest priority, it should be given the biggest block of time. Someone prone to a certain kind of scrupulosity could develop a very unbalanced routine if she or he accepted this. A seasoned hermit reminded me that she did not need to spend nine hours in prayer in order to prove she valued it more than the tasks which consumed eight hours of her day. It is the quality of the time devoted to spiritual practices, not its length, which counts. Giving prayer the best hours of the day effectively indicates the importance it has for the hermit. Life in a hermitage should fall into an easy rhythm with the hours spent in prayerful exercises "flavoring" all the tasks and duties of the day, be they work, meals, or relaxation.

One final consideration about furnishing a hermitage addresses the question of communication. Should one have a phone or Web connection? How much availability does one want or need? Most hermits find a telephone useful, and thanks to answering machines and a muted ringer, it need not be intrusive. One female hermit let family and friends know that she only answered her phone or returned calls during the early evening. If the call was urgent, they could leave a message, and she would respond when she could. Cell phones must also be handled with similar discretion. The major value of a phone, especially for a hermit who lives far from others, is to provide access to help if an emergency arises. In the U.S., being able to call 911 from home is very reassuring. Similarly, if one meets up with a critical situation while driving, being able to punch *77 into a cell phone and have immediate access to the state police affords a welcome sense of safety.

Many hermits use their phones for ministry. Those who are experienced offer spiritual guidance to clients who call at prearranged times. Others establish Web sites which list readings and reflections, prayers and religious poems, for those who are searching for spiritual inspiration in their lives. Still others post newsletters, such as *Raven's Bread,* or host chat rooms where seekers can share their concerns and find support in a spiritual atmosphere. Each hermit must determine, based on need and means of income, what forms of communication are most helpful to their solitary lives.

The "phone connection" that all hermits should foster is a spiritual version of the old-fashioned party line. Early on, callers knew that their conversations were often being stealthily monitored by some nosy neighbor. Today, when someone calls a hermit, they too know that there is another Listener, one who is not just intrusively curious but genuinely concerned. The hermit also tunes into that silent Listener when on the line and may find him or herself prompted to offer words of advice or encouragement, of warning or insight, which do not arise out of their own thoughts or experience but from Another. In such instances, the hermit becomes the voice of the unseen Listener, a humbling task which a solitary understands is never undertaken on one's own but only when (literally) called. Their job is simply to keep the lines open and clear. Nothing more; nothing less.

Hermits also serve as "towers" which pick up signals and direct them to their ultimate destination. Most of the time, the solitary is unaware of being so used; only on rare occasions are they asked to be conscious intermediaries. Throughout their quiet day, hermits focus on the spiritual realm, bringing it closer to the secular world around them. Through their hidden lives of sacrifice and attentiveness to the Holy, hermits help to create more "thin places" in the world, allowing influences from the spiritual realm to more freely touch human lives.

Solitude: Alone or Shared?

Merriam-Webster's Collegiate Dictionary defines a hermit as one who retires from society and lives in solitude, especially for religious reasons; a recluse. The same volume defines a recluse as a person who leads a secluded or solitary life; a hermit. Checking out a "solitary," we find: one who lives or seeks to live a solitary life; a recluse. A collection of synonyms: solitude, isolation, seclusion, offers varying nuances to the state of one who lives alone. Solitude implies a condition of being alone, often chosen for a purpose such as uninterrupted work or for deep thought. Isolation stresses detachment from others often because of circumstances not under one's control. Seclusion suggests a shutting away or keeping apart from others, often connoting deliberate withdrawal or hiddenness from public view.

The foregoing implies that hermits can live in varying degrees and forms of alone-ness. We are warned against a narrow stereotyping that would restrict a "true" hermit to someone who never interacts with another human being and who goes to great lengths to avoid being seen. Such total withdrawal from human contact is virtually impossible to maintain for any length of time unless one has a support network or possesses unusual survival skills. It did not apply even to the legendary desert fathers and mothers, who met with one another on a regular basis and frequently had a disciple living with them for instruction in eremitical life.

However, hermits lived alone most of the time, each following their own daily rule. Thomas Merton wrote of them. "There was nothing to which they had to conform except the secret, hidden, inscrutable will of God which might differ very notably from one cell to another!"[5] Abba Nisteros is quoted as answering a brother who asked, "What good thing shall I do, and have life thereby?" by pointing out that God alone knows what is good for each hermit. "Therefore, whatever you see your soul to desire according to God, do that thing, and you shall keep your heart safe."[6]

With this in mind, an aspiring hermit has the option to consider whether she or he is called to live entirely alone, with one or two others, or with a group. If a person finds a congenial group, other questions will surface. Will there be communal buildings, such as a chapel, a kitchen, or work rooms, in addition to the hermit's own cell? Or will each hermit have a complete hermitage and only meet rarely with other members of the laura?

Over the years, *Raven's Bread* has become a source that many aspiring hermits consult as they begin dealing with the practical questions of setting up their life in solitude. A surprising pattern emerged among these individuals. Initially, most of them were searching for a hermit community with individual hermitages available. Such "lauras" (as these eremitical groupings were called in the early centuries) do exist today, each with its own spirituality and particular practices. Some were grouped around a chapel or other shared buildings, such as a communal kitchen and/or workroom. Others maintained stricter solitude, with members living entirely on their own.

Most of the men or women who feel a call to solitude already have an attraction to a particular spirituality and its accompanying practices. The difficulty for many is finding a group with a compatible spirit. For instance, one group may be strongly marked by the Carmelite ideal of individual solitude, while another may model its daily life on the extreme simplicity of the Franciscans. Some groups are more monastic in their orientation, while others style their daily lives on that of the desert fathers and mothers.

It is a rare group that is so open-minded that an individual who joins them is completely free to follow his or her own version of eremitical life. Does every member of a particular hermit community have to be Christian? Or practice zazen? Or attend Mass daily? Slowly, it dawns on the aspiring hermit that there are dozens of ways of living the solitary life, and it may not be easy to find a congenial group.

Over the years, it has been noted that most hermit groups have a stable core of two or three members who have lived a clearly defined lifestyle together for several years. A hermit-to-be who joins them may be rather innocent about the degree to which they will be expected to conform to the established routine. But within six months to a year, the new member begins to assess whether he or she is comfortable with the prevailing practices and spirit of the group he or she has joined. Questions begin to arise. The stumbling block may be something as inconsequential as being required to remove one's shoes upon entering the chapel or can be as crucial as determining how fully the individual's financial resources are to be blended with the communal "pot."

The advantages of group living include greater security; assurance that if one falls ill, help is at hand; and shared labor that can make many jobs, such as putting in a garden, much easier. Living in a hermit laura can be especially helpful for someone who, due to poor health or a disability, could not live entirely on his or her own. Communal life can eliminate duplications of such costly items as automobiles or septic systems. One vehicle can be used by all the members with the understanding that everyone contributes their fair share toward maintenance, insurance and fuel, etc. "The devil is in the details." This applies just as truly to spiritual undertakings as it does to secular.

Here at *Raven's Bread*, we are no longer surprised to learn that an aspiring hermit who had consulted us about finding a hermit colony is now a former member and the two core hermits of the laura continue living the regimen they have developed over the years. Hermit lauras remain very small, as a consequence of such turnover. Hopefully, many of these recognize this is as it should be. Their goal should not be to grow into a sizeable community but to be a space where beginning hermits learn the basics of eremitical life from experienced "elders" before moving off on their own.

One stumbling block that hermit groups encounter is differing expectations on how the shared life should be lived out on a daily basis. History has shown that what was originally a group of hermits can evolve into a community, and the original charism of the group shifts, with the eremitical base disappearing entirely. That is why a group of hermits must wisely protect its primary inspiration by keeping to a minimum such practices as meals in common, shared recitation of the Office, recreation, and, most delicate of all, a common purse. Too much togetherness can destroy the original inspiration of solitude, silence, and independence that marks genuine eremitical life.

Some solitaries seek to live on the grounds of a monastery, convent, or abbey. This can be beneficial as far as security and maintenance goes, but there are some inherent disadvantages. The members of the community may take to visiting their resident hermit and unless one is very careful, the solitary may end up involved in the internal affairs of the order. Or members of the community can turn against the hermit for reasons as varied as the monks or nuns themselves. Or the understanding reached with the superior when the hermit first moved in will not be honored when another administration is elected. A hermit should aspire to be as simple as a dove, but it proves helpful to employ the cunning of a serpent when moving into a situation that involves so many "voices."

Agreements should be formally drawn up and witnessed, as protection not only for the hermit but also for the community offering hospitality. More than once, a generous community may find themselves saddled with someone who is not so much a hermit as a misfit; a person who flits from one place to another with a plausible, even heart-rending account of why they were so cruelly turned out of their previous situation. Individuals such as these could potentially cause scandal via words spoken out of turn, or actions unbecoming to a committed religious. The attitude or personality of the "hermit" can reflect poorly on the hospitable community, causing misunderstandings which are hard to explain. Additionally, the guest solitary is not subject to obedience to the superior but many lay people unconsciously expect that they are and wonder why this "holy hermit" is allowed to live as she or he does. Occasionally, a solitary may solicit alms from visitors to the community, putting it and the innocent caller in awkward positions.

In a Commentary on Canon 603, we find this helpful clarification about eremitic life styles: "Today, besides the public witness of the hermits through their abandonment of the world, austerity of life, and external solitude, there are also hermits who remain in the world, live in reserve, supporting themselves by common manual

167

labor. They are almost unknown, and in their cities, they pray and work to the praise of God and for the salvation of the world ... some, even, live in a laura (a colony of hermits) under the direction of a spiritual director without being bound to the same rule or institute and without constituting a community."[7]

A form of eremitical life which has already been alluded to is that lived by married persons. From a certain point of view, married hermits are a contradiction in terms. But for those who are called, it proves to be a rich development of a shared life already sacramentally blessed. If both spouses are drawn to silence and solitude, they can live together peacefully, respectful of each other's space and rhythm. If only one spouse is attracted to eremitical life, the other can provide the practical support which frees their partner to devote more time to prayer and solitary pursuits. We have read some very frank accounts of how marriage and eremitical life have or have not worked for a particular couple. The crux of this unusual form of life is the recognition that both spouses are called to a new way of living their commitments—to one another and to God—even if only one actually embraces the eremitical life. There are various ways of sharing space while still living in authentic solitude, but the majority of hermits today live alone ... until someone knocks on the door or the phone rings!

Some hermits who responded to the *Raven's Bread* survey of 2001 wrote that he or she was looking after an ailing parent, often in their own home. Not too surprisingly, this situation provided the hermit with good reason to avoid social engagements and to live a very "retired" lifestyle. A few identified themselves as "hidden hermits," solitaries known as such only to their confessors or spiritual guides. The majority of hermits who subscribe to the newsletter are individuals with the strength of character and courage to "go it alone," except for (perhaps) a spiritual guide. They have found that they do not need formal recognition of their vocation and feel confirmed in their calling by the fruit of divine peace it produces, hidden as that may be.

Hospitality: How Much and How Little

One experienced hermit writes: "For the hermit, hospitality is sacred. The hermit sees visitors as Christ presenting himself. The model to imitate is the Lord Jesus himself, who washed the feet of his disciples. The hermit is the servant of those who come. Just as Abraham did, he or she is there to greet the visitors, to make them rest, to give them to eat and drink, to share with them all that he or she has."[8]

This is the underlying spirit which should guide the hermit when dealing with the delicate question of hospitality. The committed hermit is not trying to entice people to drop by but rather accepting them when they do come, as God-sent. Neither is the solitary required to welcome any and all visitors without distinction, giving them carte blanche to their time, space, and goods. The hermit is not running The Dew Drop Inn! Discernment is required, especially when the visitor is a family member. Hospitality is one of those virtues that most hermits pray to be spared. It is required that a hermit keep an open heart but not always an open door.

Once the hermit has dropped the curtain through which she or he has peered deciding whether or not she or he is "at home," the door, if opened, should be done so generously. It is a safe assumption that the guest arrives knowing they are visiting a man or woman whose life is centered on spiritual realities. Unless the caller is selling Avon products, his ultimate goal in calling on a hermit is to partake of the spiritual peace he senses emanating from the hermitage. Therefore, it is not only admissible but desirable that the conversation be centered in God. The hermit should not whip out a prepared monologue delivered on cue like a wind-up preacher. But, after listening with care while the visitor unburdens his heart, the solitary may offer a deeply apt "word," a word that the hermit has heard in his or her inner ear and passes on to the often troubled guest. In such conversations, the hermit should "disappear," allowing the visitor to commune with the Sacred. The hermit unselfishly becomes a compassionate listener who, so far as the guest knows, has no personal problems or cares and so is free to empathize with his woes.

One must be cautious of visitors who show undue curiosity about life as a solitary. Why do they ask? Are they interested in such a lifestyle for themselves? Or so the guest can later entertain friends by delivering a first-hand description of their visit with a "real hermit?" Genuine solitaries have no wish to impress people with accounts of visitations from angels (or demons, as the case may be), of the prolonged fasts or the extended hours of prayer that the uninformed imagine to be their daily routine. When the guest leaves (hopefully soon!), it should be in peace, with the blessing of God ringing in their ears and the unction of the Spirit sweet in their heart.

Hermits who are both gifted and trained in the art of spiritual direction may offer individual guidance to those they judge to be sincerely seeking a closer relationship with the Holy. Some clients may come to the hermitage; others may speak with the hermit over the phone at a prearranged time. The latter method does not allow the spiritual guide to pick up on the many unconscious cues projected through body language, but a skilled listener can usually learn a great deal about the feelings and desires of the speaker by concentrating on what is *not* said as well as how things are phrased. The advantage of spiritual direction via phone is that it is less intrusive and can more easily be limited to agreed-upon time limits.

Occasionally, an experienced hermit may be asked to advise a person who feels God is drawing them to the eremitical life. It is a matter of utmost charity to offer guidance and support as the neophyte negotiates the first rocky shoals over which he or she is launching into a new life. But such assistance does not include throwing wide the hermitage door and offering food and lodgings indefinitely to the potential solitary. Rather, one offers the "shelter" of encouragement and discernment to those seeking their way amid the clamor of astonishment and disapproval that such a strange turn usually generates among friends and relatives.

A hermit in West Virginia, who initially offered spiritual direction and retreats to whomever requested it of her, eventually narrowed her ministry to only those who were discerning a calling to eremitical life. Much of her guidance was offered via taped "letters" recorded in response to the questions the neophyte posed to her. Only those hermits who know they are gifted with the abilities and background to offer spiritual direction should venture into this ministry. Being a deeply spiritual person does not always include the talent to serve as a spiritual guide.

Many hermits have been married at some point and have adult children who will want to visit, along with their spouses and children. If they live relatively close by, visits should be scheduled so the hermit's daily rhythm is least disturbed. If the family does not understand or approve of the lifestyle a parent has chosen, they may urge them to become more "social." Now the tables are turned. Instead of the young adult struggling to break free from the parental nest and expectations, it is the parent who must firmly insist on the right to live the life to which he or she feels called. It must be made clear to both family and friends that the choice to become a hermit is a vocation and must be honored as such. Some grandparents have discovered an unexpected boon when they have formally undertaken eremitic life—they are no longer required to provide free babysitting services at a moment's notice!

Away: Visits and Vehicles

Just as visitors bring some unwanted problems into the hermitage, the hermit him or herself can do the same after time spent outside the hermitage, no matter how necessary and legitimate the excursion may have been. There are some hermits, particularly those who are required to write a Rule to satisfy a canon lawyer, who attempt to foresee all the reasons when she or he would leave the hermitage and its grounds. Life being full of endless surprises, the list itself soon becomes endless. There is no way that every possible reason can be anticipated. For instance, I had not expected to be the person who would have to pick out my father's coffin, but there I was, faced with an unavoidable reason to leave my hermitage at a moment when I most longed for time alone to grieve my loss.

One writer cautioned that trips out of the hermitage can become a source of temptations, a way by which demons can creep through the purity of the eremitic walls and sully the atmosphere. The images this evokes can be amusing, but there is some truth in it as well. Most of the outside "temptations" which beset me during my years as a hermit are with me today. And they were encountered in the same place ... Wal-Mart! That vast assemblage of every imaginable kind of goods, cunningly arranged to attract my eye, has always been a source of struggle for me. Eventually, I grouped my visits to the supermarket and drug store and "big box stores" to coincide with other necessary appointments, thus limiting the number of times I left the hermitage. Moreover, I was without the psychological "conditioning" that daily exposure to TV, radio, and catalogs gives to most people in this land of plenty. I found myself overwhelmed amid the thousands of items beckoning for my attention. Instead of making the best use of this shopping expedition, I found myself so distracted I couldn't make the simplest of decisions. Eventually, I learned to wear mental blinders, focusing on finding only my intended purchases. God help the manager who had once again rearranged the stock, presenting unwanted goods to my unwilling eyes. My major temptation was converted into an impulse to flee screaming from the store rather than to indulge in impulse buying.

The same internal distress can erupt when visiting friends and family. Life spent in the sweet peace of one's hermitage fosters a contentment which far surpasses the stresses and chaos that one encounters in a home where children of varying ages are "in process." I have heard that even the most doting of grandparents heave a sigh of relief as the taillights of their son's or daughter's family vehicle disappear down the road.

Most hermits choose to shop for their own daily necessities rather than depend on others to supply them. Although it may seem that one keeps silence and solitude more perfectly by staying in the hermitage and asking others to supply daily needs, this doesn't accord well with the poverty and humility that should mark a hermit. If the hermit chooses to take care of errands personally, he or she will have need of transportation, usually a vehicle he or she owns. The city hermit can use public transportation, ride a bicycle, or walk, all methods which work well for appointments, banking, mailing letters, etc. But for the hermit who plans bi-weekly trips for food and other supplies, bringing all the provisions home on a bus or balanced on a bicycle could prove, at the least, awkward, if not downright hazardous. Donkeys were in vogue with desert fathers and mothers but are not ideal trotting along an urban thoroughfare!

Even the suburban solitary will find a vehicle a necessity, not to mention one living out in the country. Few doctors make house calls, and we have yet to meet the traveling dentist. It is possible to ask a friend or neighbor for a lift now and then but certain errands, such as going to a session with one's spiritual guide, are so personal that one hesitates to ask someone else to accompany them. Hermits who work part-time will need transportation, especially if they have a personal service job such as housecleaning or yard work with widely spaced clients.

If the hermit decides that a vehicle (automobile or pickup? gas or hybrid?} is needed, then it will be important to deal with it according to the vow of poverty. Who expects a hermit to drive up in a Lexus, even a donated one? (Some gift-horses are not acceptable unless they are given with no strings [bridle?] attached!) And, of course, with a vehicle comes maintenance, insurance premiums, registrations, and licenses.

When the beginning hermit meets with his or her spiritual guide for the monthly session, a list of trips outside the hermitage may be required. This accountability allows the director to have a clearer understanding of the good sense (or not) that the novice hermit exercises—what errands he or she judges necessary and their frequency. An overzealous eremite may try to lay in a year's supply of goods and foodstuffs, only to find that few staples remain usable beyond the first few months. Consider weevils, mice, and that "use-by" date. Hopefully, fervor is moderated over time and experience teaches the "young" hermit what is feasible. Eventually, only an unusual trip will need to be discussed with the director.

When it comes to family obligations, an especially sensitive discernment is required. The hermit will pray for family members and will find ways to sustain these relationships in a manner consistent with a primary commitment to solitude. Some solitaries arrange structured times for visits, trying to keep them as infrequent as family ties permit. A hermit with family nearby may find it necessary to visit with them more often, particularly if elderly parents require attention. Charity is always the supreme rule for all spiritually oriented people and, as always, it begins at home.

If visiting is not handled with wise discretion from the beginning, a hermit may find it difficult to later modify expectations they have unwittingly created. During my years as a hermit, I welcomed anyone who wished to visit me—because callers were not numerous and mainly came seeking some spiritual guidance. The same was true for phone calls, which I usually accepted. Only later did I realize that some of my visitors expected that I would reciprocate their visits and phone calls. I hurt some feelings when I didn't drop over for coffee or initiate phone conversations. Solitaries must make it clear from the beginning that the eremitical life is one of withdrawal, one which places serious constraints on social interaction.

One hermit employed an unusual system which made this quite obvious. On the edge of his property, he had erected a small bell tower where callers could announce their arrival. The hermit would greet his visitors at the bell and politely request that they respect the atmosphere of silence surrounding his hermitage by not speaking once they had passed the bell. Conversations were confined to the gate, where they could discuss whatever had led them to seek out the hermit. (Hopefully they did not choose a cold or rainy day to drop by!) I suspect this hermit made his point and visitors who did come had no unrealistic expectations about the length of their visit.

Media: TV, CD, DVD, AM/FM, WWW, etc.

Almost all hermits wrestle with the question of whether or not to have a TV or radio in the hermitage. Numerous ways of handling this issue have been discussed in the pages of *Raven's Bread*. Many solitaries choose not to have a TV at all, while others have one but severely limit their use of it. One hermitess, living in the wild

Orkney Islands, kept a small set in a cupboard and used it only on the rare occasions when a religious service was televised, such as Christmas Midnight Mass from Vatican City. Other solitaries in remote areas tuned in for Sunday Services when the roads were impassible.

During my years as a hermit, I did not have a TV but found a radio very useful, mainly for following the news. National Public Radio presented the news without much commercial interruption and with sufficient in-depth analysis that I did not need additional newspaper coverage of world events. And like my sister in the Orkney Islands, I took great pleasure in tuning in to certain religious programs, such as the annual Christmas Eve Vesper and Carol Service from Kings' College Chapel in Cambridge, England.

What about periodicals and newspapers? Each hermit will have to discern for him or herself whether these will prove an advantage to his or her spiritual life. Not all religious journals are of equal quality, and some are more applicable to the eremitical life than others. As for secular publications, periodicals such as *National Geographic* or *The Smithsonian* can provide enrichment without the seductive advertisements found in many other magazines. Daily newspapers tend to pile up only partially read, unless one has a woodstove for which they provide excellent starter material!

Access to the World Wide Web can prove both attractive and entertaining to solitaries, but also vastly time-consuming unless one develops personal "ground rules" about when and why and how much one is going to make use of this window on the world. The Web is priceless for the information it can give a hermit who needs to research a topic she or he is studying or writing about. It can assist a stay-in-hermitage shopper to purchase needful goods without leaving home. But such an option requires rigid self-control, because it is so easy to browse not-so-necessary items, compare, and finally buy with a click and an unfelt (at the time) nick to the credit card.

Another computer allure, in addition to e-mail and shopping, is games. These can provide an hour of healthy relaxation to the hermit who has no wish to bounce a basketball off a backboard yet needs to unwind after a day of serious prayer and work. "All work and no play make Jack a dull boy" applies to solitaries as well as to the dedicated student. As with other forms of the media, it is a matter of personal taste.

For some hermits, a computer is anathema, a pandering to the consumer culture and something which has no place in their hermitage. For others it is an essential tool, useful for the work, writing, and study it enables, as well as connecting with others in a quiet, non-intrusive way. Hermits who do craft work can offer their products for sale to the world without leaving their hermitage. Used with care, the computer develops new skills and keeps the user mentally keen. Nothing of itself can cause a hermit spiritual harm if used with purity of heart and discretion.

Abba Mark once said to Abba Arsenius: "It is good, is it not, to have nothing in your cell that just gives you pleasure? For example, once I knew a brother who had a little wildflower that came up in his cell, and he pulled it out by the roots."

"Well," said Abba Arsenius, "that is all right. But each man should act according to his own spiritual way. And if one were not able to get along without the flower, he should plant it again."[9]

Daily Prayer Schedule

One of the bonuses of eremitical life is being able to design one's day according to one's personal rhythm—eating, sleeping, praying, and working when one is at her or his best for each of these activities. It may take awhile to discover what times are ideal, but the benefits are worth the effort. When a daily schedule is first developed, it should be expected that it will require fine-tuning for the foreseeable future, ideally in the direction of more simplicity. Gradually, one's own biorhythms are discerned and times for rising and retiring are scheduled accordingly. However much one may wish to greet the rising sun with joyful praise, some individuals may find they are simply not mentally alert that early in the day. Forcing oneself out of bed at 5:00 a.m. may be a fine discipline but will do nothing for prayer and may only leave the hardy soul sleepy for the rest of the day. It is far better to stay with the pillow until one can waken refreshed and then pray, alert and responsive.

Some individuals may benefit from a midday siesta—most cultures around the Mediterranean observe this practice with great profit. St. Benedict, who lived as a hermit for many years before founding his Order, even prescribed a midday rest in his wise Rule. Trappist communities still observe this sensible practice. It is particularly needful because the monks interrupt their night's sleep to pray the Office of Vigils at 2:00 a.m.

In a culture where the majority of adults are sleep-deprived, it may be difficult to recognize the symptoms in oneself. If anyone should be well-rested, it should be hermits, who are engaged in a singularly demanding way of life requiring one to be hyper-alert to spiritual realities. One is endeavoring to be aware of very subtle movements in one's soul; of openings onto and advances from the spirit world. If one is dulled from lack of sleep, even mildly, it may not be possible to perceive the *"still, small voice"* whispering in the ether. In addition, one will be more susceptible to "down days" and could end up living in a state of near depression merely from lack of adequate sleep. Being alone adds to one's vulnerability. One may either sink deeper into lethargy or fall prey to the temptation which promises that some (possibly inappropriate) entertainment will lift the spirits. Whether found within or outside the hermitage, these can prove very seductive. After all, who wants to live continually amid gray clouds of drowsiness or wander around in a mild torpor, discouraged and depressed?

The foundation and framework of the hermit's schedule is prayer. For many Christians, the eremite's day is structured around the Liturgical Hours, modeling the routine of a monastery. As noted before, the Liturgy of the Hours is intended to sanctify the day by taking "prayer breaks" at regular intervals. Some hermits develop the habit of dividing their night's rest by rising after an initial period of deep sleep for a time of prayer during the calm of the night. They then return to bed for another few hours of rest before greeting the morning with praise, initiating their daily routine.

This practice sounds so idyllic that one must be wary of turning what is a method of sanctifying the day into a rigid ritual of clock-watching. One can mistake a means for an end and turn prayer periods into mindless exercises, struggles to "get in" every single word in the Breviary. Meanwhile, a line or even a single word grabs the heart, begging one to sit and listen to the Author. Instead, one plows on, intent on covering the "assigned reading." When reciting the Liturgy of Hours in common with others, one can drift into deeper prayer, allowing the group to carry one along. The "train" does not have to stop for the pray-er to savor a particular view. As solitaries, however, one must exercise the option of stopping the train itself and absorbing the vista for as long as one pleases. The moment has come to simply sit still; the goal has already been reached.

In addition to the Liturgy of the Hours (and at times, in place of its recitation) are periods for meditation or contemplation, wordless and silent. Those new to this practice may start with fifteen minutes twice a day and gradually increase the time to one or two hours daily. Reading from a spiritual book beforehand can serve to focus the mind and provide something to ponder. However, this is only a springboard to launch one into the waters of quiet listening, communion, and adoration. No matter how difficult at times this practice may be, such silent interchange with the Lord is the heart of hermit life.

For solitaries belonging to a church with a sacramental tradition, weekly attendance at Mass is a sacred practice. Some hermits include daily Mass in their schedule, especially if they live in a laura with a resident priest, on the grounds of a religious community, or near a parish church. When *Raven's Bread* collated the responses to the survey, we noticed that many hermits started their eremitical life attending daily Mass. But after a period of time, they discovered that going out of the hermitage so frequently was disruptive to the gentle flow of prayer now coursing through their days. They wisely decided to remain at home and cut back on attending outside services. This was more often true for hermits who were going to their parish church where they were inevitably drawn into social interaction with other attendees.

Some hermits are granted the singular grace of reserving the Blessed Sacrament in their hermitage chapel. This is a privilege rarely granted and only if special conditions are met. The Bishop of the diocese must not only approve the hermit's request, but also ascertain that the Sacrament will be reserved in a safe and reverent manner.

Other forms of prayer favored by hermits include recitation of the Rosary and the Jesus Prayer. The rhythm of such practices helps to settle the mind and creates an atmosphere of continual communion with God. After a while, the prayers themselves may fade away, leaving the soul quietly awash with a sense of Presence, much like a shore where ocean waves roll rhythmically in and out. As time passes and the hermit matures, everything becomes an expression of prayer—from walking out for the mail to washing the dishes.

By now, it must be obvious that an atmosphere of silence is essential in the hermitage. Initially, one may enjoy having tapes of chant and sacred song playing in the background while praying or doing quiet work. Many long-time hermits have discovered that eventually even these became unnecessary or even slightly irksome. Urban solitaries, and those living where outside noise penetrates the walls of the hermitage, may use recorded music to establish a shield of "pink noise" that protects their prayerful atmosphere.

Providing Adequate Income

One writer on hermit life raised the question: Must hermits work? He discussed the point of whether a hermit should live on alms. The desert fathers also considered this question. "A noble man whom nobody knew came to Scetis carrying gold with him, and asked the priest of the desert to distribute it to the brothers. The priest said to him: The brothers do not need it. But he was very insistent and was not satisfied, so he put the whole sum in a basket at the entrance of the church. And the priest said: Whoever needs it may take some. But nobody touched it or even looked at it. Then the old man said: God has accepted your offering.   Go, and give it to the poor. "[11]

The answer to the question: Must hermits work? is clearly yes! Once we have established our prayer routine, we can schedule the hours we wish to spend working, either within or outside our hermitage. Although it is ideal to be able to work from home, this is not always possible. Any hermit can find work to do at home—the sticking point is making a living from it! The following examples of remunerative tasks performed in the hermitage have been culled from extensive correspondence with hermits: arts and crafts such as icon writing; hand-painted or computer-designed cards; wood carving, pottery, weaving, quilting, basket-making, soap and lotion production; custom sewing; sale of garden produce and herbs, including potpourri; babysitting or after-school child care; translation of texts or books; writing poetry, biographies, and spiritual reflections; computer work such as publication of newsletters for groups, editing, and ghostwriting.

Many hermits try to find part-time employment which generates sufficient income to sustain them. Some with special training, such as nurses or paralegals, can command an adequate salary so they can make ends meet while working "out" only two or three days a week. A priest or deacon can take on part-time ministry. Others find solitary jobs such as housecleaning or yard work, fishing, maintaining a fire watch or overseeing state or federal parklands, which allow them to arrange their work hours so they can give prime time to their prayer. Ideal situations permit the hermit to remain in solitude as much as possible.

Finding suitable and adequate work is often the component that initially causes the would-be hermit the most concern. It can seem like the make or break point—hermits, too, must eat, maintain house and vehicle, and cover daily expenses just like everyone else. However, those who were genuinely called to eremitical life will, sooner or later, stumble upon a way to make ends meet. They may start out going through some lean times of "enforced simplicity," but eventually, their creative minds will cobble together adequate means of income. Among respondents to *Raven's Bread's* survey, a few hermits chose to depend on alms and reported that God came through with amazing regularity ... so long as they were content with a "sufficiency" and accepted that things might get down to the wire before needed funds came in. But come in it did, often from unexpected sources. The old adage holds: "Put God first and the rest will be provided."

One commentator on this topic observed that hermits who are capable of working should not apply for welfare or disability since this could be construed as "counter-witnessing," giving scandal to persons who resent seeing an able-bodied person availing him or herself of funds intended for the truly incapacitated. However, many begin their eremitical life about the time they are due to retire. They plan to live on the Social Security benefits and pensions they have earned earlier in life. A point that deserves consideration: All debts should be cleared before an individual embarks on the hermit vocation. If at all possible, house and vehicle payments should also be covered, or the hermit may be forced to work more hours then desired to meet monthly payments.

Hermits who apply for recognition under Canon 603 may be required to submit yearly budgets to a diocesan official demonstrating their ability to cover all personal expenses regarding maintenance of their hermitage and vehicle as well as debits incurred for "travel, recreation, and education." Auto, home, and medical insurance, as well as annual property taxes, must be paid by the hermit. In addition to medical insurance, one diocese asked that the hermit show how they plan to meet "costs of medicine, eye care, foot care, chiropractor, hearing aids, etc." Canonical hermits may also be asked to put aside funds for future retirement, including paying social security withholding taxes.

Kenneth Russell summed up his article on hermits and work with the following reasons why it is better for hermits to earn their own living. "First, working for a living introduces a sobering penitential dimension into their lives. Second, working enables them to share in the lot of the rest of humanity, particularly of the working poor at the bottom of the economic ladder. Third, it gives them the wherewithal to aid the needy. Fourth, working for a living forces hermits to shape their solitary life to conform to the realities of our time."[12]

Penance and Mortification

In 1996, Pope John Paul II wrote: "Men and women hermits, belonging to ancient Orders or new Institutes, or being directly dependent on the bishop, bear witness to the passing nature of the present age by their inward and outward separation from the world. By fasting and penance, they show that man does not live by bread alone but by the word of God (cf. Mt 4:4). Such a life 'in the desert' is an invitation to their contemporaries and to the ecclesial community itself never to lose sight of the supreme vocation, which is to be always with the Lord."[13]

The major penance in a hermit's life is fidelity to the life itself, allowing the inner passion for the Lord to shine out in visible form. Hermits choose a hidden life which, paradoxically, is a witness to everyone. It is an austere life that testifies to the richness of God's grace. The austerity that should mark the hermitage as well as the hermit has such stark beauty that people everywhere are fascinated by it. They may be somewhat simplistic in their expectations of how a hermit really lives, but this very naïveté forces the hermit to live with integrity. Religious solitaries know that anything in their lifestyle which suggests ease or superfluity clashes with the heart of their eremitical vows. Authenticity and integrity demand they live a life which celebrates the One Thing Necessary.

The only abundance that should be found in the hermitage is joy. Because dedicated solitaries have learned how to live "without care," they can patiently bear their part of the struggles, anxieties, and failures inherent in human life. Nothing is a total loss which urges one to re-focus on the goal of "alone with God alone." Daily, the penitential hermit renounces anything which turns him or her from that goal. Nothing is claimed for oneself. The hermit is rich in love and everything else is superfluous. She or he joyfully returns to the Lord all she or he has received, holding nothing back, refusing nothing, and accepting whatever hardships may come. Penitential practices walk hand in hand with the vow of poverty; simplicity and joy are the inevitable result of embracing life on life's terms—on God's terms.

Most of the hermits interviewed for the *Raven's Bread* survey of 2001 were very reticent when it came to naming their specific penitential practices. This privacy was respected, but we were able to collect enough information to learn that most hermits focused on the classic forms of penance, in vogue since the first days of the church—prayer, fasting, and almsgiving. Collated results from the survey yielded the following information: more than half of the respondents observed periods of fasting; many practiced almsgiving in either money or kind; and one-third observed the practice of Vigils or rising during the night for prayer, particularly during special seasons of the Church year such as Lent. About a quarter of the hermits responding were vegetarians; others severely limited the amount of meat they ate.

Contemporary forms of asceticism are often quite pragmatic. Maintaining a healthy diet and getting adequate exercise take the place of scourging and prolonged fasts; giving generously of one's time becomes a meaningful form of almsgiving; limiting the use of media becomes another form of fasting; and choosing to do with less rather than more contributes to a more equitable sharing of the world's limited resources. Moderation is particularly challenging in a culture where more is always better and where consumerism is touted as an expression of patriotism. By conscientiously limiting their use of basic resources such as water and fossil fuels, and by recycling paper and plastic, glass and metal, hermits offer a modest counterbalance for the waste and exploitation which characterizes contemporary culture.

By curbing acquisitiveness and restraining desires for luxuries, hermits help make reparation for the fact that one-tenth of the world's population consumes nine-tenths of its bounty. By disposing wisely of garbage, packaging material, and worn-out goods, they seek to prevent further trashing of our beautiful planet. By expressing their outrage about how large corporations exploit the land, not to mention their abuse of the working poor, they try to call them to account for such appalling inhumanity to their brothers and sisters. By taking time to be informed about political affairs and voting their consciences, they fulfill their obligation as citizens. Some of the foregoing may not be labeled penance and mortification by "strict constructionists," but they are practices which meet the goals of sacrificial living and giving.

Many hermits tithe—either money or goods. They also sacrifice time (a most precious commodity) by writing to elected officials or local newspapers; by informing themselves about how to treat the earth and their own bodies with intelligent care; by walking or cycling instead of driving when possible; and by keeping the small portion of the world entrusted to them clean and cared for. One hermit makes it her Lenten practice to pick up trash along the sides of the road near her hermitage; another devotes considerable energy to promoting the clean-up and protection of a river that feeds an important watershed in his area. Others refuse to buy or eat food and consumer goods grown or packed by underpaid laborers. Some boycott chain stores that don't offer workers fair benefits, thereby having to use more time and money to acquire everyday items. Many hermits devise personal ways of making practical reparation for the rape of our planet.

"Assiduous prayer and penance" are the final words in the initial paragraph of the Canon for hermits. When the Bishops of France composed statutes for the hermits under their jurisdiction, they defined penance this way: Penance "includes corporal ascesis (self-discipline) as well as spiritual warfare without which the former would be useless."[14] They offer a comprehensive strategy composed of work, stability, and perseverance that, together with silence and solitude, compose a hermit's penitential life. The allusion to spiritual warfare highlights the energy that a hermit should give to his or her penitential practices. Such vitality requires careful discernment for blind enthusiasm, for mortification can easily do more harm than good. Here, as with most things, one size does *not* fit all. Penitential practices appropriate for a male hermit still in his prime may be unwise twenty years later. A hermit who has had a literary bent all her life may find that rigorous outdoor activities are beyond her strength, however healthy she may be. These words of Pope Paul VI: "Where there is rigor, there is vigor" can have a place in every hermitage but only when balanced with moderation.

Habits for Hermits?

Many beginning solitaries have inquired if *Raven's Bread* knows where they can find the pattern or model for a hermit's habit, believing that Rome has legislated one. Actually, Rome has stayed out of prescribing eremitic fashions, wisely leaving the subject untouched. Therefore, each hermit has the liberty to wear whatever he or she feels is appropriate to life in the culture and climate where he or she lives. A long woolen robe would be most penitential but hardly suitable for a hermit in the tropics. Similarly, a hermit in the northern latitudes should not try to wear only the single tunic and cloak the desert fathers espoused.

Additionally, the type of work that a solitary engages in should also determine what is worn. A hermit wielding a chain saw or weed eater could endanger his or her life if she or he attempted to do so while wearing a long robe with wide sleeves! Even Trappist monks wear denim overalls when operating their tractors and harvesters. A hermit potter, who uses clay and paints daily, would need washable garments, while the solitary bent over a loom several hours a day would be wise to avoid fabrics which attract lint.

The aspiring hermit should be wary of falling into the trap of "image." Many carry a picture of the ideal hermit somewhere in their unconscious, an image composed of many elements absorbed over the years. When taking the first tentative steps toward living the eremitic life, it is needful to sort out the essential from the stereotypical. Clothing is part of the picture (hermits are not nudists!), but what sort of garments are appropriate? Because there is nothing prescribed, hermits are free to dress in a manner that expresses their identity as religious solitaries. What is essential? What immaterial?

There is a section in the Rule of St. Albert (1206) which highlights the elements of the "perfect habit":

> "You must use every care to clothe yourself in
> God's armor so that you may be ready to withstand
> the enemy's ambush (cf. Eph 6:11). Your loins are
> to be girt with chastity (cf. ibid.14), and your breast

fortified by holy meditations (cf. Prov 2:11). Put on holiness as your breastplate (cf. Eph 6:14) and it will enable you to love the Lord your God with all your heart and soul and strength (cf. Dt 6:5) and your neighbor as yourself (cf. Mt. 19: 19,22,37–39). Faith must be your shield on all occasions, and with it you will be able to quench all the flaming missiles of the wicked one (cf. Eph 6:16). There can be no pleasing God without faith (cf. Heb 11:6). On your head set the helmet of salvation (cf. Eph 6:17), and so be sure of deliverance by our only Savior, who sets his own free from their sins (cf. Mt 1:21). The sword of the spirit, the word of God (cf. Eph 6,17) must abound (cf. Col 3:17, 1 Cor. 10,31)."[15]

These military images (beloved of St. Paul) may not be appealing to some, but it does "cut to the chase" when it comes to essentials. What one wears is an outward sign of a spirited dedication to eremitic ideals. What one wears not only informs others about hermit life and values; it also influences how the solitary regards him or herself.

Before all else, a hermit's clothing should be simple, inexpensive, and modest. Some hermits so cherish the essential hiddenness of their vocation that they do not wish to be noticeable in any way. They live their solitary lives quietly blending with their surroundings. For such as these, a habit would be counterproductive and a betrayal of their intention to live a hidden and unknown life. Their ideal choice could well be some simple garments off the rack of the local secondhand shop. In the U.S., many hermits wear jeans and simple tops, their personal symbol of consecration, such as a ring or cross, small and unobtrusive. For attendance at Mass or on a special occasion, their garments may be more "formal" but still as simple and unadorned as possible. Nothing about their appearance draws special attention or questions.

Other hermits value the witness that their dedicated life gives to the world and wear clothing that is identifiable as a habit. It certainly need not be modeled on garments from earlier centuries, but rather can be a simple outfit that is worn most of the time. Hermits in India would likely wear a sari or robes modeled on that of Buddhist monks. Someone in Ireland or the U.S. might choose a belted tunic with hood in earth tones. Often, female hermits wear a small veil in place of the hood. Since hermits spend the major portion of their days within their hermitage, the main value of wearing a habit is the easement it affords to their clothing budget.

Wearing special garb for prayer, such as a hooded cloak or robe, can help the hermit become more centered and focused. Donning a prayer shawl or cape is a means of preparation for prayer, similar to a priest vesting for the celebration of Mass. It claims the body as well as the soul, reminding the pray-er of his or her purpose, much as lighting candles, burning incense, or using holy water does. We are not pure spirit, and making use of material elements to remind ourselves of who we are and what we are about should not be underestimated.

Under the caption "Outward Symbols of Eremitic Life," one male hermit wrote the following into his personal Rule of Life:

> "While in the cell during prayer or while attending the Liturgy of the Eucharist, the hermit will wear a simple habit made of a plain, twill-type cotton material (this hermit lives in the southwest USA) of a natural or brown color. The habit is made up of a simple robe, belt, scapular, cowl, crucifix, rosary, and sandals. During winter, socks and a cape or a coat may be worn. While working at manual labor or going into public to take care of certain needs (e.g. employment, doctor appointments, etc.), the hermit will wear a plain, solid-color work uniform, crucifix around the neck, and small rosary suspended from the left side and sandals with socks. This arrangement for limited wearing of the full habit during times of work is to insure the comfort and safety of the hermit, in conformity with the Second Vatican Council document

Perfectae Caritatis 17: 'The religious habit, as a symbol of consecration, must be simple and modest, at once poor and becoming. In addition, it must be in keeping with the requirements of health and it must be suited to the times and place and to the needs of the apostolate.'"[16]

Occasionally, a hermit has received some "flack" for appearing in public in full habit (i.e. a medieval style garb with veil and long scapular, etc.). One woman in New Zealand wrote that she was verbally attacked by one parishioner for wearing a long habit and labeled a "show-off"; at the same time, other parishioners were drawn to her, believing she would be a good listener to their woes and would pray for them. It would seem that a habit which draws a lot of attention, especially in public places, has some drawbacks. If the main witness of the hermit is his or her withdrawal into solitude for the sake of finding God more fully, a habit which acts like a beacon attracting others may not be appropriate for the solitary vocation.

As a member of a cloistered community for many years, I rarely went out of the monastery. Once, after a doctor's appointment, I had to wait on the street corner for my driver to pick me up. In my long brown robe and scapular, with a hip-length veil and golden emblem prominent below my starched white guimpe, I drew stares, honks, waves, and thumbs-up from drivers and pedestrians alike. I felt I like I was waving a sign proclaiming, *"Try the Catholic Church. It saves!"*

This incident occurred after many active communities had already modified their habits, a move which obviously bothered many people, Catholic and non-Catholic alike. We sisters pondered why this change, peripheral as it was to the vowed life, aroused distress and even ire in numerous laypersons. Apparently, many people find a curious comfort in seeing a nun in full medieval attire, perhaps as a reassurance that some things never change. I can only hope that those who wore such habits, with all their discomforts and time-consuming care, may be forgiven for being relieved when Rome directed a change into clothing consistent with the place and century in which the nun lived.

Although church authorities do not have any actual power to decree what sort of clothing laypeople wear (hermits are members of the laity unless they are ordained), some priests and even bishops take exception to hermits appearing in public in "full habit," meaning traditional medieval regalia. They reason that uninformed people may believe that the hermit represents the Church in some official capacity and acts or speaks with its authority. Naturally, they worry that a hermit whom they have not personally "vetted" may take advantage of the respect given them and inadvertently cause some scandal. This fear is most often unfounded, but a wise hermit, who wishes to be known as one, will make certain that she has acquainted her bishop and pastor of her presence and purpose before appearing in church in striking garb.

If a hermit decides to wear a habit, she or he should examine her or his motive. For what purpose is special garb chosen? How will he or she respond to the inevitable attention it will attract? Where and when will it be worn? Has thought been given how not to take advantage of people's reverence for garb identified with religious dedication for centuries? Although people may extend courtesies with a sincere heart to persons in religious garb, the hermit needs to check the purity of his or her own motives in accepting these gestures.

Solitaries are attracted to a variety of spiritualities: Carmelite, Camaldolese, Franciscan, or Benedictine, among others. Each of these religious families has particular symbols which identify them. Many hermits incorporate these into their personal garb. Such symbols can be a specially designed ring, pin, or medallion. The hermits' daily garb can also make use of certain colors associated with various religious families, such as the familiar brown of the Franciscans or the black and white of the Dominicans.

As we noted, *Raven's Bread* readers from around the world have asked us many things, including where to find "the" pattern for a hermit's habit. But so far, no one has asked permission to model their garb on Wood B.'s tunic!

Wood B. Hermit

"Not by appearance, shall he judge..."

Study: Spiritual and Secular

In *The Guide Book for the Vocation to Eremitic Life,* published by the Diocese of La Crosse, Wisconsin, we find that serious preparation is expected before a person will be accepted for canonical recognition as a hermit. Recommendations include a study program designed to acquaint an aspiring hermit with the history and spirituality of eremitical life, as well as providing him or her with a scriptural and theological foundation on which to build a solid spiritual life. For hermits who plan to make vows, it is also necessary that they fully understand the requirements of the evangelical counsels.

Recommended for particular study are the various spiritualities of the Church; the writings of the church fathers and mothers, as well as significant women and men mystics; the documents of Vatican Council II, especially *Gaudium et spes, Lumen gentium, Perfectae caritatis* and the post-synodal document *Vita Consecrata*; and moral theology. The aspiring hermit should be informed about the history of eremitic life and the various early Rules for hermits such as those of Pachomius, St. Aelred of Rievaulx, St. Albert, St. Romuald, St. Francis of Assisi, and the Ancrene Rule.

Every hermit should include a period of study and/or spiritual reading in his daily schedule, a time to feed both the mind and the soul. Books recommended for every hermit's shelf include the foundational teachings of each one's belief system. For Christians, these would be the Bible and a good commentary; the writings of the desert fathers and mothers; spiritual classics such as *The Way of The Pilgrim*, *The Philokalia* and the *Cloud of Unknowing*, as well as works by the great spiritual teachers such as St. Augustine, John Cassian, Francis de Sales, John of the Cross, Teresa of Avila, Julian of Norwich, Thomas Aquinas, and John Chrysostom. For Catholic Christians, a good history of the Church, as well as an updated Catechism of the Catholic Church can provide a solid foundation and answer many questions. The lives of the saints offer inspiration, especially those who lived the eremitical life or who were members of the spiritual family to which the hermit feels special attraction.

For serious study, the solitary can take advantage of correspondence courses such as those offered by The Catholic Distance University based in Hamilton, Virginia, or look into offerings now available on CD or DVD, as well as those which can be found on the Web. Exercise of the mind as well as of the body should be an essential element in a hermit's life.

However, the most important and valuable type of reading that a solitary should include in their daily schedule is *Lectio divina*, an ancient and fruitful practice in which the reader slowly reads Scripture passages, savoring them sentence by sentence, stopping frequently to "suck the juices" from a verse through which the Spirit is speaking to one's heart. This practice grew naturally out of the work which occupied many monks in the early centuries, that of copying the Scriptures by hand. Today, this slow reading of the Word of God, sometimes still combined with writing the passage, can be particularly useful when a hermit is suffering through a dry period in his or her spiritual life.

Hugh Feiss, noted Benedictine author, offers this helpful explanation of how to approach *Lectio Divina*: "Medieval readers, monastic and otherwise, were very flexible in their interpretation of texts. In particular, the Bible was thought to have several layers of meaning—literal or historical, doctrinal, and moral—so that readers found moral and spiritual guidance in the strangest places. Each helpful interpretation was thought to be inspired by the Holy Spirit. Hence, the interpretation of texts was a very creative process in which the reader was personally involved."[17]

For example, one may be perusing the Old Testament account of how Queen Esther prayed in desperate fear before she took the unprecedented step of approaching the king without being summoned. "My Lord, our King, you alone are God. Help me who am alone and have no help but you, for I am taking my life in my hand." (Esth.4:14,15) For a solitary man or woman experiencing a moment of acute vulnerability, these words may well become a comforting mantra. The Spirit vividly shows them how another human being struggled with the terror of aloneness and poured it out before the Lord.

The Book of Lamentations provided me with much comfort during a period of darkness, when I stumbled across these verses: "But I will call this to mind, as my reason to have hope. The favors of the Lord are not exhausted, his mercies are not spent; they are renewed each morning, so great is his faithfulness. My portion is the Lord, says my soul, therefore, will I hope in him."(Lam.3:21–24) Although these were the words of a woebegone prophet, praying centuries before the birth of Christ, they comforted and strengthened me in an hour of need.

In an age when books were rare and precious, many hermits memorized large portions of the Bible to nourish their souls as they went about their quiet routines. It was written of St. Anthony, the Father of Hermits, that "he was so attentive at the reading of the Scripture lessons that nothing escaped him; he retained everything and so his memory served him in place of books."[20] Palladius reported of the monks at Tabennesi that "they repeat by heart the entire Scriptures."[21] It was not uncommon for the hermits of the desert era to add the recitation of the one hundred fifty psalms to that of the Office, a practice still in vogue when Thomas Merton joined the Trappists in 1941.

Merton cited another form of Lectio in his collection of sayings of the early fathers. "One monk, Serapion, sold his book of the Gospels and gave the money to those who were hungry, saying: 'I have sold the book which told me to sell all that I had and give it to the poor,'"[22] and "A certain philosopher asked St. Anthony: 'Father, how can you be so happy when you are deprived of the consolation of books?' Anthony replied: 'My book, O philosopher, is the nature of created things, and any time I want to read the words of God, the book is before me.'"[23]

Food: Fasting and Feasting

Feeding the mind and nourishing the body are both essential for the healthy hermit. The first rule to follow when it comes to food is that each hermit should eat in accordance with his or her genuine needs. *Needs*, not wants! Determining genuine need is not difficult if one is authentically attentive to his or her own body. But how many can say that they are? A lot of attention is given to the practice of mindfulness so as to cultivate a deep prayer life. How many make the connection that physical health also benefits from mindfulness, an awareness which should include not only the body but also the food eaten?

Present-day society cultivates an ambivalent attitude toward food. On one hand, more often than not, people eat on the run or combine eating with other activities such as reading, watching TV, studying, browsing the computer, driving, or chatting on a cell phone. Bodies are treated like machines to which food is supplied with little or no consideration of whether or not it is needed or appropriate. In America, food of some sort is nearly always at hand, and people tend to dip and sip throughout the day. Eating should be a sacred activity, whether done alone or in companionship with others. Instead, it has become an unthinking panacea for all distresses. The result is that either people overeat, inviting a hatred of a bloated body, or else they fast and purge so unwisely that they endanger their health.

Hermits should not only recover a sense of the sacredness of their bodies but also of the holy act of eating. By doing so, they not only praise the Creator for the wondrous marvel that is the human body; they also make reparation for the abuse and waste of food that is rampant in the world. Spiritual writers have reflected on what they call Jesus' "table ministry," pointing out how often shared meals and feasts turn up in the Gospel stories. Hermits seldom share their tables, but that doesn't mean that eating should not be a time of particular awareness of the goodness of God and the gifts he offers. Quite the contrary! Thoughtful planning, careful preparation, and attractive serving of each meal should be holy activities, as important as praying the liturgy.

The word "liturgy" means a "body of rites" connected to worship. Food preparation is also a sacred rite, as exemplified in many Eastern cultures. In some restaurants, meals are prepared in the presence of the guests by a special chef. As a culinary artiste, he carefully places the most attractive vegetables, meats, and seasoning in a gleaming wok, and then with movements worthy of a celebrant, stirs, tosses, and bastes the mixture, cooking it to a point of perfection only he recognizes. Watching the process is a preparation for eating, a form of celebratory prayer that honors the giver of such good gifts. Many discover that such meals are often more easily digested.

The Japanese Tea Ceremony requires much training before it can be performed well and partaken with educated reverence. Key to the ceremony is deliberate timing. Placement of each item, the arrangement of the few floral decorations, and the handling of each object from the tea leaves to the cushion upon which the participant sits has its own proper form and requires a particular state of mind. Everything has it own place in the sequence of preparation; nothing is hurried; each movement is deliberate; each sip savored. Should not the hermit approach his or her meals with similar intentionality?

Food is beautiful, holy, and meant for a life-giving purpose. Studies have shown that a meal wolfed down thoughtlessly while standing or with minds engaged elsewhere will not nourish the body. Quite the opposite! How many keep a bottle of Tums at hand to calm the acid indigestion which hasty eating has provoked? How many eat much more than they would if they were fully aware of the amounts already devoured? It takes time for the brain to register what the stomach has taken in, and even longer for the body to feel the effects of food properly metabolized.

Life in solitude should allow one a great deal of flexibility regarding the type and amount of food eaten as well as when and how. A recent book, *The Slow Down Diet*, could become the hermit's "food bible," because it not only stresses healthful food but how to eat it in a manner which maximizes metabolism, energy, and, yes, pleasure! The author, Marc David, is a nutritional psychologist and lists the following eight universal metabolizers which contribute to healthful eating: *relaxation, quality, awareness, rhythm, pleasure, thought, story, and the Sacred.* Clearly, these are all appropriate to life as a hermit. If they are not present, more spiritual work is in order.

Marc David links his personal awakening to having taken up the practice of yoga, with its emphasis on breathing and body awareness. The major eating "discipline" that he recommends to his clients is: *Slow down!* Most aspiring hermits discover early on that they must make a very conscious effort to slip out of overdrive and settle into idle, even when sitting down to a solitary meal—perhaps even *especially* then. Some hermits are still in the mentality that eating is an activity to get past so we can focus on the more spiritual practices of the day.

A piece of advice which my spiritual director gave me when we were evaluating my initial months as a hermit surprised me. I had mentioned in passing that I usually read while eating. My director frowned. If I was launching into a lifestyle which emphasized fuller awareness of everything I did, a life that did not advocate "multi-tasking," what was I doing here? In effect, I was blocking my ability to genuinely savor my food by trying to absorb information from a book along with my meal.

I had set the table simply and attractively; I had taken time to prepare something nourishing ... but I had failed to share it with my Host and Guest. I have been in a restaurant and observed a couple eating opposite one another but focused on various sections of the newspaper. They are eating and drinking without thought and also without sharing anything with each other. At the other end of the spectrum, I have observed two people sharing a meal while deeply involved in conversation, occasionally touching hands and sometimes encouraging their companion to taste something from their own plate. I was impressed with how they leaned toward one another, watched the other's eyes, and shared their companion's pleasure in eating. Instead of a wall of newsprint between them, a distance no one cared to bridge, I felt the deep bonds between them.

Living alone, one can still relate to the divine table Companion during a meal. Every forkful of food is a gift, a delight that one can share with God. Sitting down to a meal, consciously grateful for the invisible companionship of the One who enjoyed eating with his disciples, can turn every meal into a moment of celebration. If the table is set attractively, the food prepared with care and blessed with a moment of prayer, eating becomes a time of holy exchange. Types of food change with the seasons; so can the blessings which accompany it. The liturgical life of the Church, as well as nature's rhythms, are observed with even greater awareness when combined with each day's meals. Table prayer should also invite to the solitary's meal those throughout the world who are also eating at the same time, as well as the many who have little or nothing at all to eat.

No longer should hermits fast so severely that they destroy the gift of a healthy body. Instead, disciplined eating can be formulated so that meals enhance vigor and honor the Sacred inherent in all food. Preparing and eating fresh and wholesome foods can demand as much sacrifice as fasting. One may not always be able to buy top-of-the-line produce, but one can at least buy fresh food when it is in season. Even solitaries should expend time on thoughtful preparation of meals and then consume them with awareness, genuinely savoring the tastes and textures teasing the palate. Eating hastily is not only bad for digestion, it is a form of blasphemy, failing to honor the food, the body, and Giver of both.

In his book *The Slow Down Diet,* Marc David makes another point that is seldom connected with healthy eating. He writes that "forgiveness is the most potent and sacred means for healthy eating."[24] If a hermit is looking for a meaningful penance, she or he could hardly do better than cultivate the habit of heartfelt forgiveness. David writes: "I'm still amazed at how those who've had long-term eating disorders, chronic fatigue, digestive complaints, and a host of debilitating symptoms see miraculous relief when forgiving people from their past and present. If you've ever been betrayed, abused, or wounded in any way, the anger, blame, or judgment you hold is toxic. Indeed, it doesn't matter how right you are and how wrong the perpetrator is. The most poisonous chemicals on the planet are the ones we self-produce deep inside our beings. Though our poison is intended for another, it nevertheless lives within us, corroding the body with acidic intent. Forgiveness heals, big time. Our most intelligent strategies in diet, exercise, medicine, and healing are ultimately ineffectual in the cloudy chemistry of the unforgiven."[25]

Most hermits realize the importance of cultivating a habit of forgiveness, but not all connect this with optimal digestive health. Most know that eating under stress causes discomfort and so try to relax before taking a meal. But perhaps not all connect long-standing digestive problems with long-held grudges. To forgive those who have caused harm in the past requires a special gift of grace, one that can be prayed for at every meal. If one is open and willing to cultivate a habit of daily forgiveness, one may soon be able to spend more on good food and less on Tums and other digestive aids.

In addition to fasting, feasting is an important element in eremitical life. All good things are meant to be celebrated, from a sweet peach or a lovely flower to feast days—holy and secular. An event as simple as the joyful sighting of the first trillium in spring deserves to be toasted. Life as a hermit is not meant to be grim and gloomy. Even austerity can be joyous, because it allows us to taste the simple goodness of the here and now.

Health Care: Medical Insurance

Before embarking on eremitical life, it is prudent to have a complete physical examination, even if one is in good health. By having tests done that are normally recommended when one reaches mid-life, anything that is amiss will be discovered and taken care of in timely fashion. Even if all turns out well, it is good to have an established baseline that doctors can refer to later. Furthermore, it will not be necessary to leave the hermitage later for frequent exams once a solitary routine has been established.

Most dioceses will ask for a behavioral assessment as well as a physician's report if one is applying to be received as a hermit under Canon 603. In their Statutes for Hermits, the Bishops of France write: "Prudence demands that special attention be given to the equilibrium of emotions since solitude presents special dangers for fragile psyches."[26] They also note that a person who seeks to live the eremitical life should have sufficient maturity and a temperament suited to such a way of life. During the first year or so of eremitical life, a novice hermit should see a spiritual guide frequently so he or she can observe his or her ability to cope with the difficulties of adjusting to solitude. As mentioned before, there is not just one temperament compatible with solitary living. So determining a person's aptitude for solitude isn't as simple as taking a test. The best proof of psychic and emotional stability is time. If the call is genuinely "of God," the hermit will come to live the eremitical lifestyle with increasing joy. Many hermits find their physical health actually improving as they settle into their vocation. The body as well as the soul thrives when one has found his true place.

Given the present medical system in the U.S., one concern of an aspiring hermit is obtaining medical insurance. For those not eligible for Medicare, health insurance is sometimes provided by an employer. However, most hermits either work part-time jobs or are self-employed. Since most employers offer benefits only to full-time employees, many hermits, after looking in vain for affordable medical insurance, must take a leap of faith and do that which most of the world (it seems) heartily disapproves. They can choose a two-tier insurance plan: dependence on God and establishment of a special "medical fund." Instead of sacrificing their solitary life in order to meet exorbitant insurance premiums, they regularly put an affordable amount of money into a "medical" savings account to use when they must see a doctor or dentist. Since most are in relatively good health, this can provide adequate "coverage." When some large bill is inevitably incurred, most medical clinics and hospitals allow patients to pay it off in monthly installments. As long as payments are met regularly, everyone is satisfied … except those gloom-and-doom relatives who seem to believe that insurance is a guarantee of good health.

A hermit who has been received by a bishop and made profession of solitary life under Canon 603 may be covered under a diocesan insurance plan if one exists, but not necessarily. More than one hermit has found herself in the dilemma of not being granted permission to make a vow of poverty until she can prove she is able to purchase medical coverage! This requirement alone has discouraged more than one hermit from choosing to be recognized publicly under Canon 603.

Most hermits will find ways, with God's help, to meet necessary expenses, but not many can provide proof of this beforehand. St. Albert ended his Rule for the hermits of Mount Carmel with the following: "Here are the few points I have written down to provide you with a standard of conduct to live up to; but our Lord, at his second coming, will reward anyone who does more than one is obliged to do. See that the bounds of common sense are not exceeded, however, for common sense is the guide of the virtues."[27] One can only hope that our Lord at His Second Coming will not ask if one has carried medical insurance as proof of common sense!

Health Care: Advance Directives

An evidence of common sense that all hermits should demonstrate is the preparation of advance directives regarding health care.

This may be a formal, statutory document, or it may be an informally written statement of what one desires if a catastrophic event makes it impossible to express one's wishes. Although it is not required to record this information on a specific form, it will be easier for others to understand exactly what you want if you use a document that is clear, complete, and witnessed. Most states in the U.S. have such documents with various designations such as a living will, a medical power of attorney, a declaration to physicians, etc., all of which are legally binding when properly filled out.

A hermit may not be living near family members, and if a sudden health problem develops which requires a decision of literally life or death consequences, the next of kin (no matter how far away geographically) will usually be asked to make that decision. They may have little or no idea what their solitary relative would desire unless there are advance directives already written and available.

No one knows what the future may hold. It is a matter of charity, as well prudence, to state in writing if one desires to have life extended should an irreversible health crisis such as a major stroke or a severe injury require continuous life support measures. The Catholic Church recognizes that it is not necessary to employ every medical means simply to keep a heart beating in a body that has little or no chance of recovery. More often than not, the victim is either unconscious or so mentally disoriented that an informed decision at this point is virtually impossible. Thus, having a written statement naming a qualified person to make such decisions is crucial.

Every hermit should find out what documents are required and complete them prayerfully. The person given medical power of attorney should be consulted about whether he or she is comfortable fulfilling what the hermit desires. Copies of these documents should be kept where they can be easily found if needed. Another extremely important decision which should be prominent in a medical chart is the do not resuscitate (DNR) order, which clearly specifies what is desired should the patient suffer sudden cessation of vital life systems. Ordinarily, hospital personnel will automatically resuscitate a patient, even if there is little hope that the person will be able to continue living on his or her own. To prevent being subjected repeatedly to measures which are actually quite brutal, one should give the person with medical power of attorney the right to sign a DNR order.

If one has a primary-care physician, it is wise to have a copy of these advance directives entered into his or her medical records. Reviewing with the physician what options exist is helpful, for then the solitary will be fully informed, will know what is considered normal emergency treatment and what is in fact palliative care. CPR (cardiopulmonary resuscitation) is almost always attempted when a person's heart or breathing stops suddenly, unless it is clearly futile. Such would be the case if a person is only found several hours after death, as happened with a female hermit in West Virginia who suffered a massive heart attack late in the evening. Another hermit on the same property found her body the next morning. If a person is already close to death, he or his surrogate can request that no extreme measures be taken when Sister Death is clearly knocking at the door.

Prolonging life through artificial means is merely extending the existence of an organism from which humanity has departed. It is more than an unpleasant ordeal; it is an affront to a person's basic rights to life, liberty, and the pursuit of (ultimate) happiness. The dying person may be largely unaware, but those around him or her are not. When there is clearly no possibility for recovery, the designated person should make the difficult decision which will allow nature to follow its inevitable course and free the person to pass into the next stage of his or her life journey. Death, when not thwarted by some rather barbaric means such as a ventilator, can be a gentle transition, aided by spiritual presences from the "other side."

I had the experience of being the "designated person" for both my priest-uncle and my father when each was dying. Before I could reach my uncle's bedside, medical personnel had already hooked his eighty-two-year-old body to a ventilator, a process which included inducing total paralysis so that he would not "fight" the machine forcing air through his lungs. I understood that he could be aware at times, wakening to a terrifying inability to move or communicate, unable to even blink an eyelid. To me, he appeared to be already a corpse but one whose chest was rising and falling to the rhythm of the pump by the bedside.

Although he had earlier declared his desire to remain at the nursing home where he had lived for eighteen years, his request had not been honored and he had been transported to the hospital with instructions to do everything possible. With nothing in writing to guide them, medical personnel, fearing to be sued for lack of proper care, proceeded to subject this clearly dying man to treatment he emphatically did not want. Eventually, his heart gave out and the DNR order, which I had signed as next of kin, prevented the hospital from getting out the paddles to jump-start that tired organ.

In stark contrast, my father died in the room and the bed at the nursing facility where he had been living for seven years. When I arrived, he was slipping into a light coma but still able to give a sign that he was aware of my presence. Over the next twenty-four hours, nurses monitored his vital signs but otherwise offered no further intervention. Since he was not in obvious discomfort, there was no reason to disturb his final hours with uselessly invasive procedures. Not even oxygen or an IV were ordered since these would only have prolonged the dying process for no good reason.

I kept a silent vigil, hoping that my presence gave him some strength and comfort. When I observed a significant change in his breathing pattern, I notified the personnel and a nurse stepped in to wait with me. I watched his carotid pulse weaken and then stop as his heart gave out. The nurse checked for any vital signs and noted the moment of his passing on the chart. My grief was softened by the easy way he had died. Such a simple, natural death was possible because of steps taken in advance.

Even if one has signed such documents, there is always the option of changing one's mind and countermanding the earlier request. If one is sufficiently alert, medical personnel will always inquire what one's wishes are regarding further medical treatment. Written directives take effect only if someone is unable to express their desires him or herself.

When issues of life or death are being weighed, the *quality* of life possible should be given serious consideration. Would the hermit want to spend his or her final days tethered to a respirator, for example, or living in a health care facility which permitted little, if any, solitude? What sort of life is being prolonged? Quite possibly, the hermit is more than ready to move on to the next stage of his or her life journey. In the early Middle Ages, someone who committed him or herself to an anchorhold was presumed to be doing so as a proximate preparation for death. More than one used a rough hewn coffin as their bed. "Sister Death" was not a feared visitor but someone expected with a certain amount of anticipation.

Death is a friend that every hermit should be ready to meet. St. Francis of Assisi composed this final verse to his famous "Song of Brother Sun" immediately after his doctor confirmed that he had only a few weeks left to live: "Praise for our sister, Death of the body, Gateway to woe or gateway to glory, No one alive can flee her embracing. Happy are those she finds in Your friendship."

Provisions for Death and Disposition

As was just noted, in the early Middle Ages, the consecration ceremony for a hermit-to-be was a funeral, complete with shroud and coffin, indicating the solitary's total death to the world. Today the emphasis is, as the Statutes for Hermits of France states, "the sign of gift, for more clearly than other forms of monastic life, eremitical life is a sign of liberation." As Dom Jean Leclercq expressed it, "The hermit is the person who in the church is united to God with a minimum of structure."[28]

This "minimum of structure" allows the hermit to be fully liberated from the cares and concerns of the world, to live as consciously as possible on the threshold of eternal life. Only death remains as the "final bar to be crossed" before the eremite attains his or her ultimate goal. Therefore, it makes eminent sense that hermits make all the necessary preparations for this journey—writing a will; purchasing a grave site or contacting a crematory; leaving directives for funeral arrangements and a memorial service.

Ideally, a hermit will not have much to dispose of through a will, but having a valid final testament with an executer appointed to carry it out can prevent some disturbing legal problems. Unless the hermit has obligations to family members or outstanding debts, it is commendable to direct that the bulk of whatever goods he or she possesses at death goes directly to benefit the poor or to some charitable organization that the hermit favors.

If possible, the hermit should set up a burial trust with a funeral company so that final expenses are already covered and do not fall to someone else. Such a trust can direct what kind of funeral or memorial service is desired, as well as how and where remains shall be interred or cremains disposed. Unless there is a family plot where the hermit can expect to be buried, he or she may wish to minimize expenses through cremation and scattering of the ashes in some appropriately hidden site.

As a final form of charitable giving, the hermit can will his or her body to medical science by naming a specific laboratory, clinic, or other facility that performs viable research to receive their remains immediately after death. Once studies are completed, many of these clinics will either appropriately dispose of the body themselves or return it to the family for burial. A hermit may also wish to donate any body organs in suitable condition to waiting recipients. Such charity is a kind of total disappearance that accords well with the eremitical ideal of complete hiddenness.

An unnamed Camaldolese hermit, whose work is collected in the small volume *In Praise of Hiddenness,* sums up the goal of eremitical life thus: "It is just to this grace of annihilation, in the death-resurrection of the well-beloved Son, that the hermit aspires all along his path of perseverant waiting. And I must confess that it is not that rare that one can discover in our hermitages those brothers who through their whole transfigured being greet you: 'What joy! Christ is risen!' There you have, I think, the most beautiful fruit of our life. Hiddenness has finally come to its harvest."[29]

Ermitage des Nations (Hermitage of the Nations)
Extreme North Cameroon, Africa

Chapter 7

Horizons for Hermits

The holy Fathers came together and spoke of what would happen in the last generation, and one of them especially, called Squirion, said: "We now fulfill the commandments of God." Then the Fathers asked him: "What about those who will come after us?" He replied: "Perhaps half of them will keep the commandments of God and will seek the eternal God." And the Fathers asked: "Those who come after these, what shall they do?" He replied and said: "The men of that generation will not have the works of God's commandments and will forget his precepts. At that time wickedness will overflow and the charity of many will grow cold. And there shall come upon them a terrible testing. Those who shall be found worthy in this testing will be better than we are and better than our fathers. They shall be happier and more perfectly proven in virtue."[1]

The horizon is the point beyond which one cannot see; the apparent juncture of earth and sky. Everything seems to emanate from it or converge toward it. During the past half-century, a sun has appeared on the horizon of eremitical life—is it rising, or is it setting? Are the figures silhouetted against the light growing larger and more clearly defined? Or are they slowly fading into an idyllic haze? Is the allure of eremitic life an enduring aspect of humanity's search for meaning, or is it a passing fad, a fashion only intermittently in vogue? There is no crystal ball to consult, but there is the witness of millennia from which to draw some tentative conclusions about present trends.

The Future: Is There One?

People of power often regard artists as among the most dangerous of individuals. The work of a genuinely creative person mirrors the world around him or her with uncomfortable veracity, revealing truths which often prove prophetic. Few of us, powerful or not, enjoy the shocks which such windows of revelation can evoke. A great work of art rises like a tsunami from the depths of the human spirit. A prescient artist detects subtle changes on the subconscious level, similar to the slow creep of tectonic plates far below the surface of the earth. Like seismographers, creative individuals often give advance warning when a social earthquake is at hand.

Not all of us really want to hear a prediction of looming catastrophe, preferring to remain cocooned in ignorance. Some want to believe the problem will go away if we but shoot the messenger! Consider how often in a totalitarian regime the prophetic voices—the poets, painters, and playwrights, the sculptors, singers and songwriters are among the first to be targeted for persecution.

Hermits are often regarded as equally dangerous. The medium through which solitaries express their vision, the truths they see, is their own lives. They are prophets without a voice, so it would seem easy to ignore them. But their silence itself speaks, implying a secret knowledge that makes people profoundly uneasy. By their very lifestyle, hermits highlight uncomfortable (and often frightening) truths. For instance, before scientists were willing to admit it, those who live in close communion with the earth (as hermits and seers do) knew that the planet was on the verge of drastic changes, and not for the better. They heard it, saw it, smelled it, and fell on their knees.

Climate changes were imminent. Animals were already adjusting or dying out. The first to speak openly of global warming were ridiculed. No one laughs these days, even though no one can yet say *why* our atmospheric temperature is rising. Is it a cycle of nature, as inevitable as the rotation of the planet? Or is it the result of unwise and selfish choices humanity has made in recent centuries? That is for scientists to thrash out. What solitaries proclaim is that such "overheating" also results from anger, greed, and cruelty, the hot and frenzied emotions that generate toxic fumes, much like the greenhouse gases which, as they build up, trap solar energies and prevent normal cooling.

Climate change, which affects everyone, is a symbol of how interrelated our small globe has now become. The increasing number of hermits alerts us to the social systems that are breaking down. Men and women are absenting themselves from society, not because they hate people but because they are profoundly uncomfortable in a culture that derides their deepest beliefs. Very little appears to be truly valued; everything is disposable; any place can be trashed; appalling amounts of food are wasted; anything can be replaced, even human body parts.

Relationships are superficial because everyone is moving away or simply moving too fast. Does no one stand still? Who lives even five years in one house? People seem bored with their very existence. In a restless search for meaning, they change jobs, relocate, find a new partner, again ... and yet again. Politicians seek to arouse followers by promising change, envisioning a new life beyond not just their country, but even the planet. With little to advocate for that won't arouse opposition, they offer fantasies about colonizing the moon or even Mars! Who will dare to promote staying put, sinking roots, deepening an inner life, exploring the world of the spirit? Only hermits and lovers of solitude appear to fully embrace such a counter-cultural path.

Eremitical life can be an incomprehensible option to society at-large. But more and more people are being drawn toward its healing silence and genuine connection with the earth. By their life choice, hermits hope to shock society into accepting responsibility for what is happening to our world and to initiate intelligent solutions. However, denial has become such an ingrained way of life that anyone who challenges a culture's carefully constructed house of lies is considered dangerous, and as such, profoundly frightening. Where is honesty or ethical living to be found? Who can be trusted?

In the Sermon on the Mount, Jesus outlined the features of the ethical person, and, to date, no one has improved on that portrait. He spoke of people who are non-acquisitive, who know how to grieve, who are meek, who thirst for justice, who are merciful, clean of heart, and peacemakers. What would a society look like if the majority of its people embraced this ideal? Genuine hermits aspire to these virtues whether or not they are Christians. The model Jesus portrayed, in words and in his life, is simply the finest and best that human beings can attain. Is there a future for such people?

Blessed are those persecuted for holiness' sake ...

Like the "anawim," the little poor ones in Biblical language, hermits and solitaries are often ignored and insulted, persecuted and imprisoned. Why? Because by their lifestyle, they speak truth to power. Secretly and subversively, they are the visionaries and prophets who proclaim that a new world is possible ... but at a price the wealthy refuse to pay and the poor are too overwhelmed to envision. Only when the "developed" nations stop claiming unfair privileges and start sharing resources with the other two-thirds of the planet will there be a chance for humanity to flourish. The earth itself will survive only if there is a more equitable distribution of its natural riches.

Hermits are symbols of liberation; images of how life on this earth could be lived if people put spiritual values first. A self-centered (and frightened) soul hears popular slogans, very often promulgated by the ruling elite, and mindlessly ingests them. The hermit of today and tomorrow is called to reject these mind-numbing platitudes and to promote new paradigms. By living them, they dare others to take them seriously. Solitaries take on the work of all creative persons—a prophetic work. And a dangerous one. Being different is never safe.

Astronomers have taken pictures of stars exploding—quite a glorious sight. But have many wondered if the same fate awaits this beautiful blue-green planet? People know that time is ticking faster, as nuclear weapons multiply. How many seconds are left on the global clock? Where are those who hunger and thirst for saving justice? Who will be the peacemakers? Whose hearts are simple and pure enough to weep healing tears over this world?

The cyclic popularity that eremitical life has experienced throughout the ages has long been recognized. In some periods, hermits were held in high esteem; at others, they were feared. Certain eras considered all loners to be strange and abnormal, while other centuries revered solitaries as sages. The person who gave all his or her time and energy to seeking spiritual realities was honored when the dominant values of an age were religious; when the ethos of a period was materialistic, hermits and contemplatives were tarred and feathered.

This is an age when, for the first time, one nation is capable of exterminating all life on the planet. If someone set off the right (or terribly wrong) chain reaction, all life can be wiped out within an incredibly short space of time. Never before has it been so crucial to foster peace on earth, to re-design the social order. For such a major change to be affected, the world needs people who explore the frontiers of the human spirit. It requires hermits and solitaries who live the Beatitudes, who care for the earth and all its citizens.

What would a future hermit look like? Many eremites will live close to the earth, in peaceful, quiet places such as mountains and deserts, in forests and on islands. Others will dwell where they directly experience the heartbeat of the world—in the great cities where they are hidden in plain sight. Many will serve in humble, hidden tasks, as did the hermits of the Middle Ages. Some may be the healers or sages whom the "movers and shakers" of this age will consult, aware that only these hold the healing vision capable of guiding the world in these critical times. Some hermits might be highly visible but most will seldom, if ever, be seen.

Many will live an eremitical life outside any particular religious denomination, while others will be models of the spirituality within their chosen creed. Current trends suggest that a fair number of solitaries will develop a uniquely personal combination of spiritual traditions and practices, and by so doing will draw humanity closer together. Religious prejudice is one of the most potent elements for igniting wars and prolonging civil discord the world has ever seen. Future hermits can (and must), within their own spirits, break down these destructive patterns which have ruled human behavior to its own ruination since before Abraham struggled with the Hittites.

Hermits and solitaries of the future must expand their sense of responsibility. When once they might have felt accountable only for people within their own culture and immediate vicinity, they now must feel answerable even for the trash cluttering the solar system. They need hearts which extend compassion to villagers in Thailand, care to the teeming slums of New Delhi, and concern to the slowly dying victims of the Chernobyl disaster. By striving for communion with the Divine, hermits can introduce a new dimension of holiness into the world, one which can transform the threat of certain disaster into a promise that human hearts can be changed and charged with caring love, with divine compassion.

Such compassion can plunge one into cosmic solitude and demand the courage to face the fear of the universe. The genuine hermit burns with the passion of a God who bears the pain of all ages and becomes, in the words of Father De Foucauld, a *"universal brother or sister."* This means living in vital communion with all people, with all beings. To grasp even the parameters of so vast a vision demands a heart that will not be daunted or deterred. To accept that the world is always in flux; that it careens continually from natural to man-made disasters; that all things pay the price of the human penchant for conquest and control—such acceptance threatens the hermit with profound despair.

God-touched hermits have nightmares about polar bears drowning because the northern ice cap is shrinking from one year to the next. They fret about seals and penguins in Antarctica who have no place to raise their young as glaciers break up and float away. They fear the future rushing toward us, one where snow packs continue to shrink in the Rockies and the Himalayas and once-lush plains turn into deserts. Some continents are drying out, while others are drowning. How will there be sufficient food to feed the children born today? Far from burying their heads in the sands of their chosen desert, hermits of the future must proclaim that "humankind has not woven the web of life. We are but one thread within it. Whatever we do to the web, we do to ourselves. All things are bound together. All things connect." (Chief Seattle)

The world needs more and better visionaries; prophets who can light the way in the growing gloom and point out the direction that leads to fuller life. It need guides who, by their lives, can connect people to the spiritual energies which alone can transform the selfishness that is killing the earth into the compassion which can save it. What sort of person can shoulder such a burden and not be crushed by its weight? Who can save this sorry world? Who can deliver the earth from the ugly fruits of violence and passion? It is only through one who believes in the power of love that humanity can cease to be its own worst enemy. The hermit is called to be a channel of that passionate (and saving) love. Contemplative prayer opens the human spirit to receive and transmit the salvation born of love. As their contemplative spirit matures, the hermit realizes, as did St. Francis, that every element, every sentient being is a relative; e.g., Brother Fire, Sister Water, Brother Wolf ... and because they accept persecution for love's sake,

... the reign of God is theirs.

Blessed are the poor in spirit ...

In little more than fifty years, eremitic life has steadily and silently grown in the western world, affecting cultures on many continents and countries. Who is preaching it? What institution is advertising it? Why are increasing numbers of otherwise "normal" human beings seeking a lifestyle defined by silence and solitude? What are they doing "out there?" Something is happening that is transcending all language barriers and religious traditions. No one knows the precise number or can identify all the hermits and solitaries. But neither can anyone deny that their numbers are increasing.

Anyone taking the eremitic vocation seriously is bound to feel helpless, quite impotent, in fact. Hermits are determined to help, to make a positive difference, but how? What can one person do, hidden and alone? Often, a solitary will feel herself blameworthy because she lives a life which shelters her from much of the suffering that so harshly mars the existence of her brothers and sisters. Love and compassion well up in them ... but is it enough? What should one do and how? This is where passionate intercessory prayer and supplication spontaneously arises.

The challenge is to live a life given over to praying for others while accepting that one will seldom, if ever, see any results. No one will be able to ascertain *how*, or even *if*, their devoted prayers are efficacious for others. It is a terrible kind of poverty—to live dedicated to helping others, yet never know what good one may be doing. All that hermits can hope is that they are doing no harm. Believers leave all results to the mercy of their God. Others rely on their convictions about the interconnection of all humanity, trusting that what affects one, touches all. This is a form of intercession expressed less by words than by a way of life.

A Camaldolese monk once wrote: "Prayer is not only speaking to God on behalf of humanity, it is also 'paying' for humanity." Suffering is part of the hermit's vocation. One of the most acute forms is to never know whether or not one's chosen lifestyle is worthwhile or has any value for others. Hermits enter into the darkness, the dusky cloud of unknowing, and walk without any light beyond that which is in their own hearts. Often, unbeknownst even to themselves, they have become beacons for others.

The small English-language newsletter for hermits based in North America, *Raven's Bread*, has subscribers in twenty-eight countries outside the USA, as well as readers in every state of the Union. More than one thousand hermits or individuals interested in solitary life subscribe to the paper edition; uncounted others find the Web edition on Internet search engines, where it is consistently listed among the top three sites for hermits.

Numbers reveal very little when one is dealing with a movement which spiritually links like-minded people around the globe from New Zealand to Ireland; from India to Canada. How can one measure a prophetic power rooted in contemplation and compassion? A creative vision that transcends disparate cultures and traditions? Commonly held goals unify these people who seldom, if ever, meet one another (though they are acutely aware of one another.) As editors of *Raven's Bread*, we have the great privilege of communicating with literally hundreds of hermits and have discovered one thing which both sets them apart and unites them—a marvelous freedom and joy born of poverty of spirit. Hermits have little or nothing to lose. Their riches are in the spirit world, which they access through their focused life of prayer and meditation.

In the western hemisphere, the word meditation usually evokes the idea of a journey inward in search of the Divine. It suggests a spirituality that is a flight from the world toward a self-centered existence where only oneself and God are the dominant players. The spirituality that is usually found in hermitages is dramatically different. Contrary to common opinion, those who spend long periods of time in solitude learn to celebrate togetherness. They also develop a compassionate caring for the least as well as for those who consider themselves the "great." The hermit embraces all and judges no one. No one is greater or lesser, holier or more sinful, in the view of the solitary because, as one who is poor in spirit, she or he cannot condemn anyone. Intimately aware of their own weaknesses, hermits develop a humility which prevents them from ever looking down on others. "Understanding" literally means "standing under." From such a position, it is impossible to look anywhere but up. Standing there, looking up toward all, hermits exercise generous compassion.

Hermits can be alone in the desert or anonymous among a crowd on a subway. No one may notice them, but everyone is touched by them. Their joyous freedom, their poverty of spirit, radiates peace. The kindly compassion of the solitary silently announces that heavenly gifts are present, mysteriously touching others, bringing freedom from fear. Because the poor in spirit have nothing to lose ...

...the kingdom of heaven is already theirs.

Blessed are they who mourn ...

How does a silent, unknown, and unseen person proclaim that a new future is possible, that the reign of God is already at hand? For one thing, this person is someone who knows how to listen deeply to the pain of another. Only when one literally embodies the suffering of the many and allows that pain to be imprinted on one's soul, can one truly mourn. The hermitage is not the place where grandiose plans to save the world are dreamed up accompanied by brass bands. Rather it is where the pain of the world, its despair, its darkness, and its desolation is simply accepted ... accompanied by tears.

In the twenty-first century, the attitude toward hermits is ambivalent. Where should deeply concerned people invest their energies and whatever resources they have, when even the richest country in the world has nearly 36 million people living below the poverty level, twelve million of them children? While many people are either unaware or simply do not care that a country which raises more food than it can eat is rife with households where children suffer malnutrition, the hermit chooses to look squarely at this inexplicable tragedy. Agencies that supply aid to these families report that this poverty, this hunger, is increasing despite all the assistance programs, all the new methods of growing, preserving, and delivering food. "What has caused this?" the hermit prayerfully asks.

Requests for emergency food assistance increased by an average of 14 percent during one recent year, and appallingly, 20 percent of these requests went unmet. Forty percent (nearly half!) of these requests were from working families. In the 3.5 percent of U.S. households that experience hunger, some members frequently skip meals or eat too little, sometimes going without food for a whole day. Meanwhile, official surveys indicate that every year more than 350 billion pounds of food is available for human consumption in the Union States. But of that total, nearly 100 billion pounds—including fresh vegetables, fruits, milk, and grain products—are lost to waste by retailers, restaurants, and consumers. In other words, up to one-fifth of America's food ends up in landfills each year. The value of this lost food is estimated at around $31 billion annually. The saddest part of this story is that roughly 49 million people could have been adequately fed by these lost resources.

What does the foregoing have to do with hermit life? The hermit hears "the cry of the poor" as clearly as does the God in his or her heart. The solitary grieves over the human diminishment that hunger causes, especially to the children whose minds and bodies are stunted for lack of adequate nourishment. But these silent weepers do not believe that their tears are useless. They live on a level of mystical awareness which profoundly unites them with those for whom they grieve. Their lives become one with the God who also mourns for his suffering children. They achieve a mysterious union with the Divine which consecrates grief; which transforms tears into saving love and turns prayer into a powerful means for good.

By losing their lives in God, hermits let go of the panaceas that promised comfort, easy answers, and false security. They refuse to turn away from unpalatable truths and distressing facts. Hermits do not insulate themselves from raw misery, whether close at hand or across the globe. Their hearts are opened by their intimacy with the God who cares for all his or her children. If at times they feel their hearts are breaking, they know it is only so they will be enlarged to hold more of earth's shattered ones. Hermits die to their past narrow concerns. In their intense desire, they search for new means of absorbing the griefs that multiply in every direction. What they discover is that when others go hungry, so do they. When others are homeless, so are they. When others are cold or naked, without dignity or even a name, so are they.

While living in my West Virginia hermitage during the Gulf War of 1991, I had no TV. However, I closely followed the daily developments via radio. Vivid reporting, combined with my lively imagination, created a sense that I myself was dodging bombs in Kuwait or marching across the torrid sands, tortured by thirst and fear. Each death reported represented a grieving family, lives changed forever, and I was cut to the quick. I felt outrage that our country should choose war when it was not necessary. Other means could have resolved that conflict, had people been willing to invest their energy in negotiations rather than invest their capital in a military machine which crushed peoples indiscriminately. So far as I knew, no war had ever achieved a good end.

On February 28, 1991, I was sitting on the floor before the altar in my hermitage when the harsh screams of rockets and the thunder of explosions suddenly ended. Once again, I heard the peaceful murmur of spring peepers in the run beside my cabin. Overcome by the awesome silence, my mind reeled. With the cease-fire came my own liberation. I celebrated the moment by journaling a spontaneous bit of poetry:

> Evening thickens and candle-glow brightens.
> a great Quiet descends
> where bombs racketed only last night.
> Among the stark trees, silhouetted on the ridge,
> Venus (Goddess of Love) appears,
> her entourage shimmering over my hollow.
> Behind the shoulder of the eastern hill,
> the sky whitens where a huge moon
> heaves itself up and over the edge,
> spilling softly down the now silent slope.
> Across the muddied, still bloodied, land
> where I live,
> a great Quiet descends
> where bombs racketed only last night.

Rabbi Heschel wrote a few days before his death: "There is an old idea in Judaism that God suffers when man suffers. There's a very famous text saying that even when a criminal is hanged on the gallows, God cries. God identifies himself with the misery of man." Hermits and solitaries also cry when a criminal is hanged, for through their immersion in the spiritual world, they don the heart of love which God shares with them. It is a painful burden, one beyond the strength of anyone who tries to carry it alone. The solitary who is growing into the mystic realm, however, soon discovers that she never walks alone; each day deepens her relationship with the Divine, its power and strength.

The wonder of this mystical exchange is not that God helps the pray-er bear the burden of human suffering but that God seeks human help to enable him bear the anguish that exists on earth! Hermits and solitaries help God reduce human misery by the way they live. They consider that their work is to keep God and humanity together. How? By allowing God and humanity to embrace within their heart. There is no separation between the God who loves and the world that exists because of that love. The prophetic hermit says by his or her life that what one does to another human being, one does to God. Hurting any living being injures the God who gives it life.

The hermit shares the conviction of St. Paul: "We know that all creation is groaning in labor pains even until now, and not only that but we ourselves, who have the first fruits of the Spirit, we also groan within ourselves as we wait for adoption, the redemption of our bodies ... for creation itself will be set free from slavery to corruption and share in the glorious freedom of the children of God." (Rom 8, 21–23) Because they choose to mourn ...

... they will be comforted.

Blessed are the lowly and meek ...

Genuinely meek individuals are rare in a culture which encourages everyone to climb to the top and to use every means available to get there. A book called *Hope for the Flowers* by Trina Paulus is a parable in which hundreds of caterpillars are trying to reach the peak of an endlessly squirming caterpillar pillar. They believe that the only way to the "top" is by climbing over one another. Eventually, one somewhat battered caterpillar gives up the struggle and listens to its own inner wisdom. Yes, getting to the top is the goal, but climbing over others is not the way. Instead it realizes that the way leads through spinning a cocoon out of its own resources and losing itself in a deep, transformative sleep.

In due time, it awakens metamorphosed into a glorious winged creature which drifts easily from flower to treetop, sipping nectar and leaving life-giving pollen in its wake. Blessed are those who go down and deep ...

Hermits are those who hear the call to do and be *less,* rather than more. Instead of climbing over others to achieve a goal defined by norms they cannot believe in, they seek the depths of solitude, not just for themselves but for others. They intuit that the way for them leads through hidden silence, a spiritual cocoon that will take them in the opposite direction from the rest of the world. Where others seek to overcome, they accept being overcome. They will let the world take advantage of them and not seek retribution because their life is focused on hidden service. Only those who are truly meek, who are not in competition with others, can embrace and live out a covenant of kindness and compassion.

The hermit of the future has the immense challenge of rediscovering and accepting his or her own creature-hood, something that the technological age has made unpalatable. To be a creature means to have been created by another. In a world where the self-made person is the most admired, few people bow their heads and acknowledge the truth that such a thing cannot exist. People cannot invent themselves, let alone reinvent themselves. They exist thanks to those who preceded them. Additionally, as creatures, human beings are dependent on limited resources with senses that are fragile and easily abused. It may be argued that the advances of technology make it possible for humans to transcend these limitations. However, without clear minds and sharp senses, no one would be able to make use of technological advances. People are only as alive as their senses are keen.

The solitary is someone who has recognized the great need to reconnect with his or her senses ... and the world his or her senses are designed to apprehend. In the present-day culture, senses have been slowly dulled due to continuous assault and over-stimulation. Only by living in such a way that eyes and ears, smell and taste and touch, are both exercised and protected can people recover their intended keenness.

I was quite surprised by what happened to me after I had lived some years in a cloistered monastery. People would frequently leave gifts for the sisters, which would be placed in the community gathering room. Often, I knew even before entering the room that something from "the outside" had been delivered. My sense of smell had been so cleansed that the faintest of new fragrances was immediately noticeable. Other sisters said they experienced the same phenomenon. Once, someone sent me a box of colored embroidery threads in silky, rich shades. As the skeins spilled over my brown skirt, I could actually feel my irises reacting, expanding, absorbing and caressing the colors. Such delight! Living in an environment where only the natural world offered me any bright colors, my vision had been purified, allowing me to experience pleasure in ways that many others, bombarded by electronically enhanced sights and sounds, had lost.

Hermits of the future will need to recover the responses they had as children when color and texture, scents, sounds, and tastes were so bright, so beautiful. In doing so, they will recall their creaturely limitations. One can only ingest a certain amount of information and stimulation at any one time. Instead of true multi-tasking, all a person does is screen out what cannot be absorbed from the multiple claims on one's attention. In the process, one spontaneously erects protective barriers, nature's way of guarding a person from dangerous overload and burnout. One may joke about children's selective hearing but be unaware of how badly impaired one's own hearing has become. The same is true for sight and smell, taste and touch. Many people have become benumbed to all but the most intense of sensory experiences. This applies equally to minds and emotions. Exposed daily to scenes of horrific violence, continually assaulted by accounts of cruelty and carnage, people eventually are unable to be moved by the simply sad, the small sorrows of everyday life.

Life in the healing silence of a hermitage allows minds and bodies to recover their original depth of feeling and keenness of perception. A solitary re-learns how to respond to the present moment, and multi-tasking is unmasked as the impossibility it really is. Why do several things poorly when one can do a single thing well and with deep pleasure? Background music, instead of soothing nerves, can become a defense against really hearing. It prevents one from appreciating the subtler sounds of the natural world—the silky whisper of leaves in the wind, the gurgling of water after a rain shower, the commotion of birds and insects and other small creatures. Only with senses fully alive can we be "reduced" to the naiveté of childhood and recover the age of wonder.

A "meek" solitary learns not only to *hear* more keenly but to *listen* as well. She or he not only hears the beauty of natural sounds but also responds with quiet attention to anyone who speaks. It does not take people long to discover that the hermit down the road will listen when no one else has time. Does it really matter that the speaker communicates merely mundane events important only to him or herself? The hermit hears the loneliness beneath the chatter and responds with both perception and patience.

More than one hermit may find he is called upon to exercise some form of telephone ministry. Discernment is required lest he find himself merely a sounding board for anger or self-pity. Or he gets caught up in the local gossip circle. Worse yet, he could become regarded as the local oracle dispensing wisdom to the unenlightened. The truly meek are never arrogant. They listen deeply but speak little. They may find themselves taken advantage of and will have to make discreet decisions about how far certain relationships can go. On occasion, a voice within may urge them to either decline any further communication or, on the other hand, let themselves be used for reasons as yet unknown.

During my years as a hermit in West Virginia, I would occasionally receive phone calls from a younger woman who suffered from multiple problems, not least of which was alcoholism. She generally called me when she was profoundly inebriated to either cry on my shoulder or berate me for not loving her sufficiently. She needed to know she was special to me, cherished above all others, and she was suspicious of any other relationship I had. These rather one-sided conversations gradually turned into a no-win situation, an endless request for proofs of love I could not give. Any assurance I offered was not accepted, because my friend could not believe in her own loveliness. When her doubts turned to anger and abusive language, I knew it was time to break the cycle. I told her yet once again how much I cared for her but that, for both our sakes, I would no longer accept phone calls from her when she was in this frame of mind. Though I had refused to talk to her, I continued to hold her in my heart, praying that a Love stronger than mine could break through her profound self-doubt.

More than a year passed without my hearing another word from her. I grieved; I wondered if I had failed her, but knew that all I could do now was trust a Lover wiser than I. Then one day, the phone rang. It was my young friend, her voice strong, her thinking clear, and, to my wonderment, profoundly thankful for my love for her! The past year had been one of grace for her. She had gone through a detox program, received much needed counseling, and was now in college, completing coursework for degrees in sociology and psychology. Her reason for calling me was to share a paper she was writing, illustrating her belief that love was the most potent "method" any psychologist could employ. She had come to accept her self-worth through remembering those long, often frustrating, frequently angry conversations we had had. On the surface, it had appeared I had failed her; giving up on her when she most needed me. My inadequacy, when admitted, had opened a door in her heart through which the Lord had walked with transforming love. Blessed are the meek who frequently fail...

... for they shall inherit the earth.

Blessed are those who hunger for holiness ...

The "holiness" for which a hermit hungers has been variously translated as "righteousness," right living, right relationships. It is not only a total communion with the divine but also with all "relations," in the sense that the Native Americans use that term. They begin or end all their serious writings or orations with a salutation to "all our relations," evoking the image of a reverential bow to the trees, to the coyote and deer, as well as to all members of the human family. Not forgotten are the Spirit Guides who watch over all their comings and goings, protecting and directing their steps.

Matthew Fox insists that authentic holiness generates peace. Not merely sweet tranquility but a peace based on justice, a justice painfully realized by those who dare to *have* less, to *be* less, so that others may have more and be more. Justice is achieved only where people choose to give rather than take. The Native Americans have a tradition called Potlatch or the Give-Away ceremony. A person or a family proves their right to a position of regard within the tribe by how lavish a Potlatch or Give-Away ceremony they sponsor. The more a person can give to his or her neighbors or friends, the more worthy he or she is to hold a prestigious position among them. But the main purpose of these ceremonies is the redistribution of wealth. The status of any given family is measured not by their having more resources but by how fairly they redistribute them. The propagation of such an attitude may well be the saving hope for our world, presently on a self-destructive course, with the rich getting richer and the poor growing poorer.

Celtic spirituality has a similar sense of justice and fair distribution of God's gifts, both material and spiritual. One of their teachers is Pelagius, who taught that there are three types of people: those who have enough, those who have not enough, and those who have more than enough. "Let no man have more than he really needs," he warned, "and everyone will have as much as they need, since the few who are rich are the reason for the many who are poor."[3] Pelagius urged that there be a redistribution of the gifts of nature in imitation of the utterly fair distribution by God of the gifts of grace. This was for him the heart of Gospel righteousness. Small wonder many of his teachings were condemned as heretical!

God prescribed through Micah. "You have been told, O man, what is good and what the Lord requires of you: Only to act justly and to love mercy, and to walk humbly with your God."(Mic.6,8) Another translation of that verse reads: "Only to act fairly, to love tenderly and to walk lowly with your God." The variety of translations results from the richness of the original Hebrew words. Justice in the Hebrew mindset is a matter of loving kindness and fairness, not condemnation based on an assumption of guilt. The psalmist meekly begs God to render true justice in the confidence God would grant the good expected from a loving judge. In Zechariah, a similar verse urges everyone to: "render true judgment and show kindness and compassion toward each other." Zech.7,9

Today's hermit, like those of the past, cherishes his or her solitude because it affords opportunity to become more and more transparent to the spiritual world. Not all hermits are Christian. Before the revival of eremitism in the West in the mid-twentieth century, most hermits were found in Asia and India, where spiritual practice was based on beliefs outside Christianity. The Chinese yinshih was a scholar-recluse, with little or no thought of religion. What they had in common with all other people who cherish solitude was that they had renounced the "red dust of the world," making them dead to worldly ambition and desire for success.

The righteousness that is an eremite's goal need not be overtly religious but, in the West, hermits are nearly always those who are fascinated with the divine and who long to be immersed in God. The genuinely holy person finds joy in the beauty of life presently around him or her, not merely in the promise of future happiness. Their joy is rich because they are content with what they have; their joy is secure because they know that what they most value can never be taken from them.

The word "holy" derives from an Old English term for "wholeness." The whole-hearted person is someone of integrity, a person with a single focus, a whole heart. By shedding everything which could impede union with God, the righteous person is freed to dance with the divine wherever that may be found—in a flower or a cathedral, in sacred writings or a cloud-strewn sky. The holy man or woman is transparently honest. One can depend on him or her to tell the truth, pleasant or not. At the same time, they are gentle, never brutal with the truth they know. One can trust them to not bruise the broken reed nor smother the smoky flame. In their presence, everything flourishes.

The hermit of the future must be a profoundly passionate person whose hunger and thirst for true justice will consume anything contrary to their goal. One of the things which must fuel such passion is the recognition that the planet is on the verge of self-destruction unless spiritual ideals overcome the materialistic values which currently govern the world. Past civilizations have been wiped out when greed or lust for power weakened the original inspiration of the group. What would happen now that the entire world is linked through technology? More than just a single country or one continent or even a hemisphere will be destroyed. The hermit of the future hungers and thirsts for holiness so that Planet Earth may be preserved as one of God's more beautiful creations.

Holiness is keeping the commandments, all of which are love. The first commandment is to love God; the second is to love one's neighbor as oneself. They are actually only one decree, because it is impossible to love God without loving his creation. The holiness that Jesus taught is not simply refraining from evil but actively doing good, as the story of the Last Judgment in Matthew 25 highlights. It is not just those who do harm who are condemned but those who fail to do good—who do *not* feed the hungry, welcome the stranger, or clothe the naked. The future hermit must find ways to mirror the goodness of the God she or he worships. There are many ways to live out the righteousness of God—the important thing is to be passionate about it, to hunger and thirst to see it realized.

Instead of being cut off from society, isolated from the "messiness" of real life, the future hermit must deliberately expose him or herself to raw reality. Rather than being always well-shod, warmly clothed, and adequately fed, the future solitary will need to model him or herself on the monks and nuns of Asia, whose bare feet connect frequently with the earth; whose hands hold begging bowls to experience dependence on the charity of a passing stranger; whose bodies are shielded from the weather by only one cloak. It would be tragic if hermits were to one day become highly revered members of society instead of standing shoulder-to-shoulder with the outcasts, as they have so often in past ages.

The "new heavens and new earth" promised in the book of Revelation depends on people who, as John wrote, "have endurance and have suffered for my name and have not grown weary … nor have they lost their first love" (cf. Rev. 2,3–4). The spiritual solitary is the one who has "ears to hear what the Spirit says." What he or she hears may well inspire fear or awe, another connotation of the word "holy." Alone in their hermitages, future hermits will struggle with the same demons as the early desert fathers and mothers dealt with, although they may not label them demons. The God they seek is not a tame reality, and living in proximity to the Divine is not always safe.

Once hermits have been "burnt" by the nearness of the Holy, they are scarred for life. No one will elect them as a national leader, nor shall they win any fame. The hermits of the future will be profoundly hidden, from themselves as well as others. They will not measure their progress—it is utterly impossible to do so, since hermits dwell where there are no mileposts to mark the distance they have come or note the miles remaining to their destination. Moving deeper into God involves letting go of any sense of where one is. If hermits read about mystical experiences, about the ladder of perfection or the dark night of the soul, it is for pleasure in the poetry, not to determine if they have entered the second dark night or have arrived at the fifth or sixth mansion.

Thomas Merton dramatically describes the essential lost-ness and lowliness of the hermit vocation in his poem on St. John the Baptist:

"Night is our diocese and silence is our ministry
Poverty our charity and helplessness our tongue-tied sermon.
Beyond the scope of sight or sound we dwell upon the air
Seeking the world's gain in an unthinkable experience.
We are exiles in the far end of solitude, living as listeners
With hearts attending to the skies we cannot understand:
Waiting upon the first far drums of Christ the Conqueror,
Planted like sentinels upon the world's frontier."[6]

In the Celtic tradition, hermits are among those who live at a "thin place," a point where the veil between this world and the spirit world is particularly fine-spun. Here, the barrier which separates the two worlds can be more easily penetrated. In addition to thin places, there can also be thin times, such as All Hallows Eve, when the spirits of the dead may visit the living for a brief period. Those who "pass through" are not just friendly spirits with kindly intentions, a fact which creates a certain ambivalence towards these thin places or times.

No matter how sophisticated our belief system may be, we still sense the eeriness in an ancient cemetery as evening falls and the owls call. Something shimmers like a dusky haze among the ruins of old monasteries and churches. The abandoned cells of hermits on Mt. Athos still seem inhabited, still seem imbued with an aura that stirs archetypical responses in our psyche. It takes courage to live in a thin place, where spirits hover close. Even Wood B. Hermit appears anxious as his lantern illumines a sign near a graveyard marked "Spirit Xing". One task for hermits of the future will be to stand as guardians of the thin places, for without a doubt, the barriers are thinning. Alexander Scott describes creation itself as "a transparency through which the light of God is seen." Hermits are those who knowingly live at those places in creation where that Light penetrates most strongly because they are hungering for holiness.

... for they will be satisfied.

Wood B. Hermit

Blessed are the merciful …

One of the rarest attitudes found in the world is mercy. Mercy is so misunderstood that many people feel it is a sign of weakness to either ask for it or to extend it. While pondering how a hermit might be merciful, a sketch of Wood B. Hermit came to mind. The stereotypical hermit is preparing for winter by laying in a supply of birdseed, dried corn, and apples in order to provide for "visitors" during the harsh months ahead. Many of these creatures no doubt caused Wood B. grief during the warmer months, but when they are in need, Wood B. will open his hand and heart to them … as well as the supplies they raided during the growing season.

"What goes around comes around." Few people, reviewing their lives, have much reason to expect exceptional rewards for how they have treated others. When it comes to the Great Commandment, most people focus on how they would have others treat them, rather than on how they have treated others. Mercy is hoped for but seldom expected. Anyone could be among those who dragged the adulterous woman to Jesus in order to point their fingers in righteous indignation while, at the same time trying to entrap the Man known for his mercy. Clearly these scribes and Pharisees felt that the Law which they understood so well was not compatible with the kind of mercy Jesus practiced.

Jesus foiled their attempt to ensnare him when he said, "Let the one among you who is without sin, be the first to cast a stone at her." (Jn.8.7) Deuteronomy prescribed that the person who cast the first stone had to be an eyewitness to the offense, and that would have been …? Since women were not permitted to bring an accusation of this gravity, the witness had to be male. Thus, the man who tossed the first stone would practically be admitting his participation in the adultery and hardly be without sin!

"If you only knew what this meant, 'I desire mercy, not sacrifice,' you would not have condemned these innocent men."(Mt.12,7) In another Gospel incident, the ever-present Pharisees have accused Jesus' hungry disciples of breaking the Law by plucking some ripe grain heads on the Sabbath and snacking on them as they walked through a field. Note that they did not charge the disciples with stealing, or even trespassing, but of doing what "was forbidden on the Sabbath," namely, working. It was such a flimsy application of the prescription against working on the Sabbath that Jesus challenged it with examples where mercy trumped the prohibition. But in addition to his teaching, Jesus also *showed* mercy, not only to his disciples by defending them, but to their accusers by attempting to open their eyes to the true meaning of the Law. It was one of the rare times when he openly proclaimed his identity and authority. "The Son of Man is Lord of the Sabbath." (Mt.12,8)

Matthew shows Jesus quoting this same Scripture passage about God's preference for mercy over sacrifice when he is at table in a tax collector's home, a man officially outside the Law. Jesus is breaking the law himself by sitting down among the guests who were other "tax collectors and sinners," people the law-abiding Pharisees would *never* fraternize with. Interestingly, Jesus did not challenge the labeling of these people as sinners but instead used it as a reason why they deserved mercy. "Those who are well do not need a physician, but the sick do. Go and learn the meaning of the words. 'I desire mercy, not sacrifice.' I did not come to call the righteous but sinners." (Mt.9:12,13) The truly merciful person not only refrains from punishment but also from condemnation.

The desert fathers understood this (at least some of them did some of the time!), as we learn from this story about Abba Moses, who was invited to a council called to censure one of the brothers in Scete. Abba Moses first declined to come but when urged, he took an old basket filled with sand along with him. When the brothers pointed out that his basket was leaking sand, the old man said, "Here I come, with my sins trailing out behind me and I do not see them, yet I am asked to pass judgment on another!" The brothers understood his actions and pardoned the brother they had intended to condemn.[11]

How does a person who lives alone show mercy? Mercy is a disposition of mind and heart which inclines a person toward compassion and kindness. The hermit of the future will continue the service that solitaries of the past have always rendered—she or he is a listener and a friend to everyone who calls upon him or her.

Fr. Cornelius Wencel, er.Cam, writes: "A friend is a person who provides us with the shelter of love and who brings us the gift of peace and tenderness. The hermit is called to be the friend of every one of his brothers and sisters ... When he listens with love and silence to all the troubles and secrets that others entrust to him, he does not want to judge, evaluate, or condemn them. On the contrary, he lets their words flow, so that they can be freed from any anger, fear, or sorrow, and so be transformed into a natural and spontaneous joy. The only thing that is really needed here is a simple presence of love that brings warmth and peace to the deepest levels of the human personality."[12]

In today's climate of pandemic loneliness and cultural crisis, many a hermit will be called upon to be a spiritual guide. In the past, people seeking God had a person in the social structure to turn to—their pastor or minister or rabbi. Sadly, the future promises fewer of these institutional spiritual guides. It may well be the consecrated layperson, known to live a life of prayer, who will be required to step in and fill the gap. By deliberately making her or himself available to spiritual seekers, the hermit of the future can become a model of true mercy.

In this very delicate and complex calling, a solitary offers him or herself in service to every one of his or her brothers and sisters, never asking in advance if the seekers are in "good standing" with the religious authorities. More than likely they are not, which is why their cry for help is so poignant. If they have been labeled as a "tax collector or sinner" by a representative of a religious denomination, their pain may be even deeper and their wound more critical. Lying robbed and injured by the side of the road and passed up by the priest and the Levite, their sole hope may be in a Samaritan, someone who may not be acceptable at the great Temple in Jerusalem. This hermit may worship on a mountain beyond the Jordan but prove she or he is among those whom the Father seeks, those who worship in spirit and in truth, in the mercy she or he bestows.

The hermit of the future will be a spiritually mature person who is spontaneously gentle and discreet, capable of displaying great empathy for those who seek his or her support. Human society is changing at such a rapid pace that people often find themselves without a sense of their own identity. The solitary who has gone into the desert to recover his or her own self is most qualified to assist others to do the same. The hermitage of the future should not be an enclosed fortress cutting the prayerful hermit off from others but rather have an open door inviting those in need to "stop and rest awhile." It is the place where the sign *"No Trespassing"* has been converted to read: *"Trespassers Will Be ... Forgiven."*

Hermits live in a world that transcends differences and are persons of dialogue and reconciliation, of understanding and friendship. The mercy shining from the solitary's heart is a reflection of the mercy she or he continually receives. The gift he or she offers is one he or she has already been given. When the Judge asked the woman taken in adultery, "Where are they? Has no one condemned you?" she replied in wonder, "No one, sir." Then Jesus, the only person present who *was* without sin, simply said, "Neither do I condemn you. Go and from now on do not sin anymore." (Jn.9:10,11) We can only hope that this was one woman who never forgot how she had been saved through sheer mercy and who extended that mercy to others.

... for mercy shall be theirs.

Blessed are the single-hearted ...

The "single-hearted" has been variously translated as pure of heart or clean of heart—a perfect description of what a hermit should be striving to become. Being "single-hearted" is the goal of the eremitic lifestyle because it enables the solitary to live free from the endless distractions which are afflicting and exhausting modern society. Like some plagues, this disease which scatters the mind is spread by the technological gadgets which both claim and divide our attention simultaneously. Few people these days are allowed to focus on only one thing at a time. How often do people feel guilty of wasting time unless they are doing at least two things at once: e.g., listening to educational tapes or catching up on phone calls while driving, or doing the laundry and watching TV while cooking. "Time-saving" devices, instead of freeing people up for more leisurely living, merely make it possible for them to attend to three tasks at once! The genuinely single-hearted are made to feel like the simple-minded because they prefer to focus on only one thing at a time.

People enter solitude in search of truth, simplicity, and peace. They know instinctively that the desert is an enemy of any artifice or pretence. By choosing to renounce all manner of duplicity, the hermit enters into a new reality and experiences a different dimension of time and space, an order of being that is unfathomable and intangible to most. As the solitary matures, she or he discovers a realm where the glory of God is revealed in everything and at every moment. This revelation becomes increasingly entrancing as the chaff of the secular world is shaken out and blown away, leaving only the pure grain of simplicity and truth. This "moment" of revelation is not just one dramatic visitation but is rather a continual conversion—an endless turning away from insincerity, hypocrisy, and lies.

The complexity of contemporary culture is confusing, calling for re-evaluation and change. One failure of modern society is that values are increasingly perceived only on a horizontal level, in a secular and purely humanistic way. Human dignity and solidarity are seen only as secular goals and achievements. Seeing them thus limits what can be accomplished. These and similar values can even revive atheistic communism unless they are set against the backdrop of the absolute and universal.

The future hermit will seek to live as have Native Americans for centuries past, seeing all that exists as "my relations" and drawing a thread of reconciliation between God and humanity, between human beings and their planet. While involved in this universal reconciliation, hermits discover their true and mysterious name, the one by which the Divine alone knows them. This discovery of one's true name creates a singular bond, much like a marriage, between the solitary and his or her God, explaining why a hermit so seldom feels lonely when alone in the hermitage. Their minds are focused on seeking God; their hearts are satisfied with finding God.

The single-hearted hermits of the future will seek to live in a spirit of humility and service, allowing the redemptive power of love to transform them and to flow through them in self-giving sacrifice. Such focus will give their lives authenticity and make them effective for good.

A story dear to many Jungian analysts is that of the rainmaker. A rainmaker is a person whose very presence allows good things to happen. The operative word is *allow.* The rainmaker doesn't make things happen; she or he allows good to come into the world. Irene Claremont de Castillejo writes:

> "We have forgotten how to allow. The essence of the Rainmaker is that she or he knows how to allow. The Rainmaker walks in the middle of the road, neither held back by the past nor hurrying towards the future, neither lured to the right nor to the left, but allows the past and the future, the outer world of the right and the inner images of the left all to play upon him or her while she or he attends, no more than attends, to the living moment in which these forces meet ... In those rare moments when all the opposites meet within a person; when all are allowed and none displaces any other ... then that person is in an attitude of prayer. Whether she or he knows it or not, such receptive allowing will affect all those around him or her (for good)."[13]

This is the task of the single-hearted—to allow the world to enter their souls with all its tragedy and triumph; its beauty and baseness. The pure of heart will let people be ... lovingly, trusting in the goodness which will result if they but refuse to meddle or even pray for any preconceived outcome. They have no ulterior motive but to allow good to happen, however it is meant ... with single-hearted love.

... for they shall (even now) see God.

Blessed are the peacemakers ...

The Russian hermit, St. Seraphim of Sarov said: "Be at peace yourself and thousands around you will be saved." Peace is at the heart of the eremitic ethos. It is what gives the hermit vocation its universality and its power to transform. It restores original relations, the original grace at the heart of all humanity. The hermit of the future bears the burden of recovering the peace which has been lost since humanity first refused to accept that liberty has limitations.

By initiating a dialogue with the universe deep within him or herself, the hermit hopes to promote a sense of human solidarity, longing for unity and peace within the whole human family. No hermit is permitted, by the fact of his or her solitary way of life, to escape from the world. What she or he should strive for is not to avoid the world, but rather to minister to it, encourage its development, its progress, and finally, its salvation. She or he understands the eremitic calling to be one of service rendered with a unique empathy and compassion for the whole of creation.

The great charge that every hermit receives as part of his or her vocation is to shield the tiny spark of divine fire barely flickering at the heart of our sterile civilization. Each hermit performs this service in a different way. Some do so through the purely spiritual channels of prayer and sacrifice. Others make themselves available as spiritual guides, assisting people to find paths of peace. Still others reveal the beauty of God's world through the arts or the written word.

Once people begin to perceive the world around them as beautiful, they can also recognize it as benevolent and will be able to trust it. Trust opens the way to peace. People who trust each other are those who talk to and are close to one another, who through simple gestures of kindness and compassion create an atmosphere where peace is nurtured and cruelty, hatred, and war are simply not permitted.

Hermits and solitaries contribute to peace around them by cultivating it first of all within their own hearts, a long-term and arduous task which is never fully achieved. It is the effort that counts—the continual practice of prayer, the rigors of solitude, silence, and penance, the daily renewal of belief that peace is possible. The peace of the desert has nothing to do with a shallow psychological composure but rather with the power of the Spirit dwelling in a humble and quiet heart. It is tranquility emerging where all is in right order.

The hermit who prays for peace is not seeking a precarious balance of power achieved by military might (or exhaustion), nor is it the control of the lesser by the mightier. It *is* born of struggle but not of violence. It is the fruit of a "revolution" which recognizes that everyone is our relation and deserving of our respect. Until everyone is free and has a sufficiency of worldly goods, no one has peace. Only when no one is plotting to obtain a surplus can everyone have enough. Only when everyone is satisfied with *enough* can there be an abundance of peace.

The way of peace that is paved with solitude and silence is not the way of the sword but the way of the Gospel. It is the Good News which announces that in the end, love will still be standing, offering bread to those exhausted from wielding the sword. Having renounced all violence him or herself, the hermit delicately and mercifully removes the swords from the hands of his or her "relations," beats them into plowshares and pruning hooks, and returns them with the seeds of peace to be sown in the ground fertilized by tears and prayer.

... for they shall be called children of God.

Consider the Ravens

To you, readers, hermits and would-be hermits, we address these final words. Eremitical life is available to *all* who are attracted to silence, solitude, and simplicity. It is like the treasure hidden in a field. Once found, the finder sells everything she or he has in order to buy that field and the treasure it holds. You need no one's permission to follow your heart. To you who have found this treasure, we add this.

Let no one rob you of this jewel or convince you it is fake or counterfeit. Rather, it is a gem of untold value, a diamond dug from the heart of the earth and polished by the praying hands of thousands before you. Do not listen to anyone who tries to tell you that you have chosen a selfish way of life, that you are running from your responsibilities to the world. It is because you see no better way to serve that you are seeking solitude where, in prayer and deep silence, you can balance our dizzily tilting planet.

As for personal qualities and lifestyles, remember that no two hermits are alike and that there are as many ways of living hermit life as there are hermits doing it. There is no single "type" or personality better suited to eremitic life. You need only be a self-starter, someone who can maintain a routine without anyone to nudge you out of bed in the morning and into your prayer space at regular intervals. Do be a person of passion who finds deep delight in the prayer and spiritual exercises around which your day will turn.

The diverse forms of hermit life are each valid in their own way, as long as they are lived with sincerity. Do not let yourself be misled by a stereotype of what a hermit is. Hermits are not angry recluses living in the wilderness abhorring ordinary conveniences. The Spirit blows where it will and will ask many of you to live in ways that defy any categories.

Each time you must leave your accustomed seclusion, take your peace with you. Share it generously with friend and stranger. If you do so wisely, it will increase like a flame passed from candle to candle. Your own fire will not be diminished.

Without doubt, you will endure periods of deep loneliness. Befriend it and learn from it. You will be stronger for having faced that fear directly. Be patient with the process of discovering your inner friends. A four-legged companion may add another dimension to your life and give you someone to care for directly. Do not neglect the wild ones.

Strive for balance in your daily routine, a pleasing round of prayer and work and relaxation. Eat wisely and with moderation; give yourself adequate sleep; find your pleasure in the small things of life—with them, you can fill each day with beauty and contentment. Honor time from dawn to dusk. At each turning of the seasons, smell the air, touch the leaves, taste the new foods that it offers. Cherish all the changes of the ever-circling year—those without and those within.

Often, you will feel you are walking in the dark with just the radiance from your own flashlight to illumine the ground for your next step. Take that step, and only then will you see if there is a place ahead for your next footfall. If not, know that you have found the spot where you are to stay. Put down deep roots. Hermit life is nurtured by stability. Our world desperately needs hermits to "just stand there" as sentinels on our world's frontier, watching for the Coming One. Do not try to explain this to others. Those who would understand already know this; those who don't understand never will.

You are unlikely to hear a voice out of the clouds, although you shall likely encounter a Cloud of Unknowing more often than you would care to! Maintain a perspective that allows you to discern what is to be done today and what is better left for the morrow. As much as possible, possess your soul in patience. Look kindly on everyone, yourself first of all.

Above all, remember this word from Leon Bloy: "Joy is the most infallible sign of the presence of God." Write it on your walls; carve it in your heart, and *claim* your heritage! There are great riches to be had in the eremitic life if you are satisfied with a sufficiency (as St. Paul says). The Lord will provide for you out of his mysterious resources if you but allow him. His timing will be exquisite— usually just at the moment when you give up!

You will find joy beyond all imagining once you have entered fully into the charism of your vocation. Be solitary, silent, and alone, cherishing your portion with gratitude. Be still and know that:

> "Life is more than food and the body more than clothing. Consider the ravens: they do not sow or reap; they have neither storehouse nor barn, yet God feeds them. How much more important are you than birds! Do not be afraid any longer, little flock, for your Father is pleased to give you the kingdom. Sell your belongings and give alms.

Provide moneybags for your selves that do not wear out, an inexhaustible treasure in heaven that no thief can reach nor moth destroy. For where your treasure is, there also will your heart be." (Lk.12:23,24,32–34)

About the Authors

Paul and Karen Fredette live on a secluded mountain slope north-west of Asheville, NC with their border collies, Neill and Cynda, and their magical white cat, Merlin. They minister to hermits world-wide through a quarterly newsletter, Raven's Bread, and a web presence through which they offer eremitical resources and guidance. See www.ravensbreadministries.com

Endnotes

Introduction
1. Open Letter to *Raven's Bread.*
2. *ibid.*
3. *ibid.*
4. Winters
5. Ward, *The Sayings of the Desert Fathers: The Alphabetical Collection*, 104.
6. Nomura, *Desert Wisdom: Sayings from the Desert Fathers*, 92.

Chapter One: Solitaries: Sages or Psychotics?
1. Lassus, OP, *In Praise of Hiddenness*, 8.
2. *The Catholic Herald,* March 15, 1989.
3. *Newsweekly,* February 17, 1989.
4. *Raven's Bread,* vol. 8, #3.
5. Ibid., vol.8, #4.
6. Merton, *A Search for Solitude*, 287–293.
7. Ibid., 293.
8. Unpublished reflections offered to *Consider the Ravens.*
9. *L'Eremittisme en Occident jusqu'a l'an mil,* 173.
10. Jones, W. Paul, pers. comm.
11. Wencel, *The Eremitic Life: Encountering God in Silence and Solitude*, 23.
12. Ibid., 24.
13. Open Letter to *Raven's Bread.*
14. Jones, pers. comm.
15. Anonymous, *Raven's Bread,* vol.8, #3.
16. Loree, Sharron, *Raven's Bread,* vol. 8, #2.

17. Jones, pers. comm.

18. Swan, *The Forgotten Desert Mothers*, 25.

19. Wencel, *The Eremitic Life: Encountering God in Silence and Solitude.* 15.

20. Stockton, privately circulated writings.

21. Nomura, *Desert Wisdom: Sayings from the Desert Fathers*, 82.

22. Jones, pers. comm.

23. Merton, *The Wisdom of the Desert*, 54.

24. *Raven's Bread*, vol. 7, #4.

25. Merton, *The Monastic Journey*, 159,160.

26. Eliot, *Ash Wednesday VI: Collected Poems*, 95.

Chapter Two: The Reawakening of Hermit Life in the Twentieth and Twenty-First Centuries

1. Baker, *Paths in Solitude*, p10,11.

2. Wencel, *The Eremitic Life: Encountering God in Silence and Solitude*, 6.

3. Merton, *The Monastic Journey*, 156.

4. Simonelli, *Mountain Base Road*, vii.

5. Lisa Miller, "Life in Solitary," *Newsweek*, June 20, 2005.

6. Swan, *The Forgotten Desert Mothers*, 42–43.

7. Merton, *The Wisdom of the Desert*, 5.

8. *The Statutes for the Hermits of France*, 1989.

9. www. The Hermitary.

10. Ibid., #5.

11. Clay, *The Hermits and Anchorites of England*.

12. France, *Hermits: The Insights of Solitude*, 89.

13. Karper-Fredette, *Where God Begins to Be*, 6.

14. Cirino, *The Cord*, July-August 1991.

15. Merton, *The Monastic Journey*, 155.

16. Code of Canon Law, 226,227.

16. Nomura, *Desert Wisdom*, 15.

17. Merton, *The Monastic Journey*, 157.

18. Ward, *The Sayings of the Desert Fathers*, 42.

19. Denny, David M., a privately circulated study.

20. Lassus, OP, *In Praise of Hiddenness*, Appendix.

21. *Raven's Bread,* vol. 8, #3.

22. *Raven's Bread,* vol. 7, #4.

23. Ibid.

24. http://www.op.org/ravensbread.

25. *Review for Religious*, March-April 1989.

26. *Raven's Bread* Hermit Survey 2001.

27. Ibid.

28. Ibid.

29. Ibid.

30. Ibid.

31. Ibid.

32. Ibid.

33. Ibid.

34. Ibid.

35. Ibid.

36. Merton, The *Wisdom of the Desert,* 74.

Chapter Three: Don't Just Do Something ... Be There

1. Swan, *The Forgotten Desert Mothers,* 47.

2. Ibid., 47.

3. Jones, *A Season in the Desert: Making Time Holy,* Prelude.

4. **Hermit. Anonymous. pers.comm**

5. *Raven's Bread,* vol. 11, #3.

6. Merton, *Search for Solitude,* 3.

7. Eliot, Burnt Norton, *Collected Poems,* 177.

8. Merton, *Search for Solitude,* 32.

9. Hanh, *The Miracle of Mindfulness,* 4–5.

10. Hahn, *Living Buddha, Living Christ,* 204.

11. Griffin, *The Hermitage Journals,* ix.

12. Jones, *A Table in the Desert: Making Space Holy,* Prelude.

13. Merton, *A Search for Solitude,* 185.

14. Merton, *Conjectures of a Guilty Bystander,* 157.

15. Ward, SLG, *The Sayings of the Desert Fathers,* 237.

16. Merton, *The Wisdom of the Desert,* 73.

17. Ibid., 25.

18. Ibid.

19. Nomura, *Desert Wisdom: Sayings from the Desert Fathers*, 64.
20. Merton, *The Wisdom of the Desert*, 51.
21. *Raven's Bread,* Vol. 10, #3.
22. Merton, *The Wisdom of the Desert*, 76.
23. Julian of Norwich, *The Classics of Western Spirituality*: *Showings*, 226.
24. Ibid., 183.
25. Ibid., 229.
26. Ibid., 229.
27. Merton, *A Search for Solitude*, 31.

Chapter Four: A Solitary Canon

2. MacDonald, *Hermits: The Juridical Implications of Canon 603*, 1.2.
3. Ibid., 1.2.1.
4. Ibid., 1.2.1.
5. Ibid., 1.2.1.
6. Beyer, SJ, *The Law of Consecrated Life: Commentary on Canons 573–606*, 139.
7. Grace Izzynuff, pers. comm.
8. Anonymous,
9. Ward, *The Sayings of the Desert Fathers:, Alphabetical Collection*, 198.
10. Swan, *The Forgotten Desert Mothers*, 72.
11. Beyer, SJ, *The Law of Consecrated Life: Commentary on Canons 573–606*, 139.
12. Macdonald, *Hermits: Juridical Implications of Canon 603*, 1.2.2.
13. *Raven's Bread,* vol. 10, #3.
14. *Raven's Bread,* vol. 11, #2.
15. *Raven's Bread,* vol. 11, #2.
16. Merton, *Wisdom of the Desert*, 29.
17. Nomura, *Desert Wisdom*, 33.
18. Merton, *Wisdom of the Desert*, 68.
19. Ibid., 68.

20. Macdonald, *Hermits: Juridical Implications of Canon 603,* 1.2.3.

21. Ibid.

22. Russell, "Dangers of Solitude," *Review for Religious,* November-December, 2000.

23. Ibid.

24. Ibid.

25. Nomura, *Desert Wisdom,* 12–13.

26. Weisenbeck, *Guidebook for the Vocation to Eremitic Life,* 10.

27. Ibid., 26.

28. St. Athanasius, *Ancient Christian Writer:, The Life of St. Antony,* 22–23.

29. *Raven's Bread,* vol. 9, #4.

30. Nomura, *Desert Wisdom,* 104.

31. Canon 603 §2.

32. Macdonald, *Hermits: The Juridical Implications of Canon 603,* 2.1.1.

33. *Catholic Star Herald,* October 26, 2001.

34. Anonymous, Pers. Comm.

35. Macdonald, *Hermits: The Juridical Implications of Canon 603,* Part 3,.Par. 2.

36. Unpublished Work

37. Source unknown.

Chapter Five: Helps and Hazards

1. Anonymous Sayings of the Desert Fathers

2. Ward, *Sayings of the Desert Fathers: Alphabetical Collection,* xxvi.

3. Simonelli, *Mountain Base Road: Exploring a Life of Engaged Hermitage and Contemplation,* 112,113.

4. Russell, "Acedia—The Dark Side of Commitment," *Review for Religious,* Sep. 1988.

5. Ward, *Sayings of the Desert Fathers: Alphabetical Collection,* 3.

6. W. Paul Jones, Unpublished Writings.

7. Nomura, *Desert Wisdom: Sayings from the Desert Fathers*, 95.
8. Ibid., 82.
9. Swan, *The Forgotten Desert Mothers*, 68.
10. Nomura, *Desert Wisdom: Sayings from the Desert Fathers*, 60.
11. Ibid., 96.
12. Ibid., 104.
13. Swan, *The Forgotten Desert Mothers*, 58.
14. Ward, *The Sayings of the Desert Fathers*, 140.

Chapter Six: Practical Points

1. Ward, *The Sayings of the Desert Fathers: The Alphabetical Collection*, 148.
2. Thompson, *The Hound of Heaven*, Lines 9–12.
3. Nomura, *Desert Wisdom, Sayings from the Desert Fathers*, 42,43
4. Merton, *The Wisdom of the Desert*, 34.
5. Ibid., 6.
6. Ibid., 26.
7. Beyer, SJ, *The Law of Consecrated Life*, 138.
8. Pers. Comm
9. Merton, *The Wisdom of the Desert*, 67–68.
10. Nomura, Desert Wisdom, Sayings From the Desert Fathers, 72.
11. Russell, "Must Hermits Work?" *Review for Religious*, March-April 2000.
12. John Paul II, *Vita Consecrata*, #11.
13. Canonical Committee of Religious, *Statutes for the Hermits of France*, 4.4.
14. St. Albert, *The Rule of St. Albert*, #15.
15. Name Withheld, *Eremitic Rule of Life*, III. C.
16. Feiss, *Essential Monastic Wisdom: Writings on the Contemplative Life*, 23.
17. St. Athanasius, *The Life of Saint Antony: Ancient Christian Writers*, 21.
18. Ibid., 108, ftnt 23.

19. Merton, *Wisdom of the Desert*, 37.
20. Ibid., 62.
21. David, *The Slow Down Diet: Eating for Pleasure, Energy and Weight Loss*, 176.
22. Ibid.
23. Canonical Committee of Religious, *Statutes for the Hermits of France*, #8.
24. St. Albert, *Rule of St. Albert*, #20.
25. Canonical Committee of Religious, *Statutes for the Hermits of France*, #2.
26. Lassus, O.P., *In Praise of Hiddenness: The Spirituality of the Camaldolese Hermits of Monte Corona*, 76.

Chapter Seven: Horizons for Hermits

1. Merton, *The Wisdom of the Desert*, 48–49.
2. Newell, *The Book of Creation: An Introduction to Celtic Spirituality*, 42.
3. Merton, "The Quickening of John the Baptist," *The Collected Poems of Thomas Merton*, 201.
4. Merton, *The Wisdom of the Desert*, 40.
5. Wencel, er.Cam, *The Eremitic Life*, 194.
6. de Castillejo, *Knowing Woman: A Feminine Psychology*, 133.

Select Bibliography

Athanasius, St. *Ancient Christian Writers: The Life of St. Antony*, newly translated and annotated by Robert T. Meyer, PhD, Copyright 1950 by Rev. Johannes Quasten and Rev. Joseph C. Plumpe, Copyright 1978 by Rev. Johannes Quasten Rose Mary L. Plumpe. Paulist Press, Inc., New York/Mahwah, NJ. Reprinted by permission of Paulist Press, Inc., www.paulistpress.com.

Baker, Eve. *Paths in Solitude*. Eve Baker Middlegreen, Slough: St Paul's, 1995.

Beyer SJ, Jean. *The Law of Consecrated Life: Commentary on Canons 573–606*. Paris: Tardy, 1988.

Camaldolese Hermit, A. Ed. Fr. Louis-Albert Lassus, OP. *In Praise of Hiddenness: The Spirituality of the Camaldolese Hermits of Monte Corona*. Bloomingdale, OH: Holy Family Hermitage, Ercam Editions, 2007.

Cirino, Andre. From a re-edited article first published in *The Cord*. July-August 1991.

Clay, Rotha Mary. *The Hermits and Anchorites of England*. London: Ben Baker, Fellowship of Solitaries Edition, 2000.

Coelho, OFM, Christopher. *A New Kind of Fool*. Secunderabad, India: Amruthavani Publications, 1986.

Colegate, Isabel. *A Pelican in the Wilderness: Hermits, Solitaries and Recluses*. Washington, DC: Counterpoint, 2002.

David, Marc. *The Slow Down Diet: Eating for Pleasure, Energy and Weight Loss*. Rochester, VT: Healing Arts Press, 2005.

de Castillejo, Irene Claremont. *Knowing Woman: A Feminine Psychology*. New York: Harper & Row, 1974.

Eliot, T.S. *Ash Wednesday VI: Collected Poems, The Century Edition*. New York: Harcourt Brace Jovanovich, 1968.

Feiss, Hugh. *Essential Monastic Wisdom: Writings on the Contemplative Life*. New York: HarperCollins, 1999.

France, Peter. *Hermits: The Insights of Solitude*. New York: St. Martin's Press, 1997.

Griffin, John Howard. *The Hermitage Journals: A Diary Kept While Working on the Biography of Thomas Merton*. Garden City, NY: Image Books, 1981.

Hall, Sr., Jeremy. *Silence, Solitude, Simplicity: A Hermit's Love Affair with a Noisy, Crowded and Complicated World*. Collegeville, MN: The Liturgical Press, 2007.

Hanh, Thich Nhat. *Living Buddha, Living Christ*. New York RiverHead Books, division of G. P. Putnam's Sons 1995. Used by permission of Riverhead Books, an imprint of Penguin Group (USA) Inc.

——— *The Miracle of Mindfulness: An Introduction to the Practice of Meditation*. Boston: Beacon Press, 1987.

Harris, Paul, Editor. *The Fire of Silence and Stillness: An Anthology of Quotations for the*

Spiritual Journey. Springfield, IL: Templegate Publishers, 1995.

Hermitary, The. Web site

John Paul II. *Vita Consecrata*. 1996.

Jones, W. Paul. *A Season in the Desert: Making Time Holy*. Brewster, MA: Paraclete Press, 2000.

_____. *A Table in the Desert, Making Space Holy*. Brewster, MA: Paraclete Press, 2001.

Julian of Norwich. *The Classics of Western Spirituality: Showings*. New York: Paulist Press, 1978.

Karper, Karen. *Where God Begins to Be: A Woman's Journey into Solitude*. Bloomington, IN: iUniverse, 2004.

MacDonald, Helen L. *Hermits: The Juridical Implications of Canon 603*. Ottawa: Studio Canonica, 1992.

Matus, Thomas. *Nazarena: An American Anchoress*. Mahweh, NJ: Paulist Press, 1998.

McNamara, William. *Wild and Robust: The Adventure of Christian Humanism*. Cambridge, MA: Cowley Publications, 2006.

Merton, Thomas. *The Collected Poems of Thomas Merton*. New York: New Directions Paperback, 1980.

———. *Conjectures of a Guilty Bystander*. New York: Doubleday, 1989.

———. *Contemplation in a World of Action*. Garden City, NY: Doubleday, 1971.

———. Edited by Bro. Patrick Hart. *The Monastic Journey*. Kalamazoo, MI: Cistercian Publications, 1992.

———. *A Search for Solitude: The Journals of Thomas Merton, Vol. Three, 1952–1960*.

Copyright © 1997 New York: HarperCollins, 1997.

———. *The Wisdom of the Desert*. New York: New Directions Paperback, 1970.

Miller, Lisa. "Life in Solitary." *Newsweek*, Vol. CXLV, No. 25, 2005, 48–50.

New American Bible, The. Camden, NJ: Thomas Nelson, Inc., 1971.

Newell, J. Philip. *The Book of Creation: An Introduction to Celtic Spirituality*. Mahweh, NJ: Paulist Press, 1999.

Nomura, Yushi, Trans., *Desert Wisdom: Sayings from the Desert Fathers*. Maryknoll, NY: Orbis Books, 1982.

Paulus, Trina. *Hope for the Flowers*. Mahweh, NJ: Paulist Press, 1972.

Fredette, Paul and Karen. *Raven's Bread: Food for those in Solitude*. Quarterly Newsletter. Hot Springs, NC: *Raven's Bread* Ministries, 1997.

Rufus, Annelid, *Party of One: The Loners' Manifesto.* New York: Marlowe & Company, 2003.

Russell, Kenneth C. "Acedia—The Dark Side of Commitment." *Review for Religious.* Vol. 47, No. 5, 1988, 730–737.

———. "Dangers of Solitude." *Review for Religious.* Vol. 59, No. 6, 2000. 575–583.

Simonelli, Richard. *Mountain Base Road: Exploring a Life of Engaged Hermitage and Contemplation.* Nederland, CO: Mountain Sage Writing and Publishing, 2006.

Fredette, Fr. Joseph, Trans. *Statutes for the Hermits of France By the Canonical Committee of Religious.* 1989.

Swan, Laura. *The Forgotten Desert Mothers: Sayings, Lives, and Stories of Early Christian Women.* New York/Mahweh, NJ: Paulist Press, Inc., 2001. Reprinted by permission of Paulist Press, Inc. www.paulistpresss.com.

Ward, SLG, Benedicta. Trans., *The Sayings of the Desert Fathers: Alphabetical Collection.* Kalamazoo, MI: Cistercian Publications, Inc., 1975.

Weisenbeck, FSPA, Sr. Marlene Compiler. *Guidebook for the Vocation to Eremitic Life.* LaCrosse, WI: Diocese, 1997, 2000.

Wencel, Er.Cam, Fr. Cornelius. *The Eremitic Life: Encountering God in Silence and Solitude.* Bloomingdale, OH: Ercam Editions, 2007.

Made in the USA
Lexington, KY
13 April 2010